LOOKING BACK FROM NINETY

Also by Daniel Ford

Cowboy: The Interpreter Who Became a Soldier, a Warlord, and One More Casualty of Our War in Vietnam

Flying Tigers: Claire Chennault and His American Volunteers, 1941-1942

Tales of the Flying Tigers

Poland's Daughter: How I Met Basia, Hitchhiked to Italy, and Learned About Love, War, and Exile

A Vision So Noble: John Boyd, the OODA Loop, and America's War on Terror

The Lady and the Tigers (with Olga Greenlaw)

Glen Edwards: The Diary of a Bomber Pilot

The Only War We've Got: Early Days in South Vietnam

The Country Northward: A Hiker's Journal

Novels

Michael's War: A Story of the Irish Republican Army

Remains: A Story of the Flying Tigers

The High Country Illuminator: A Tale of Light and Darkness and the Ski Bums of Avalon

Incident at Muc Wa: A Story of the Vietnam War

Now Comes Theodora: A Story of the 1960s

Thank you for buying this book. For the photos that didn't fit into its pages, for more about the author and his work, or to sign up for an occasional electronic newsletter, visit the website at danfordbooks.com

LOOKING BACK FROM NINETY

The Depression, the War, and the Good Life that Followed

Daniel Ford

Warbird Books 2021

ISBN 978-1-7322300-2-6 paperback

The pages that follow are the truth as best I can reconstruct it. I have sometimes altered names and circumstances, to spare the feelings of others, so no character in this book can be considered the portrait of any actual person, living or dead, and any such resemblance is entirely coincidental.

Daniel Ford, November 2021

Contents

Dedication

In 1965 I dedicated *Now Comes Theodora* to my mother and father; in 1972, *The High Country Illuminator* to the woman I married; and in 1991, *Flying Tigers* to our daughter Kate. To complete the cycle, *Looking Back From Ninety* is for the two young women who have been our delight for the past twenty years or so:

Helen Serena Laird

Anna Joan Laird

1 – The Depression

NOVEMBER 2, 1931, WAS A LOVELY DAY, sunny and warm, or so Mom told me when I was in my twenties and making my own way in life. Dad drove her to Symmes Arlington Hospital, high on a hill in a neighboring Boston suburb, and there he left her in the care of a maternity nurse. (Symmes has since been replaced by upscale housing with gorgeous views of Boston and the distant countryside.) He had a reason to drive home: they'd left my two-year-old brother asleep in his crib. But I doubt that Dad cared much for baby-sitting, any more than he'd be eager to hang around the fathers' waiting room. He was Irish. His job was to earn the money, and on Saturday night to walk with the wife to the A&P store, wait by the cash register, and hand her the dollar bills to pay for the groceries, meat, or produce. The Somerville A&P was a "combination store," each with its own manager, not a newfangled supermarket with a row of cash registers at the exit.

Then they would walk back to Jaques Street in silence, a paper bag in each arm. I am assuming that Dad didn't waste gasoline by driving to the store, and I'm also assuming the silence. I don't ever remember my parents having an actual conversation. They exchanged information and the occasional recrimination, but that was about it.

Well — our house. It was one in a row of similar three-decker buildings on Jaques Street. Somerville and Arlington were linked to Boston by geography, and in the 1930s they were filled with those three-deckers and their Italian and Irish inhabitants. (Indeed they still are, though the inhabitants I suppose come from elsewhere.) I remember a photo of our house: it had an almost flat roof, with a porch facing the street on each floor. The owner of such a three-decker would himself be an immigrant, living with his family on the ground floor and renting out the apartments above. The one in the middle fetched the higher rent because it was cooler in summer and cheaper to heat in winter, when it could steal a bit of warmth from the coal stoves above and below it.

Dad owned the house, or rather shared it with the bank. In 1927 his mother had died, so Dad put the Old Lady his grandmother into a Catholic nursing home in Cork City and sold the Tullig farm to his Uncle Jack, who gave him half the money down and a note for the rest. Jack never paid the balance, and by the time Dad got around to suing his estate, the Second World War had come and gone, and the British pound – and the Irish pound tied to it – had lost nearly half its value against the dollar.

Dad came to America, rented a room from an Irishwoman on West 158th Street in New York, and worked various jobs, most often at an A&P or First National warehouse, though once he worked at an estate out on Long Island. The Irish in America were mostly farmers' sons, and they'd had their fill of country life. They flew like moths to New York and Boston, where the streets were paved with gold, and all a man need do was bend over and pick it up! Well, no, of course they didn't believe that. They expected to work hard, and they were accustomed to working hard. It was enough for them that America was the land of opportunity. It was *Tir na nÓg*, indeed, the land of youth and beauty, abundance and joy.

One day Dad was walking down the sidewalk, and who should he meet but his cousin John Forde,

Uncle Jack's son! That seems astonishing, doesn't it, two lads from the County Cork and first cousins to boot, bumping into one another on the sidewalk? But that sort of thing happens all the time when you're young. It happened to Dad in New York City, it happened to me in Paris, it happened to my daughter in Zurich, and I'm sure it will happen someday to my granddaughters in some odd corner of the world. Anyhow, the cousins met. It was Prohibition time, so they walked to the next intersection and asked the policeman — who of course was Irish himself — where to find a speakeasy. "Stand there on the corner," he told them. "I'm off duty in five minutes and I'll take you there." So they did, the three of them, and over bootleg whiskey — *poteen*, as it was called in Ireland — John Forde convinced Dad to go West with him and work on the wheat harvest. So that's what they did in the fall of 1927.

Dad by this time had come to the conclusion that the bachelor life was not for him, so he had "sent for" Annie Crowley, with whom he'd been low-key sweethearts during the Irish Civil War of 1922-1923. The Crowleys and the Fordes were fierce Republicans during the rebellion that began in 1916. Early on, Mom had a true sweetheart in Mick Walsh, like herself from Ballygarvan. But when the Bloody Damn English had enough of rebellion and proposed a truce in 1921, and Dad's hero Michael Collins went to London to be swindled by Winston Bloody Churchill, the diehard Republicans wanted nothing to do with the Irish Free State that was on offer. It was independence or nothing! And they got nothing. So the two sides went to war, Diehards and Free Staters; Annie Crowley and Mick Walsh found themselves on opposite sides, and they parted. That was how Mom and Dad found themselves thrown together.

So they'd been sweethearts of a sort. Dad knew no one else he might ask to marry him, and she was mourning the death of her favorite brother, young Willie Crowley, who had killed himself at the age of twenty. This seems to have happened a lot to the Crowley men. Mom's father died by his own hand, like the lad who would have been another of my uncles. There were no suicides among my cousins, but at least one in the generation that followed. And none of the Crowley men ever married! Uncle Jack emigrated to Australia, as did Uncle Dan for whom I was named; they lived at opposite ends of the country, and as far as I know they never met. Uncle Pat inherited the farm at Kilnahone, where he died an old bachelor. It was up to the Crowley girls to pass on the genes, but alas not the name.

Anyhow, in 1927 Annie Crowley was feeling sad about life. She wrote Dad that she would marry him and come to America; she went to Cork City and proved that she was of good health, spoke English, had a good education by British colonial standards — six years of National School — and had relatives in Arlington, Massachusetts, to guarantee she wouldn't be a charge upon her new country. These were the O'Haras, with Annie O'Hara some kind of cousin, as was their son Francis, for whom I was middle-named. Indeed, it was not long after I was born that "Francis" became the name by which I was known, and this in time became "Frank." I never cared for either one, and as soon as I found myself in control of matters, I changed myself back to Daniel, beloved of the Lord.

When Annie Crowley stepped off the boat in Boston, to be greeted by the O'Hara family, she was given a letter from Dad. It was postmarked in Vancouver! Far from meeting her as she'd expected, her future husband was *still* three thousand miles away, and in another country to boot! When Mom went to bed in the O'Hara's spare room that night, she slept with the light on, because she didn't know how to turn it off and was too shy to ask.

But it worked out okay. Mom got a job as housekeeper for a family in Cambridge and became pals with the nearly-grown daughters, who introduced her to cocktails and took her to see Harvard College and other grand sights of the city. And Dad showed up eventually. Mr. O'Hara gave the bride away, and for their wedding night they took the coastwise steamboat to New York, where they settled for a time in Hell's Kitchen. I suppose there were some arguments about that, and it would seem that Mom actually won out. If so, it was probably the only time she did.

Anyhow, they moved back to Boston. Dad took the money from the farm at Tulligmor and used it for the down payment on the three-decker in Somerville. These names — Tullig and Kilnahone — refer to what the Irish knew as a "townland." Kilnahone contained three or four small farms on the same lane outside Ballygarvan, while Tulligmor or Big Tullig was located in Ballinhassig and had only the Forde farm.

He got a job — Dad was always able to get a job, though he generally tired of it in a year or two — and they were well off by the standards of the time and the circumstances of their upbringing. What more could a young family want, than a house that paid its own way, and on Saturday evening a pay envelope containing two five-dollar bills and four singles? There was a federal income tax in 1928, but it didn't apply to the likes of Pat Forde. No Social Security or Medicare contribution, either, and no sales tax.

On their marriage certificate, Dad's name was shown as Forde, but by the time Joe was born the *e* had gone missing. It seems that the other men at the A&P warehouse kept making two syllables out of his name — Ford*ee* — so he put a stop to that by dropping the final letter. I have always been a bit sorry he did. Especially in high school and college, I would have fancied being Daniel Forde.

Joseph Patrick Ford was born in June 1929, when everything still looked grand about America's and the family's future. Joe was a Junior of sorts, since his first and middle names were a reversal of Dad's. Indeed he was a covert Pat Forde III, though that never arose because our grandfather died before Dad came into the world.

Three months later, though, the stock market began its slide that wiped out much of the country's wealth. It took a while for the tsunami to reach the A&P warehouse and the three-decker in Somerville. Dad still had the job when I came along in November 1931, though apparently he didn't go to work that Monday. I suppose Mom's labor pains began in the night, and he just took the day off. There was no obligation to telephone, since few people had phones at home in those years. He must have still owned the car, or truck; I'm sure it was a Model T Ford, not because he was loyal to the family name (and it wasn't his family anyhow) but because there were millions of them going back to 1908, and they were cheap and reliable. The Model A was then in its fourth and final year of manufacture, but that wonderful car would have been far beyond Dad's ambition. He always bought vehicles that were on the verge of expiring.

And the tenants were probably still paying their rent that year, though not, I suspect, in the one that followed. November was an important month in that respect: like bears hibernating for the winter, a family would move into a new place in November — the middle-floor apartment for choice — and buy a ton of coal to store in one of the three bins in the basement. The December rent might also come in, though perhaps not on time. It was in the New Year that the trouble began. In January there might be a bit of pleading. Yerra God, weren't they all Irish together? The man had lost his job, but surely he'd find something to do before the middle of the month, and it wasn't as if there was anyone else knocking on the door with cash in his fist. Perhaps the $10 would show up in the final week of January, and nothing at all the following month. So then the task of evicting them began. By the time Dad got the freeloaders out on the street, it was spring again. The replacement tenants of course were no better. And Dad himself was out of work as often as he was on. They struggled through two years of a worsening depression, but in 1934 the bank foreclosed and now we were the tenants.

I've said that Dad could always find a job, and even in the pit of the Great Depression, he pulled it off. He saw the advertisement in the *Boston Sunday Post*: caretaker wanted for a summer estate in Alton, New Hampshire, forty dollars a month – the equivalent of $795 today – plus a house to live in. I don't remember any of this, of course. Perhaps, despite it all, Dad still had the Model T; perhaps he packed it with the four of us and a few bits of furniture tied on top, and drove us over two-lane highways to Chestnut Cove Road in New Hampshire.

~ ~ ~ ~

Up to this point I've depended on the stories I heard about my first two years. I have no memory of

Somerville, save for an image of me in a red child's wagon on a concrete sidewalk. There were no sidewalks on Chestnut Cove Road, and no child's wagon either, so that must be Jaques Street. Perhaps I am remembering a photograph, and perhaps in memory I have colored the wagon red.

Dad's new employer was Lindsay Todd Damon and his remarkable wife Bertha. Professor Damon headed the English Department at Brown; he was sixty-two when we moved to Alton. Missus Damon was ten years younger and had married twice before, with a rather adventurous life as writer and editor before marrying Professor Damon in 1928. (One of her magazine articles told of a 1925 road trip with the soon-to-be famous Ansel Adams and his wealthy patron, Albert Bender.) In an afterword to her first book, she wrote that she also had bought houses, remodeled them, and sold them at a profit – with a tone of yearning, it seems to me, as if she missed this rather unusual profession. I find it rather endearing that today Bertha Damon has a page on Wikipedia, while the austere professor does not.

They bought 250 acres in New Hampshire as a summer home, probably after the Crash had savaged real estate prices, and very possibly in 1934, prompting the advertisement in the *Boston Sunday Post* that Dad had answered. They needed someone to care for the place when they returned to Providence in September, and a handyman during the summers.

The Damon Place was gorgeous, a vast tract of pine woods between Lake Winnipesaukee and Chestnut Cove Road, a dirt track that couldn't be navigated during Mud Season, and not always in the winter. Because there were no power lines, the trees grew as they would, so their branches met overhead, and driving the Cove Road was like going through a tunnel. We lived in the Gatehouse, with a lane leading down to the fine white Damon house overlooking the lake and an expanse of lawn. A boathouse and a pier extended out over the water, and a white-sand beach stretched off to the left.

I don't remember the Gatehouse, either, during that first year. Dad was a heavy smoker, he'd grown up in a damp climate, and he'd often slept rough during the rebellion and civil war. He came down with what was known as "the Irishman's disease" – tuberculosis. Perhaps, indeed, he'd brought it with him from Ireland. The standard treatment was bed rest and an induced collapse of the infected lung, so Dad was packed off to the state-run sanitarium in Glencliff in the White Mountains for a year, which would stretch into two and finally three.

Mom rented a camp in Alton, just behind Alton Central School, where Joe started first grade in 1935. I don't remember it at all, and after a few months we moved to a place a mile south of town called Dodier's Camp. There was a considerable French-Canadian population in Alton, whom the Yankees scorned. Dodier's Camp had a kitchen and an unfinished living room where we slept. Joe and I slept in the marital double bed, and Mom on a single bed that during the day served as our couch. There was a privy in the back yard, which had earlier been a gravel pit. Joe now had a considerable walk to school, while I ran wild. I remember once stubbing my toe and driving a splinter beneath the nail. Mom heated a needle over the flame of a match and prepared to dig the splinter out, but I screamed that she must let me fall asleep, which I promptly did, lying on the day bed. Joe and I both had that ability, which I wish I could recapture today.

I also remember visits from the County Nurse.

"Hello, Glasses!" she would say to me. "Where are you going with that boy?" So I was bespectacled even then, with a string around the back of my head to keep the glasses from falling off. And I remember one time that Mom was walking home from shopping in Alton and was given a lift in a neighbor's truck. She was mortified, because on the door of the truck was painted his profession: CESSPOOLS CLEANED. But it would have been rude to refuse.

In time, Mom rented another place, also a mile from school, before we finally settled down in the second-floor apartment in Marion Messier's House, on Wolfeboro Hill Road a bit closer to town. This may have been in preparation for Dad's release from Glencliff Sanitarium. For two years his left lung was collapsed by air pumped into the chest cavity, but the TB persisted, and finally the doctors cut out and removed two ribs, to collapse the lung altogether. We visited him at rare intervals, driven there by the County Nurse in her Model A roadster, which we boys enjoyed because we sat in the rumble seat with the air rushing past us.

For the last such visit, Mom hired Mister Buckley, the town plumber, to drive us to Glencliff, a rather long distance on the roads then in use. The sanitarium was a huge white building with a long front porch where a hundred or so patients could sit and smoke. They were all men, I think. They could buy medicinal cigarettes that were said to strengthen the lungs. Dad's room had earphones that brought in music from a central radio, which enthralled me during the visit, since we had no such entertainment at home.

The next day, Mom took us into the St. Joan of Arc rectory, to talk to the priest about something or other, and she told him about visiting Glencliff.

"Buckley?" he wondered of our driver. "That's a Catholic name." He was puzzled, I suppose, why he didn't know the family, if they ought to have been Catholics. I couldn't understand how a *name* could be connected to a religion.

By this time, President Roosevelt's New Deal had taken hold, and we were on Relief, as it was called. Mom had a small credit at the IGA Store downtown, and once a month the Relief truck stopped in front of Marion Messier's House and offloaded canned pork and bags of flour, rice, prunes, raisins, and the famous split peas that kept Americans from starving in those years. When I was a bit older and a pupil at Alton Central School, the boys' most scornful term of contempt was "*Pea soup!*" Not until I was a married man did I realize that thick pea soup with diced vegetables and a ham bone made a delicious meal.

Mom also applied for a pension from the government of Ireland when it acquired full independence from Britain in 1937. Ireland was a Free State no longer, and the heroes of the Black and Tan War could apply for a medal and in some cases a pension. When I researched Mom's medal a few years ago, I discovered that her application was supported by none other than Mick Walsh, her teenage sweetheart, parted from her by the civil war. She got the medal and the pension too, to Dad's great annoyance, for he got nothing. Mom claimed that he'd tried to blame his tuberculosis on his days on the run during the Tan War, but it may also have been his greater notoriety as a member of the Diehard Irish Republican Army. Women were equally active – Mom told stories of smuggling blasting caps inside her blouse, and of hiding Dan Crowley's revolver when the Black and Tan mercenaries searched the farmstead at Kilnahone, but nobody at that time held women responsible for a family's politics. Besides, she had Mick Walsh to vouch for her, and during the Tan War she'd been captain of the local *Cumman na mBan*, the League of Women, who acted as nurses and couriers for the IRA.

~ ~ ~ ~

Funnily enough, for a boy who grew up to be a university professor, Joe failed first grade – he was "kept back," in the phrase of the time. You must understand that the Fords were fairly exotic for Alton. We were "not from around here," at a time when people seldom left the town in which they were born, and if they did, they went to the city, not what the Depression-era *New Hampshire: A Guide to the Granite State* called "a little one-street settlement" like Alton. And we were Catholics, which put us in much the same league as the French Canadians. This wasn't as bad as being Jewish, but not entirely respectable either. I suspect that the code words "Churches nearby," which told Jewish travelers there was no room at the inn, was a hint to Catholics as well, that they ought to find a room in a more cosmopolitan town or, better yet, city.

And finally there was the extreme oddity that Mom and Dad had come from Ireland. They were foreigners! They had a curious way of speaking! I remember, a few years later, walking back to Marion Messier's House from Alton Central School, stopping to chat with Mister Drew, a neighbor, who was doing the prototypical labor of President Roosevelt's Works Projects Administration, digging ditches for forty dollars a month. (The authors of that New Hampshire guidebook also worked for the WPA.) Mister Drew rested on his shovel, wiped his brow, and asked: "What language do they speak, over there in Ireland?"

"They speak English."

"Well, that's all right, then," he said, and went back to work.

There were traces of the Irish in Joe and me as well, acquired from our parents. Probably that's what put Joe in the bad graces of his first grade teacher. I later realized that Joe spent much of his childhood in a state of terror. This may have been a hangover from a lonely year on Chestnut Cove Road, and then of course Dad was far away in a strange sort of hospital. Joe would hide if a stranger came to the house. And he got frantic if he realized that Mom had gone somewhere, and even, he later confessed, if she fell asleep and he couldn't hear her breathing. If Mom should disappear or die, we'd be alone in the world, and then what would become of us? I by contrast had no worries. Whatever happened, Joe would be there, and he'd sort it out.

For some reason – perhaps he missed a day or two of school, or perhaps he was just late on his first day – Joe was scolded by the teacher in front of the whole class, which was divided by an aisle into first and second grades. All those eyes! And there were bullies on the playground, who specialized in stomping the toes or cracking the knuckles of the little kids, and the teacher did nothing to stop it. What with one thing and another, Joe was so tense that he'd break the point of his pencil. The sharpener was at the front of the room, beside the door, and he didn't dare make the trek. In the end of all, he apparently did nothing for the entire year, and the teacher gave him a failing grade. As a result, Dad decreed from Glencliff that I couldn't enter first grade in the fall of 1937, but must wait a year, so as to remain two grades behind Joe in school. This was probably the nicest thing Dad ever did for me. Being a year older than most of my classmates was an advantage that would put me at the top of my class, then and afterward.

Meanwhile, Joe returned to school to find his nemesis gone, to be replaced by Miss Pittman, a young woman just out of Normal School. She quelled the playground bullies and actually sharpened Joe's pencil for him when he broke the point. In addition, he acquired a guardian, a third grader named Andrea Dore, whom he met walking to school on the day of his return, and who wiped a smudge from his face before he entered Alton Central School.

Speaking of terror, we both suffered from nighttime fears. There was the rampaging bear at the window that turned out to be a tree swaying in the wind, but above all, there were the Things under our bed. I don't know when the Things came to live with us, but it was fairly early, and they stayed for many years. Joe and I had many discussions about them, but we never mentioned them to Mom. We decided that they had no power to reach out and grab us, but when we knelt to say our prayers, we were careful to keep our knees from intruding into their space. The really scary thing was to wake up in the middle of the night and realize that my arm was hanging over the side of the bed, where a Thing could so easily grab it and pull me down to do whatever Things did to little boys.

I started first grade in the fall of 1938, walking down the hill from Marion Messier's House. I was a quick learner, and Miss Pittman assigned me to tutor Andrea Dore's kid brother in his numbers. We'd go out to the hall and sit at the bottom of the coat rack, cushioned by the rubbers and overshoes that were stowed there. The Dore boy was okay up to number twelve, but the teens were too much for him; he thought they should go three-ten, four-ten, five-ten, and so on. I hope I straightened him out.

I did have one weak point. Every Friday, the district music teacher came from Farmington to visit Alton Central School and go through the four elementary classrooms on the ground floor. For such lessons, the two grades in a room were combined, instead of one being put to its studies while the other did its recitations. I couldn't get the hang of the musical notes, and when we were supposed to recite them, I'd wait for a cue from the others. "We seem to have an echo in this room," the music teacher said.

And I did once get into trouble with Miss Pittman. She asked a question to which the answer clearly was "pen," a word that I promptly supplied.

"No," she said, and scanned the first-grade rows. (The second-graders had been set to coloring.) "Anyone else?"

My classmates had already decided that, if anyone knew the answer, it was Francis Ford, so the room was entirely silent. I was easily outraged then, as now, and I blurted: "But it *is!*"

"Francis," Miss Pittman scolded me, "the word is *pen*, not *pin*. You talk as if you'd just come over from the Old Sod!"

Just as Miss Pittman didn't approve of the way I pronounced words with "en" in them, I later took grief from Dad for my Yankee tricks with the language, with chimney rendered as "chimbly" and water as "wattah."

It was a very long walk from Alton Central School, through the village and up the hill to Marion Messier's House, or so it seemed to me. I especially remember coming home on a Thursday afternoon in September 1938, soon after I started first grade. The sky turned yellow. (Joe remembered it as yellowish-green.) That night the great New England Hurricane swept through, toppling a big oak that smashed our second-story porch and rendered it unusable for the rest of the time we were there.

One winter, a friend and I – his name, alas, I don't remember – came across a motorist unable to start his car. He gave us a quarter to go to the nearest fuel pump and buy a gallon of gasoline, which we did. I think we got a nickel in change. We'd have done better simply to pocket the twenty-five cents, because when we returned with a glass jug filled with bright-red gasoline, the car was gone! What would we do with the jug? In the end, we poured the gasoline into the snowbank and left the jug behind. That night I had a nightmare that Alton Central School burned down as a result of our criminality.

Another time, passing the brick town hall on the west side of Main Street – also called State Road 28 – we heard a voice calling to us. We obediently went over to see what was wanted. The voice came from a barred cellar window, and the man jailed there asked us to go to the IGA Store and buy him a box of Cracker Jack. ("Some historians consider it the first junk food," I am told by Wikipedia, to which I turned to confirm that it was mostly popcorn glazed with sweet molasses.) As a reward we could keep the prize inside. We obeyed that request, too, and I regret to say that I don't remember what bit of jimcrackery we earned for our trouble, or which of us got it, or again, what was the name of my apparent best friend.

Another memory of me and this pal: we set out to walk to Alton Bay, a mile up State Road 28, but along the railroad track that paralleled it. Our adventure ended when we reached the bridge across the Merrymeeting River, flowing north to Lake Winnipesaukee. We didn't dare cross over, for that would have required us to step from tie to tie, over the empty air and the evil black river. So we made our way out to the road and walked back toward Alton. We stopped at the little store owned by Howard Long, well known at Alton Central School to have a soft spot for little boys, who could always count on getting a piece of candy when they came to visit. He lived over the store, which was tucked against a hillside, so the glass-fronted shop was actually the basement. There was a hand-cranked gas pump out front, with a sign bearing the image of a flying red horse. We went inside to say hello. I was amazed by the quantity of candy bars beside the cash register (I had never tasted one of those) but not the open pack of Lucky Strike. I knew that Mister Drew sometimes bought his cigarettes one at a time, if all he had in his pocket was a penny.

Mister Long didn't disappoint us, and we each walked home sucking on a dissolving ball of colored sugar.

Dad did eventually come home from Glencliff, and the Damons hired him anew at forty dollars a month – what Mister Drew earned from the WPA – and no rent to pay. He had to buy a car, however. I think it was a Chevrolet. Perhaps he'd been soured by the Model T Ford, because I don't think he ever again bought a car or truck from his namesake manufacturer.

At some point in our young lives, we had acquired a dog, a mutt named Bozo. Sadly, he vanished while we were packing up for the move to the Damon Place. Joe and I walked up and down Wolfeboro Hill Road, calling, "Bozo! Bozo!" He didn't answer. Many years later, Mom told us that Dad had shot him with the little Colt automatic that he claimed to have smuggled into this country. (The serial number is correct for the Troubled Times in Ireland, but would Dad really have gambled his entry to *Tir na nÓg* for the sake of a souvenir pistol?) I suppose Professor Damon didn't like having animals around the place. Or perhaps Dad just wanted to start life anew, and without the encumbrance of a pet, especially one that reminded him that we'd survived for three years without him.

~ ~ ~ ~

The Gatehouse on Chestnut Cove Road would be marketed today as a Cape Cod cottage and priced, no doubt, at a substantial fraction of a million dollars. It was shingled, of course, and we were told that it was one hundred years old, which seemed impossibly ancient to me. The shingles however might well have been that old, for they were black with age. It was a small house, and more or less Cape Cod-like, with eaves coming down almost to the tops of the windows. There were four of these, two on each side of the front door, which was set into a vestibule or mud room for storing overcoats and overshoes, and to stop the wind from sweeping into the living room. But we never used that door.

There was a shed-roofed dormer above each double set of windows. The attic however was unfinished, so it became our storeroom and a three-season playhouse for Joe and me. Winters were cold in those years, and long, so we had no use for the attic then. In the fall, Dad built a low plank fence around the house and filled it with pine branches, which when covered with snow kept the cellar from freezing. The foundation was built from fieldstones with no mortar between them. When I travel in the backwoods of New Hampshire and Maine today, I still see homes with wind-proofed cellars, though with plastic sheeting instead of pine boughs.

I remember the Gatehouse winters better than the summers, because the summers were so easy; they just slipped by. We ran around barefoot for three months, except for shopping on Saturday evening and Mass on Sunday morning. The winters, though, were hard and seemed to last forever. As is still fairly common in New Hampshire, we entered the cottage through the kitchen door on the west side, facing the barn. There was a wood-fired Glenwood range in the kitchen, and a gray soapstone sink with a pump beside it. The water pipe came up from the cellar. When the nights were cold, the last thing Mom did before going to bed was lift the pump-handle, so the water ran back into the well, since the kitchen could get cold enough before morning that the water might freeze and burst the pipe.

The table was in the kitchen, too, its surface covered with patterned oilcloth Mom had thumb-tacked in place. That same piece of oilcloth traveled with us from house to house until I graduated from college.

Except for meals, we spent our time in the living room, which had a great fireplace that was our second source of heat. In the winter, indeed, we lived in front of the fire, even taking our dessert there, in the form of a slice of homemade white bread artfully impaled with a fork and toasted in front of the fire, then buttered and sprinkled with a tablespoon of mixed cinnamon and sugar. The tines had to enter the bread more or less vertically, so our knuckles got toasted, too, if we didn't regularly switch hands.

And we read in front of the fire, by the light of a kerosene lamp, though for me it was mostly the comics in the *Boston Sunday Post*, with Li'l Abner and Billy the Boy Artist my favorites at this time. There were also Tarzan, Dick Tracy, Flash Gordon, Buck Rogers, Terry and the Pirates, and eventually Superman, who appeared in the *Post* toward the end of our stay in Alton. The heroes were all male, you'll notice. Brenda Starr, Girl Reporter, wouldn't make her appearance for another year or two. At least twice I also read the stories in the magazine that came with the Sunday paper, one having to do with the great New England Hurricane, the other with the discovery of the Lost City of the Incas in the mountains of Peru.

Mom or Dad might play our push-button accordion, more of a concertina than the piano accordion usually seen in the United States. The notes were the same as a harmonica's: you squeezed the bellows for one note and pulled them out for another, a more physical sport than playing the larger instrument. I got no further on it than *Annie Laurie*, which I can still play on the harmonica. Years later I spotted a very similar accordion in the window of an antique store on the King's Road, as Sally and I walked from the Green Man in Putney to downtown London. I was sorely tempted, but the thought of bringing it home on a Boeing 707 persuaded us to let it go.

Mom and Dad were both masters on the accordion. Mom would play a plaintive Irish song, and accompany herself in a quiet, plain voice such as I later heard from my cousins in Ireland. Dad didn't sing. He favored lively jigs and reels, heavy on the chords and with much stamping of his left foot.

More rarely, they told stories of growing up in Ireland, and battling the Black and Tans who tried to put down the Irish rebellion – "the sweepings of English jails," as Dad said of them. Not till many years later did our parents speak of the civil war, when as Diehard Republicans they were on the losing side.

We had no other entertainment. In the long summer evenings we played outside, but in the winter we went early to bed. There were two bedrooms. Joe and I still slept in the double bed, with a rubber hot water bottle between us. Mom and Dad slept apart. This was doctor's orders, she later told me, for fear she'd catch TB. This was not entirely fanciful, for at school we were given a TB patch test every year, and I always tested positive. Miss Pittman made a great fuss the first time the patch — like a band-aid, as I remember it — was applied, and next morning I had a telltale rash beneath it. She called for the County Nurse, who calmed her with the explanation that I was exposed as a child and had antibodies to the disease.

In the morning, Dad got up first. He went to the kitchen and rebuilt the fire in the Glenwood Range, and he primed the pump with a pitcher of water so Mom could come out and put oatmeal to cook on top of the stove. When the kitchen was warm, Mom called us, and we jumped out of bed, scooped up our clothes, and ran to the kitchen to get dressed in front of the stove. In the dark of winter, this was done by the light of a kerosene lamp.

I don't think we had a chamber pot, for our bladders and bowels were young and elastic, but even at early middle age — he was not yet forty — Dad made use of a pee bottle he kept beneath his bed. We had no outhouse as such, though Missus Damon later added one when she remodeled the Gatehouse as a home for herself. Our privy was in the barn, a two-hole wooden bench with last season's copy of the Sears, Roebuck catalog hanging from a nail. I gleaned much information from those catalogs, about ladies' underwear, trusses for hernias, urinals for long-distance truckers, and other mysteries of adult life.

An old horse named Alfred lived in the barn, which otherwise contained a hay loft, a chicken roost, and some farm implements. We loved to pat Alfred's soft muzzle and feed him wisps of hay. Alas, one day he managed to get out of his stall, wander down the Cove Road, be hit by a car, and killed.

Every morning as we returned from the privy, Joe and I fetched the warm eggs from the chicken roost. In April, Mom ordered hatchlings from Sears; they were held for us in the Alton post office, which resonated with the cheeping from a dozen or so flat cardboard boxes. We took our box home and started the chicks into life in our kitchen. One became an outcast; the others pecked at his head, so we named him Baldy and made a pet of him. In today's terminology, he was our Rescue Chicken. I assume he was eventually eaten like the others.

There was a stone wall to the north of the Gatehouse property, which Joe and I used as our route to the privy, proud of our ability to balance on the fieldstones. Alas, one winter evening I fell off the wall as we were returning to the house, on the lee side where the snow was deep, and apparently I quite disappeared. Joe went into the house and settled down to read the *Sunday Post* magazine, not daring to confess he'd lost me en route. It was some time before Mom thought to ask, "Where's Francis?" Dad went out with a lantern to find me and carry me home – sobbing, I'm sure. Luckily for Joe, the whole thing seemed more funny than not, or anyhow the story was afterward told that way.

If the winters were hard on Chestnut Cove Road,

the barefoot summers were glorious. There were no other children on the road, so we had only each other to romp with, and the occasional visit to Captain Meyers who lived to the west of us, an old bachelor and Navy officer who came up from Boston each summer. He had a battery radio, and from it we learned some pop songs and advertising jingles: "*I'm Chiquita Banana, and I've come to say / Bananas have to ripen in a certain way / When they are flecked with brown and have a golden hue / Bananas taste the best and are the best for you!*" And there was Mister Woodman to the south, who while Dad was in Glencliff had done odd jobs for Missus Damon. She later featured him in a book, *A Sense of Humus*, about how "Samule" helped her restore the old farmstead's vegetable garden, where she grew her prize-winning roses. Mister Woodman's first name was actually Walter, and Dad claimed that the roses and most of the other events in the book were variations on his own years working for Missus Damon. (She gave fair warning in the book's disclaimer: "In general, any resemblance to relatives, hired men, or neighbors is purely coincidental. And just too bad.")

What impressed me most about Mister Woodman was his three Model T Ford cars. He kept one in service by cannibalizing the others. He showed Joe and me how he'd replaced a failed radiator by putting a water barrel on the roof and letting the engine coolant bubble through it. And Henry Ford's planetary transmission! The forward bands — there were three transmission bands, for low gear, high gear, and reverse, each with its own pedal — were so worn that when he came to a steep hill, he would turn the Model T around and back to the top. Or so Mister Woodman said.

We seldom went down to the lakeshore during the summer months, and we were instructed to reach up and catch a fringe of hair if we happened to meet Professor Damon, as Dad had done as a boy in Ireland when meeting the gentry. (A commoner was expected to doff his cap, but boys went bareheaded, so a tug of the forelock was the traditional substitute.) We would do this all through Dad's years as the caretaker of rich men's estates.

Missus Damon was less formidable. Indeed, I think she was fond of Dad, whom she addressed as "Ford," since surnaming the help was the custom in those years. Because he'd run the Tulligmor farm all through his young life — his father having died after a fall from a horse before Dad was born — he was extraordinarily handy around the place. He could do anything with his hands: carpentry, plumbing, electric wiring, engines. I spent one afternoon with him in the Damons' pump house while he overhauled the generator. It put out eight volts of power, which fed a bank of four huge batteries, which in turn fed thirty-two-volt current to light bulbs and other electrical gadgets, perhaps even the water pump, or perhaps it ran off the same engine that powered the generator. It ran twenty-four hours a day from June to September.

But in the fall! On warm weekends, free from school, we could go down to the beach and splash about in the lake, or walk out on the pier that ran past the boathouse. There we'd lie on our backs and watch the clouds speed past. That was a glorious way to spend an hour, when it seemed that the clouds were stationary and we were rushing past them.

Once in a rare while, some Irish friends would drive up from Boston on Sunday after early Mass. I particularly remember Nora Drinan and her longtime boyfriend Billy Conn. (Not to be confused with the Irish-American "white hope" from Pittsburgh who outboxed Joe Louis for twelve rounds in 1941, only to try for a knockout punch in the thirteenth, a grievous mistake when fighting the Brown Bomber.) We'd see the pair of them, Nora Drinan and Billy Conn, all through our boyhood, until she got tired of waiting for a proposal, and she went back to Ireland. Looking back at their sad romance, I wonder if Billy perhaps yearned to play for the other team. One Sunday, Joe and I went out with him in the red canoe from the Damons' boathouse. We were wearing our swimming trunks, and I lay down in the canoe to improve my tan. Billy reached over and pulled down my trunks. "Get a tan all over!" he joked. I now wonder about that, and I also wonder why I remember it so vividly, just as I remember how kindly Mister Long greeted my friend and me when we visited his store on our way home to Alton. Children notice things even when they don't understand them.

When I spent the Christmas long vacation in Ireland in 1954, I met Nora Drinan again. She'd made a good marriage with the village postman, so she got what she most wanted out of life, to be a wife if not a mother. Late marriages were common among the Irish then, since it was the only reliable birth control that the Church allowed.

Mister Martin's yellow school bus came along Chestnut Cove Road to collect Joe and me, except during Mud Season or after a major snowstorm. Then we had to walk out to the main road to meet the bus, almost a mile, which took us past Mister Woodman's House. This was State Road 28 from Wolfeboro to Alton, Farmington, and points south, so I am impressed to read in the WPA Guide that after passing "a superb view of Lake Winnipesaukee and its surrounding hills" – this being Roberts Cove, just north of the Damon Place – "the highway follows a curved, rolling, and winding road with extremely sharp curves, and cars should be driven with care." I was never aware of any danger, riding to and from school behind Mister Martin, or in the back seat with Joe when Mom and Dad went grocery shopping on Saturday night, or driving to Farmington for Mass on Sunday, the mission church of St. Joan of Arc having closed after the summer season. We even went to Midnight Mass at Christmas, wrapped in a blanket in the back seat, since the car heater couldn't keep up with the terrible cold. We'd be home in the wee hours, to drink a tiny glass of Port wine in front of the fireplace, then to open our presents, such as they were – clothes, invariably, that didn't excite us at all.

And one night Dad took us outside to see the Northern Lights, a rare spectacle in New Hampshire. They were entirely white, as I remember, rippling in great waves across the northern sky. I also recall that they were accompanied by a crinkly noise, though I suspect that I later added the sound track, just as I put red paint on the wagon in which I was towed down the sidewalk in Somerville.

One other thing I should say about the Damons: they supplied most of our reading material, or Missus Damon did. She gave us their back copies of *Life* magazine with its photographs, huge and informative. Thus we absorbed Adolf Hitler, speechifying from a balcony to an adoring crowd; and the Spanish Civil War with a cannon in the foreground, gradually demolishing a building across the street. (In college, I would discover that these were stills from a newsreel.) And the Polish boys and women digging trenches in Warsaw, as shelters against German bombs. And the brave Finns on skis, dressed in white, defending their country from the Russian invaders. Dad's voice trembled when he spoke of "little Finland," which alone of European countries had repaid its First World War debt to the United States – plus, of course, they were fighting the godless Russians.

There were books, too, many of them outtakes from Professor Damon's library: *White Shadows in the South Seas*, *Northwest Passage*, and *The Wind and the Rain*, which thrilled me when I was a bit older and realized something interesting happened between a boy and a girl in the orphanage. There were some Zane Grey westerns, too, which Dad would read on a Sunday afternoon, lying supine on the day bed. These books traveled with us from house to house, shelved in a hutch Dad had built from pine wood felled by the 1938 hurricane. I must have read each of them a dozen times, *Robbers Roost* and *Riders of the Purple Sage* included. Each time I learned a bit more from them. *White Shadows* had been annotated by Professor Damon, who beside a cannibal's explanation of his motives wrote in a fine hand, "The savage got the better of that argument!" As for *The Wind and the Rain*, it was written by the Englishman Thomas Burke, and subtitled *A Book of Confessions*. It was supposed to be the author's account of growing up poor in London, but by the time I was in high school I concluded it was as fictional as any of Zane Grey's westerns.

Dad also had a Modern Library copy of the *Oracles of Nostradamus*, which he consulted whenever he wanted to know how things would turn out – would Britain dare to go to war against Germany, for example, or would Wendell Wilkie manage to beat

President Roosevelt in 1940? Whatever the question, Dad could always find it prefigured in one of Nostradamus's prophecies, and he was not at all discouraged when it turned out wrong.

Joe on the left, Dad in the middle with Bozo, and I at right. This must be our house on Jaques Street in Somerville, just before we moved to Alton. A photo in those years was a special occasion, so we're wearing Sunday best.

2 – *The War*

IF YOU MUST LIVE THROUGH bad times, take my advice and do it while you're young! Not until years later did I realize that I'd grown up in the worst economy in American history. The Great Depression was everyday life for Joe and me, and likewise we thought it normal that so many Americans were out of work, and that everyone we knew was poor except the Damons and perhaps Mister Buckley the plumber. The WPA and the Relief truck and all the rest of the New Deal were part of our lives, at least until Dad was once again employed by the Damons. Nor did it occur to us then (as it has occurred to me more recently) that President Roosevelt's routine of tax, spend, and regulate not only failed to end the Depression but kept it going until the Second World War. In the end of all, Adolf Hitler and Joseph Stalin brought prosperity back to America, when Finland, France, Belgium, and especially Britain began to buy warplanes, tanks, and even rifles and bullets from American factories.

Until I sat down to write this chapter, I believed we left Alton because of the improving economy – that Dad had been offered a better salary by Mister Manning, a publisher of city directories who was developing an estate near Laconia, near the causeway leading out to Governor's Island on Lake Winnipesaukee. Money began to trickle into the American economy in 1939, when Germany and Russia started to divide Europe between them; and the trickle became a flood the following year, boosting American wages.

But perhaps that wasn't what happened. I find

that it wasn't until 1944 that the dollar regained the value it had lost during the Depression. Professor Damon died in May 1940, and no doubt he was ailing before that. So perhaps Missus Damon, seeing herself soon to be a widow, decided to sell the lakefront house and most of the land on Chestnut Cove, while refashioning our Gatehouse as a pretty summer home for herself. She wouldn't need a hired man in this new life of hers. That would explain why she and Dad parted as friends, and perhaps how we acquired those outtakes from Professor Damon's library.

However that may be, we moved to Gilford in the fall of 1939 – not, you'll notice, to Laconia, meaning that we'd have to change schools again when Dad finished building the caretaker's cottage that was Mister Manning's first task for him. All through our boyhood, Dad seldom thought to schedule these moves during the summer, which would have eased the transition from one school to the next. Joe was two years older, and still very shy; I think the moves affected him more than they did me.

Dad had rented a house on Dockham Shore Road, running along the south bank of Lake Winnipesaukee. I suppose it was a summer place at an attractive off-season rate. I don't remember much about it, except that it had a rocky shore and that, for the first time since leaving Marion Messier's House, we had electricity. Dad accordingly bought a second-hand washing machine. It was powered by an electric motor on a platform beneath the tub, from which it dribbled oil on the kitchen floor. Mom also got an electric iron, so her work was much reduced from what it had been at the Gatehouse, cleaning clothes by rubbing them against a zinc-plated scrub board, and smoothing them with a heavy flatiron heated atop the Glenwood range. That was good, because she had developed a goiter, the first of the many ailments she suffered while we were growing up. She had the goiter removed at Lakes Region Hospital in Laconia, and for years afterward she took iodine drops in a glass of water.

While Mom was in the hospital, Breda Sexton took the bus up from Boston to look after us and the house. Breda was a kind of a secular nun, who helped out at Irish families when the mother was absent or sick. We would see a lot of her over the years. She was a rough cook whose specialty was creamed salt codfish on boiled potatoes, and she banged the pots and pans a lot.

Dad also bought us a console radio that stood as high as my chin. Among other excitements, Joe and I could listen to a weekly serial called *I Love a Mystery*, and the mystery that autumn was "Blood on the Cat." Breda was astonished. "Blood on the cat!" she cried as she slammed a pot into the sink. "Glory be to God, blood on the cat!"

And we had an electric toaster, there being no fireplace at Dockham Shore Road. All this stuff was secondhand. The toaster was a marvel: there was a flip-down panel on each side that held a slice of bread; you flipped the panels up, waited a minute or two, then opened the panels again, whereupon the bread neatly flipped over, so you could toast the other side. This required great attention, for otherwise the bread would blacken and burn. We were by this time buying Wonder Bread at the store; it was fortified by vitamins and didn't require an hour of baking. Mom now limited herself to the occasional loaf of Irish bread, with citron and raisins, for a special occasion, and never in the summer.

We still had the old icebox. It was not at all

unusual in the 1940s for families to rely on blocks of ice for cooling perishables. And nobody, not even the Damons and the Mannings, had air conditioning. That's why they had their estates in New Hampshire!

Dad drove to the Manning Place each morning to work on what would become the caretaker's cottage, on the left side of the access road to Governor's Island. The Mannings lived on the right side of this road, with a beach somewhat smaller though just as white as the one at the Damon Place. Dad and a Gilford farmer named Clarence Dame, plus a carpenter who worked with them when they needed an extra hand, had the cottage framed and enclosed in a very few weeks.

Joe and I were playing in the sand one Saturday when the three men were shingling the roof. It was a hot afternoon, and Dad had his shirt off. The carpenter asked him about the great scar running down his back, and to our secret giggles Dad began to tell how he'd stormed a Lewis gun emplacement and been seared by a British bullet during the Irish rebellion. We knew of course that the scar was from Glencliff Sanitarium, when two of his ribs were taken out.

They had the house closed up before Thanksgiving, so they could build a wood fire in the stove and finish the interior during the winter. Dad and Clarence Dame did all the inside work, even the plumbing and the electric wiring.

While this was going on, Joe and I took the school bus from Dockham Shore Road to the modern brick school in Gilford village. As a treat for us new kids, the bus driver stopped by the side of the road and showed us where Howard Long from Alton had raped and murdered a ten-year-old boy. Indeed, it turned out that Mister Long had had quite a run as a molester and murderer, beginning in 1924 when he assaulted a girl who escaped by biting his face, her teeth marks later identifying him. He was eighteen at the time, so he was sentenced to what was optimistically known as a "reformatory," where bad boys were supposed to learn a trade and become useful citizens. He was soon paroled through the influence of his wealthy mother.

In 1930 he raped a boy, was caught, and was committed to a mental asylum. This time his mother gave the judge thirty thousand dollars, perhaps half a million dollars today, to set up and manage a trust fund for her son. It was an obvious bribe, which sufficed to get the young man – he was now twenty-five – released. The judge then bought him the convenience store on the road to Alton Bay.

In 1936, Mister Long molested and killed a boy in Dover, getting away entirely, and a year later he committed the Gilford rape and murder. It was at some point between these two killings that he treated me and my unremembered friend to a candy ball apiece. I suppose we were too young for him: each of his four known victims was ten years old.

He was arrested, tried, convicted, and hanged in July 1939. I was hugely impressed by this tale. New Hampshire had no executioner of its own, so a hangman was brought down from Canada. He studied the prisoner through the cell window, to calculate his weight and build, but he must have done a poor job of it. Though the rope was cut to his specification and stretched for weeks in the Belknap County Courthouse, it didn't snap the condemned man's neck, and Mister Long took seven minutes to die. He was given the last rites by a priest from Laconia, and his last words were, "God bless you, Father Donnelly, you've been good to me."

Laconia had two Catholic parishes, known

as the French Church and the Irish Church. I assume that Father Donnelley was our parish priest at St. Joseph's.

~ ~ ~ ~

Dad and Clarence Dame finished the caretaker's cottage in the spring of 1940, and we moved to the Manning Place. This put us in the Laconia school district, and we were assigned to the Mechanic Street School, five miles away in the outskirts of the city. So Joe and I attended three schools that year, Alton to Gilford to Laconia, he in fifth grade and I in third. I remember nothing about my teachers in any of them. But in September 1941 I started fourth grade at Mechanic Street, and that teacher I remember very well: Miss Agrafiotis. We soon fell in love.

I had a locket, acquired for twenty-five cents and the seal from a canister of Ovaltine, sponsors of *Captain Midnight* on the radio each weekday evening at five o'clock. (The lads at Mechanic Street were divided into two clans, those of us who listened to *Captain Midnight* and those who listened to *Jack Armstrong*, a less warlike program. For the girls, there was *Little Orphan Annie*.) The locket had a secret compartment, and in it I kept a lock of my baby hair that Mom had saved in an envelope marked with the date and place, probably Somerville, Massachusetts. It was quite blond. In a private moment I showed this treasure to Miss Agrafiotis, and she coaxed me for half of it. I wonder if she would be fired for that today?

What Missus Damon was to roses, Miss Agrafiotis was to me, and my schoolwork blossomed under her care. She asked the principal to give me an IQ test, which came back with a score of 132. This thrilled us both, though I didn't have a clue about its significance. It was enough for me that Miss

Agrafiotis was pleased.

Mechanic Street served a hot lunch priced at ten cents. Miss Agrafiotis arranged that I got my meal coupons without cost, while Joe in sixth grade had to pay a nickel for his.

On November 2 that year, I turned ten years old – just the age to whet the interest of Howard Long, though perhaps my metal-framed spectacles would have turned him off. Joe was the handsome lad, with Dad's black hair and square jaw. I had a triangular face like Mom's, though with a bump on my nose like Dad's, a bequest of the Norman invasion, and of the Roman Legions that preceded it.

We now owned a black pickup truck, so when we went to the First National store for Saturday-night shopping, or to St. Joseph's for Sunday Mass, Joe and I rode in back. This was quite exciting, though we needed a blanket around us when the weather grew colder. One time only, I got to ride in the cab with Dad. He was going to the rectory to talk to the priest – Father Donnelly, I suppose! – and for some reason took me along. He needed a Mass said for the repose of the soul of somebody in Ireland, perhaps his Uncle Jack at Tulligmor. After settling the details, he asked the priest, "And what's the customary donation, Father?" I was much impressed by the delicacy of this. In a secular transaction, Dad would have asked, "And what's the damage?" with a guffaw. Weren't we all friends together?

On the way home from the city, Dad stopped by the side of the road. We got out, leaned against the warm engine compartment, and looked at the stars, which were bright in the sky in those years of fewer people and less money. Dad pointed out some constellations and identified them for me. Again, I was impressed by his wisdom, and I treasured that night.

I think it was the only time in my boyhood that I felt close to my father, that I felt I loved him and that perhaps he loved me. He was otherwise, starting from the day he came back from Glencliff, an intruder in the house, more feared than loved.

Or perhaps I should say *respected.* I've earlier mentioned how handy he was. Nor was this just farm work and rough carpentry. Mister Manning, or more likely Missus Manning, wanted an arched doorway between the dining room and the Great Room, as they called it, their combination library and parlor. I was in the house while Dad drew out the line on a piece of pine three feet long and two feet wide, which he had planed flat by hand. (No machine could plane a board that wide, or anyhow none in a New Hampshire mill.) Dad tacked two nails into the bottom of this board, tied a loose string between them, and used the string to restrain a flat carpenter's pencil while he drew an ellipse on the board. This required much trial and error, positioning the nails and adjusting the length of the string to get a curve that satisfied him.

It was not until I was a sophomore in high school that I understood what he had done. The nails were the focal points of an ellipsis, and the string enforced the rule that all points on the curve must be equidistant from these focal points. Dad had figured it out by himself, though his education was limited to the six years provided by the British colonial government. Joe, who was a bit of a snob, would later call this "Dad's peasant wisdom."

Not long after this, on a reasonably warm Sunday afternoon in December, he packed us all into the truck and drove to Alton to visit Missus Damon. I was astonished by the changes. Electric power lines now ran past Captain Meyers's house, the trees had been cut back, and our Gatehouse was outfitted with electric lights, electric refrigerator, running water in the kitchen, and a tall grandfather's clock in the living room. The dormers were gone from the attic. No doubt there was a bathroom, too, though I didn't see it.

While the sun was out, Missus Damon gave us a tour of her new outhouse, a splendid structure beneath the apple tree that had once provided us with fresh fruit in the summer and jars of applesauce in the winter. She was especially proud of the sign on the door, which played off a pop song of the day: *"Don't s—it under the apple tree with anyone else but me."* Joe and I giggled at the expurgated letter *h*, Dad gave his big guffaw, and Mom looked away.

Back in the living room, Missus Damon asked Dad's advice about the grandfather's clock, whose pendulum often stopped swinging on Thursday, instead of lasting the week as it should have done. Dad suggested a drop of sewing-machine oil a couple times a month. "The first and the fifteenth!" she said, and wrote it on a small card that she tucked into the window frame protecting the clock-face. To this day, I use Missus Damon's memory trick to maintain the engine on our backup generator, running it for ten minutes on the first and fifteenth day of every month. (I am dubious, however, about Dad's advice to her. There's a grandfather's clock in our hallway, which came to me along with Sally Wife, and we've never insulted it with oil.)

Finally, Missus Damon presented Dad with a copy of her book, *Grandma Called It Carnal*, telling how she and her sister were brought up by their austere grandmother. I trust there was more truth in her memoir than in Thomas Burke's stories of Limehouse and the orphanage. In any event, it had spent months on the best-seller list when it was published in 1938.

I read this book, too, every year until I went away to college, and I especially remember the story of the spinster who came to visit, and for whom Grandma provided a hot-water bottle to warm the sheets. The stopper fell out overnight, scalding the woman, who in the morning confessed that for the first time she understood St. Paul's warning that "It is better to marry than to burn!" I remembered that line from reading Missus Damon's book, and since I started college in 1950 and left it and much else behind, that's more than seventy years ago. After I wrote the first draft of this chapter, I acquired a secondhand copy of *Grandma,* to make sure I had the wording right, and I'm awed at how well it's written, both the funny parts and the sad. I am impressed too that Simon and Schuster published a memoir that requires a familiarity with *The Odyssey* for its fullest enjoyment, and despite its sly erudition became a best-seller. Somehow I don't think that would happen today.

On the flyleaf, Missus Damon wrote *To Pat Ford and the boys*, which of course hurt Mom's feelings. It's true, I suppose, that the two conducted their conversation as if Mom weren't in the room. But in that case, Missus Damon should have kept Joe and me off the inscription as well.

It was near sunset by now, and time to go home. Joe and I climbed into the back of the truck and wrapped ourselves in our blanket for the long drive along the shore of Lake Winnipesaukee. When we turned into the road to Governor's Island – it's now called Summit Avenue, though I'm sure it didn't have such a grand name in 1941 – Dad was hailed by Mister Manning's secretary, Miss Duckworth, who was out on the road with a flashlight. He stopped the truck and leaned out to say good evening. "The Japanese bombed Pearl Harbor today," she told him.

"The yellow devils!" Dad said. "And where's Pearl Harbor, for the love of God?"

"In Hawaii."

This left me no wiser, and I suspect the same was true of Joe, though he was in sixth grade by this time. But the grownups took it seriously, and we were suitably big-eyed when we went into the caretaker's cottage. Dad stoked the wood stove in the living room and turned on the console radio and searched for information about Pearl Harbor. If there was any, I don't remember it, and we were packed off to bed after a light supper. On Sundays our heavy meal was at noon, a pot roast or a broiler hen or ham or roast pork, the leftovers from which would get us through Thursday night. Friday dinner was typically creamed codfish on boiled potatoes (though more delicately done than Breda Sexton's), and on Saturday we'd have baked beans on toast before taking a sponge bath in the kitchen, to get ready for Sunday again.

Oh yes, the sponge bath! Mom heated a kettle of water on the Glenwood range or, in warm weather, on a two-burner kerosene cooker that sat on top of the range. This she poured into the enamel washbasin, which was white with black spots wherever it had banged against something, probably in Breda Sexton's hands. We stripped in turn and sat on a four-legged stool, one corner of which I had cut off in an early attempt at carpentry, and we washed ourselves with a wet facecloth. I went second, since I was the younger. I suppose Dad and Mom did something similar after we went to bed.

~ ~ ~ ~

It wasn't just Mom who visited Lakes Region Hospital that year. I kept getting sore throats, despite the tablespoon of cod liver oil that slithered down our throats every winter morning. The wisdom of the 1940s held that the cure was to have my tonsils taken out, so I was in the hospital for two or three days, in the children's ward.

And Dad has his first full-blown asthma attack, the consequence of damaged lungs and his pack-a-day habit of Camel cigarettes. ("I'd walk a mile for a Camel!" the radio assured him every evening.) He coughed year around, a rubbery explosion that sometimes turned into a hack, especially with his first cigarette of the morning. "You shouldn't smoke so much," Mom told him at breakfast one time.

Though we drank tea the rest of the day, for breakfast it was Nescafe powdered coffee, sweetened with sugar and lightened with a dollop of Evangeline evaporated milk. Dad enjoyed his first Camel of the day with a cup of this mixture. "It helps bring up the phlegm," he said of his morning cough. Which it did, of course, though without the cigarette there would have been no phlegm.

During the summer, he got wheezing spells. "*Oh God!*" he'd say as he gasped for air, an "*Oh God!*" with every breath. One time at the caretaker's cottage, gasping was not enough, and Mom ran to the Manning house and asked Miss Duckworth to call an ambulance. Perhaps it was a busy day, or perhaps it was a problem with the new system of rationing tires and gasoline, but what showed up at our door was a hearse, not an ambulance. At the hospital, Dad was given oxygen and a shot of adrenaline to speed his heart rate and thus improve his breathing, and in a day or two he returned home – I don't know how, since Mom couldn't drive.

Ever after, Dad's asthma attacks and hospitalizations became a feature of our summers, and they kept us poor. Not only were they expensive, but his employers of course didn't pay him when he didn't work. Eventually he learned to avoid the ambulance rides by injecting himself with adrenaline – today called epinephrine and used to rescue people allergic to bee stings and the like – when an asthma attack came on. As we grew older, Joe and I were drafted into this routine, for Dad shook so badly he couldn't manage the hypodermic syringe. So Joe or I swabbed his upper left forearm with a cotton ball soaked in alcohol, located the vein, slid the needle in, and depressed the plunger until the syringe was empty.

After his stay at Lakes Region Hospital, he took a battery of tests to determine the cause of his asthma. It turned out that he was allergic to pretty much *everything* – pollen, dust, mold, even eggs.

~ ~ ~ ~

I enjoyed the War. It was quite a step up from the Depression, and it gave us boys an infinite amount of games to play, both in the schoolyard at Mechanic Street – "Bang, bang, lie down, you're dead!" – and at home, deploying toy soldiers behind a defensive wall of dried-out teabags. It was Red Rose tea from Canada, Mom's favorite brand because it tasted like the tea sold in Ireland. Similarly, the Fords bought Canadian bacon, thickly sliced and less fatty than the American version.

Miss Agrafiotis, however, took the War very seriously. Perhaps she had a brother likely to be conscripted – "drafted," as Americans termed it – or even her father. Though she seemed very adult to me, I suspect she was about twenty in 1941, perhaps just out of the two-year Keene or Plymouth Normal School that trained schoolteachers at the time. Years later, we met again at a Young Republican dinner, when I was seated next to her, or just across the table. She looked at my name tag and asked, "Did you ever know a *Francis* Ford?" So Miss Agrafiotis was a Young Republican, too, and the maximum age was thirty-five. This encounter seemed very ordinary at the time, but today I'm astonished that she could spot the fourth-grader in the college boy that I had become.

Anyhow, at Mechanic Street School she led us in the Pledge of Allegiance with great fervor, with stress on occasional words – "*one* nation, *indivisible*, with liberty and justice for *all*" – as if it was a hymn of joy. (The bit about Under God came much later.) There was a considerable Greek community in New Hampshire's largest city, where Miss Agrafiotis came from, and it was important for immigrants in those years to be regarded as Americans rather than Irish or Greek or Italian. Of course our names gave us away, as did our religion. Following the Pledge, she led us in reciting the Lord's Prayer. The version used in schools was the Protestant prayer, with "debts" replacing the Catholic "trespasses," and an extra phrase about the Power and the Glory that we Irish boys omitted. I don't know what Miss Agrafiotis thought about this. If she went to Sunday services, it was probably to the Orthodox church above a restaurant on Main Street in Laconia, and she would have prayed in Greek. So perhaps she didn't even know about the Catholic-Protestant schism. I should have asked her about that, when we met again as Young Republicans!

In the spring of 1942, she collected ten cents from each of us, and in exchange gave us a red Minuteman stamp to paste into our booklets. This ceremony was repeated in the schools we attended thereafter, with the idea that, when the booklet was entirely filled, we'd exchange it for a War Bond worth $25 when it matured ten years later. But what with sick days and snow days and such, Joe and I never reached the $18.75 purchase price, so instead of a bond we eventually took the cash and added it to the account where we had saved our summertime earnings. It helped pay my way through the University of New Hampshire, hence to our reunion as Young Republicans.

~ ~ ~ ~

Sadly, I didn't finish that enchanted year with Miss Agrafiotis. Dad apparently tired of Mister Manning and moved us away from the lake that had smiled beside most of my childhood. (We were told that *Winnipesaukee* meant "Smile of the Great Spirit," though I suspect that was somebody's pretty invention.) Our new home was in Rochester, where we lived in another caretaker's cottage, this one belonging to Mister Champlin, who owned a box factory in the city, and who'd bought up a several farms along Rochester Hill Road. This is now Route 108, though in 1942 it was State Road 16, a designation that has since been shifted to the Spaulding Turnpike that bypasses the town altogether.

Driving along Rochester Hill Road, the Champlin Place was on the right side of the road, while on the left was an airstrip built by Mister Champlin's son – Bill, I think his name was – who instead of volunteering for service in the War, headed up a Civil Air Patrol squadron on his father's land. This was not just a rich man's dodge, though I suppose it also served that purpose. The CAP flew coastal patrols throughout the War, looking for German submarines; ninety planes were lost in these missions, and sixty pilots killed. Many years later, I took my first flying lessons at Skyhaven Airport, as Bill Champlin named it after the War, and it became a regular stop on my flights around Lake Winnipesaukee. From there I'd fly up to Alton Bay, then to Wolfeboro airport for a quick landing and takeoff, do the same at the Laconia municipal airport in Gilford, then to my home field, the lovely grass airstrip at North Hampton, thus circling over most of my boyhood and all but two of the schools that Joe and I had attended.

The caretaker's cottage was a small, square building just past the Civil Air Patrol runway, but on the right side of the road. Beyond it was a working farm whose former owner, now tenant, managed the farm operations on the Champlin Place, while Dad was took care of the family's buildings and grounds.

While we lived on Rochester Hill, Dad was obliged to register as an alien, receive an identity card, and carry it with him for "the duration," a term that became part of our wartime vocabulary. Joe and I were much amused by his photo on the alien registration card, with Dad glowering at the camera and looking for all the world like a German saboteur, not to be trusted near a quasi-military facility like young Bill Champlin's airfield.

We rode the school bus to a two-story brick building rather like the one on Mechanic Street, except that in Rochester the neighborhood schools only went as far as the sixth grade. So in September 1942, Joe transferred to the new and splendid Spaulding High School, which in those years housed the seventh and eighth grades as well. As the bus took us down Rochester Hill toward the little city, there was an interesting house, long unpainted, its front porch heaped with oak leaves. It was occupied by a madwoman who sometimes appeared on the porch, her hair wild and white, wearing a cotton house-dress even in the coldest weather. The boys on the bus assured us that she sometimes appeared naked on the porch, but we never witnessed this phenomenon, though we were always on the lookout for it.

The caretaker's cottage was only four miles from town, so we could have walked it, but we never did. So as before, the school bus excepted, we visited town only on Saturday night and Sunday morning, and once or twice to the movies. I saw Walt Disney's *Dumbo* while we lived in Rochester; the flying elephant gave me an awful headache. And Joe and I acquired cards at the handsome public library on South Main Street, a gift from Andrew Carnegie, who had scattered 2,500 libraries around the world in the years before and after the turn of the twentieth century. Rochester's gift equates to about $620,000 today – multiply that by 2,500! – so I do not at all wish for punitive taxes on the likes of Mister Carnegie. Thanks to him, Joe and I widened our literary horizons beyond the *Boston Sunday Post*, Zane Grey, and *The Wind and the Rain*. We also bought a sixtynine-cent hardcover from Woolworth's, when Dad gave us each a dollar to spend on ourselves at Christmas, as we had also done at Laconia. Most of these books were written by a man named A. Hyatt Verrill, with titles like *The Boy's Book of Buccaneers* and *The Incas' Treasure Cove*. Though Professor Verrill's colleagues criticized his books for their "outrageous fabrications," I treasured them, and I still think that the most important thing about a young person's literature is that it be engrossing enough to convince him or her that reading is a worthy endeavor. From Rochester forward, I was was always surprised to visit a school-mate's house and see no bookshelf in the living room. I still enjoy trash, if it's well written, by the likes of Donna Leon, Michael Connelley, Mick Herron, or Nelson DeMille.

~ ~ ~ ~

We were off again in the fall of 1942! This time, Dad put our furniture onto a moving van and loaded us into his latest vehicle, a 1934 Chevrolet sedan with a shade that could be rolled down to cover the rear window, which Joe and I enjoyed deploying. We drove over the General Sullivan Bridge, where Dad handed fifteen cents to the toll-keeper, and entered the fantastically modern U.S. Route 1, called the Boston Post Road. It boasted three lanes of traffic, with the middle one reserved for passing, and when we came to a hill sufficient to block Dad's view of the road ahead, there was a long overhead mirror that somehow showed if another car was in the passing lane. I had never seen anything so fabulous as this, and my excitement peaked at the state line. Though I was born in Massachusetts, and had spent the first two and a half years of my life there, I had no memory of the place.

We didn't go into Boston, though, but turned west to Concord, home of the brave Minuteman celebrated on our War Savings Stamps. Indeed, we turned right onto Monument Street, where the actual Minuteman statue was located – it was gray, though, instead of red like the engraving on the ten-cent stamp – and a concrete replica of the "rude bridge that arched the flood" in 1775.

It turned out that Mister Laughlin preferred to call Monument Street by the more venerable name of Old River Road. He owned a swath of land between it and the west bank of the Concord River. A long paved driveway led to a Georgian brick mansion with a kitchen wing on one side and on the other a bedroom suite for the Laughlins. That's an Irish name, pronounced *lock*-lin, and the family wealth came from Jones & Laughlin Steel Co. in Pittsburgh. Joe and I were limited to the kitchen wing, and from there, if the coast was clear, we could go upstairs, where there was a nursery, the guest rooms, and a library with shelves so high that the top ones were reached by a rolling ladder. We were allowed to borrow, one volume at a time, an encyclopedia called the *Book of Knowledge,* which had educated and entertained Henry Laughlin Junior and his sister as they were growing up. In 1943 young Henry was an Army Air Forces pilot and probably stationed overseas, since he never visited his parents while we lived in Concord. His sister was married to an Englishman, a pilot in the Royal Air Force, who did visit one time.

After the brick mansion, the driveway curved past the stable, with espalier apple trees pinned to its white clapboards. There were three stalls and three horses, a mare called Glenaree, a big gelding Dad called Charlie, and a fine young colt named Gunfire, since he was the grandson of Man O'War. We called him Gunny, and Glen was his mother. The hope had been to put Gunny to stud, but he had some defect, and in time he was neutered.

The asphalt drive gave way to dirt as it entered the woods and led to our house, a pretty Cape Cod cottage, with a *telephone*! Dad was proud of how he finessed that luxury. Mister Laughlin asked him if we wanted to keep the phone, and Dad replied, "Well, if it would be useful for you to call *me*. . . ." What could Mister Laughlin do then, but pay the monthly bill from New England Telephone? The Laughlins' number was Concord 22, but I don't remember ours. It was a private line, too, and not the two-party line common in the 1940s.

Dad drove us to Concord and registered us at Peter Bulkeley School. It was a big, handsome brick building with grades one through four on the ground floor, five through eight above, which meant that Joe must revert to elementary school from his elevated status at Spaulding High. The principal asked Dad whether I should be placed in 5A or 5B. Being Irish, Dad knew better than to praise his son, which in the Old Country was known to attract the interest of the fairies, who might then swap a sickly one of their own for the more promising human youngster. So, when asked whether I was a good boy, he'd laugh and say "In patches!" And an Irishwoman might say of Joe or me, "Ah, he's a fine lad, God bless him!" with the blessing equally likely to keep the fairies away.

Whatever Dad told the principal about my schoolwork, I wound up in the slow class, as opposed to the fast learners in 5A. I was soon sent across the hall, however. The teacher had us reading a story about a Mexican lad named José, whose name I pronounced more or less correctly, though I have no idea where that knowledge came from. The teacher corrected me; she wanted it sounded as *Josie*. I told her she was wrong, and on Monday the principal intercepted me and told me to report to 5A.

The most of my education, as always, was picked up on the playground. There were a lot of Norwegian and Italian families in Concord, as well as the Yankees of an earlier time. One of the latter was Peter Pirnie, whom I remember particularly because in 1957 I exited the Post Exchange at Coligny Caserne in Orléans, south of Paris, and met him, the former sad sack now tricked out as a first lieutenant, and instead of saluting I laughed in his face. Lieutenant Pirnie was good enough not to report me. As for the

Italians, they were "truck farmers," growing vegetables for the market in the North End of Boston. One family was *so* Italian that they named their sons Primo, Secondo, and Tercero. Primo was in Joe's class and Secondo in mine. But here's the wonder of being young: though we regarded Germans, Italians, and Japanese as monsters to be shot on sight, it never occurred to us that Secondo was anything but a good American like the rest of us. I remember once when he was being trounced on the playground, I did a swan dive such as I'd seen in the movies and rolled his attacker away, then helped him up and dusted him off to general approval.

My buddy, though, was Gordon Olson, whom his family called Asa, and who lived on a road running parallel to Monument Street. We cemented our friendship riding together on the school bus each weekday morning and afternoon. Thanks to Dad's having outwitted Mister Laughlin, we also chatted on the telephone. As with Peter Pirnie, we would meet again in France, in Gordon's case at the youth hostel in Paris. He was living behind the hostel, whose owner allowed him to pitch a tent there while he waited for a new passport from the American Embassy, Gordon having lost his to a pickpocket on the Metro.

~ ~ ~ ~

Mister Laughlin was not only rich but clever. Knowing that the War would be long, that inevitably it would involve us, and that it would bring shortages of all kinds, he'd bought two Lincoln Continental convertibles in 1941, one for himself and the other for Missus Laughlin. Not until 1946 would automobiles again be manufactured for civilian use, and they were retreads of the 1941 model year. To feed those two twelve-cylinder engines, Mister Laughlin turned his acres along Old River Road into a truck farm such as the Italians operated elsewhere in Concord. While Dad could buy four gallons of gasoline each week for the "A" sticker on our 1934 Chevy, the Laughlins as farmers each got a "C" sticker, good for eight gallons, which must have annoyed the Italians when they saw it on the windshield of the Lincoln Continental, parked at the Boston & Maine railroad station in town. And the orange Allis Chalmers tractor got an "R" sticker with an unlimited supply, though how this was monitored, I have no idea.

Two Norwegians, father and son, lived nearby and also worked at the Laughlin Place. There was a bit of tension between Dad and the "Squareheads," as he called them, for they'd worked on the place for years while he as foreman made the decisions. In addition to the three grownups, the Depression-era Civilian Conservation Corps barrack in Concord now housed high-school kids from Boston, who worked during the summer vacation for the local farmers, and they too helped with the planting, weeding, and harvesting at the Laughlin Place. So did Joe and I. We started at twenty cents an hour in the summer of 1943, with a nickel raise when we demonstrated we could keep up with the Boston lads. In 1944 we earned thirty cents an hour, and in 1945, the last summer of the War, a near-adult wage of thirty-five cents, the equivalent of five dollars today.

I especially remember haying in the dog days of August. The machinery was old and meant to be pulled by a horse, with the operator sitting on a steel seat shaped for his bottom and pierced so the rain would drain away. From this throne he handled the reins and deployed a sidebar cutter to bring down the hay, later the "tedder" that tossed hay to speed its drying, and finally a rake to put it in windrows before its journey to the barn. With Dad driving the orange Allis Chalmers tractor, I was usually the one who rode behind and operated the lever that raised and lowered the implements, since this didn't require much stature or strength. (The sidebar cutter was powered through gears that were turned by the wheels.) And as the smallest in the crew, I was also the one who stood on top of the wagon as it was loaded, catching the hay on the tines of my pitchfork as it was passed up to me by the taller boys and men on the ground. Then I sat down for the ride to the barn, where I passed the hay up to the loft, to be caught in turn by the others of the crew.

God, that was hot and dusty work! Dad believed that nothing cut the thirst like tepid tea from a Seagram's Seven bottle, so that's how the Fords did it. The Squareheads and the Boston lads made do with water from the tap. As for the dust, it collected in my hair and mixed with my sweat to become a solid. When I got a haircut in September, instead of sideburns I had a layer of hayseed at my temples, which Mom had to scrub off before I went to school.

I also raised rabbits, a profession I learned from the *Book of Knowledge*. I sold the offspring as breeding pairs to my schoolmates who also wanted to help win the War, and as meat to the butcher downtown. He worked in the cellar. I squatted by the trapdoor and handed the rabbits down; they were supposed to be silent, but they could squeal like a pig when they saw where they were going.

What with one thing and another, Joe and I banked so much money that when we asked Dad for the customary dollar before Christmas, he pointed out that we'd saved more than he had that year, so we should look to ourselves for Christmas money.

Likewise, we had to pay for the haircut if we wanted one at the barber shop, and to supply the nickel for an ice cream cone on Saturday evening, and a dime if we wanted to attend the Saturday-afternoon double feature at the movie hall downtown, which we did every couple of months. The bill included a western, a war film, and a serial adventure that was a mystery to Joe and me because we hadn't seen the previous cliffhanger and wouldn't see the one that followed.

When not otherwise occupied, we collected newspapers, tin cans, balls of tinfoil from Dad's cigarette packs, and milkweed floss to be made into life preservers for the U.S. Navy.

~ ~ ~ ~

My greatest hope of course was to become a fighter pilot, like the Laughlins' Royal Air Force son-in-law. He visited Old River Road one time, and when he telephoned from the B&M station to announce his arrival, he asked the operator for "Concord double-two," which caused great hilarity when the news spread around town. The Laughlin daughter must also have been in residence, because the baby boy was. He lived in the nursery on the second floor, with a monitor connected to the kitchen and to the servants' quarters on the third floor. When he cried, it was the cook or a maid who settled him down.

With the glamorous and well-tailored Royal Air Force pilot as my model, I spent a dollar on a cardboard cockpit to mount on the desk in Joe's and my bedroom, with a broomstick handle for a joy stick, with which I shot down hordes of German Messerschmitts and Japanese Zeros.

I also owned a pack of aircraft recognition cards. We lived not far from Bedford Army Air Field, and when a bomber roared overhead, I would run out to see whether it was a B-25 Mitchell or perhaps a

Heinkel He-111 bent on bombing downtown Concord. (In truth, I didn't need the cards, because I could recognize the handsome throb of the Mitchell's Wright Cyclone engines before I saw its twin tail and high wings.) One time, indeed, we actually visited the airfield, when General George Patton made an appearance with his famous pearl-handled pistols at his side. I don't know who drove us to Bedford. It wouldn't have been Dad, whose sympathies tended to lay with the Germans, who after all had sent rifles to the Irish rebels before the Easter Rising of 1916.

Well, all this patriotic activity of mine must have helped, because by the time I started seventh grade in September 1944, it was pretty clear that we were winning the war, with a bit of help from the British and the Russians. Not that I ever doubted we would! It actually came as quite a surprise to me when, much later, I realized that the Allies had taken an awful beating on every front for the first few years, and that the War didn't really turn in our favor until we cleared the Germans out of North Africa and the Japanese out of Guadalcanal, at the start of 1943. Somehow the really bad news never made it into the *Boston Record*, which by this time was Dad's favorite newspaper.

As seventh-graders at Peter Bulkeley School, we thought of ourselves as very grown up. We were in Junior High, and we moved between the four classrooms of seventh and eighth grade to get the benefit of the men who taught math and science. Joe by this time was a freshman in high school, so I saw nothing of him during the school day, except when we were on the bus, and there we sat apart. Sally and I have granddaughters in college, and I am astonished at how closely they follow one another's lives, one in New Hampshire, the other in Connecticut. They even do Tabata together, a brutal form of exercise, on a Zoom call across the miles. Joe and I were never like that. I've no idea what classes he took at Concord High, and I doubt he knew or cared about mine.

As a seventh-grader, too, I realized that girls weren't just competition for the role of teacher's pet. So it was at Peter Bulkeley School that I developed a habit that plagued me until I was a senior in college, falling madly in love with a girl I didn't dare approach, like Charlie Brown with The Red Haired Girl. I don't remember much about my seventh-grade Beatrice except that her family was rich enough to own a swimming pool, for in the summer of 1945 she took flight off the diving board and broke her neck, and my heart with it.

I did however manage an apprenticeship in romance. This was with a dark-haired sixth-grader who lived nearby, and who owned a Shetland pony. Unlike my Beatrice, she had no breasts that I could see, so she wasn't nearly as frightening. We had a small gang, along with Georgie Hodgedon and Winthrop Puffer who lived a bit farther up the road. Isn't it typical that I remember the boys' names but not the girls'? Anyhow, we all learned to dog-paddle one summer, splashing about in a pond on the Laughlin Place, and to ride that patient Shetland. (I don't remember his name, either.) This girl – well, let's call her Maryanne – had a tree-house, so we could clamber up and play house. She was the mother, of course, and as the oldest I was father. Georgie and Winthrop therefore were left to be the kids; Winthrop was a seventh-grader, like me, but he was a year younger, thanks to Dad's determination to keep me two grades behind Joe in school.

The tree-house, and our games in it, gave me a chance to kiss Maryanne, which I did one quiet evening, pretending I had just come home from work. And she kissed me back! These were cheek-kisses, of course, but we did hug one another. Nothing was said about it, but on the very next occasion when we were alone in our make-believe house, we kissed for real. That is to say, I kissed her on the lips, and Maryanne kissed me back, as if we were politely taking turns, and then went on about our household chores, high in a horse-chestnut tree behind the barn where the Shetland pony spent his nights.

Dad holds Glenaree, who has her ears back as usual. Mom holds Charlie the gelding, and Joe is being very cautious with Gunfire the colt. I took the photo, probably in 1943, before in secret I began to ride Gunny in circles around his stall. Almost certainly it's a Sunday, and we've just come from Mass.

3 – *The City*

WE LEFT CONCORD IN 1945, a year like no other. President Roosevelt died in April, an event so shattering that at Peter Bulkeley School we were called out to the playground as if to a fire drill, and the principal told us that the man who had run the nation for most or all our lives was gone. The janitor lowered the flag to half staff, the girls cried, and we were sent home for the rest of the day. Gordon Olson and I spent much of it on the phone, pondering how Harry Truman could possibly run the country and win the War.

But somehow he managed. In May, Germany surrendered, an event almost as astonishing as the President's death, and in August we dropped Little Boy on Hiroshima. I can still conjure up the front page of Dad's *Boston Record* for August 6, 1945:

ATOM BOMB
SLAPS JAPS

We'd spent the day bringing in the hay, so Dad must have driven into Concord to buy the paper, having heard the news as we worked. Today the anniversary of the Hiroshima bomb is an occasion for much breast-beating, but in 1945 the jubilation was so great that it sucked the air from my lungs. Nine days later, Japan surrendered, and the War was over at last. What in the world would happen next?

Well, the Fords moved on. I cried bitter tears, packing up to leave the caretaker's cottage, and I suspect Mom did as well. We'd lived at the Laughlin Place for almost three years – exciting years! The caretaker's cottage was our new normal, with its white clapboards, red shutters, and the wonderful telephone that connected me with Gordon Olson and Winthrop Puffer and Maryanne. And the neat little bathroom at the head of the stairs, with its modern plumbing, the radiator that kept it warm in winter, and the dormer window looking out on my rabbit hutch in the back yard. One time, having been sent to my room for some infraction, I locked myself in the bathroom, opened the window, crawled out, and dropped to the ground victorious. That lasted until I returned to the house and someone went to use the toilet and found the door locked from the inside. Dad looked at me, freed from my room without permission, and of course he made the connection. I was sent to the stable, to bring back a ladder, climb it, and undo what I had done. I felt very badly used.

And the stable! Charlie the big gelding had died, and Dad and the Squareheads had spent an entire day digging a hole big enough to accommodate his carcass. That left just the mare and the colt. Glen had a reputation as a biter, but I'd spent hours bringing her around, leaning against the stall with my back turned to her, until she surrendered and rested her muzzle on my shoulder. We were friends ever after. And I'd climb into Gunny's stall and pet him and lean on him, and finally I slipped onto his back. I didn't need a saddle for that; I didn't weigh much, and he didn't seem to mind having me astride. So next I persuaded him to take the bit between his teeth, and to let me put a halter and reins on him. Whenever nobody was around, we'd ride in a circle around his stall with me on his back.

A year or so later, Mister Laughlin wrote Dad in Brookline to tell him that they'd broken Gunfire to the saddle, and that he'd taken to it quite readily. It never occurred to me that if Gunny had bucked, I might have cracked my skull on the ceiling.

And Gordon Olson! What would I do without his fine open face, his grin when he boarded the bus and made his way back to where I was sitting, his broad shoulders that backed me up when I got into trouble on the playground? What Miss Agrafiotis was to me at Mechanic Street, Gordon Olson was at Peter Bulkeley, the only person I could always depend upon.

~ ~ ~ ~

I've no idea what possessed Dad to leave the Laughlin Place, or why he thought he'd be happy in his new job. He was now the janitor at St. Aidan's Church, on Freeman Street in Brookline, halfway between Beacon Street on the south and Commonwealth Ave on the north, each with a pale yellow trolley that dove underground and became a subway train when it entered downtown Boston. (The power came from an overhead wire while the car was on the surface, and a third rail in the subway.) Brookline was very intimidating, the noise especially, and having concrete and asphalt always underfoot. We lived in a three-decker house next door to the church, whose pastor was Monsignor Creagh. I don't know how he got his title, but he'd had the parish for more than thirty years, and he'd baptized Jack Kennedy and five of his siblings when the Kennedys lived on Beals Street, near Coolidge Corner half a mile south. Indeed, I see that the future president had roller-skated to Freeman Street on Sunday to serve as an altar boy.

Since the Kennedys had left Brookline in 1927, Father Creagh at that time would have been a comparatively youthful fifty-three. By 1945, alas, he had become a fierce old skinflint, who had his housekeeper cut the rectory sheets in half when they got thin in the middle; then she stitched the two sides together, to get a few more years out of that the less-worn portion. Mom "turned the sheets," too, but we didn't have a wealthy parish to support us.

I remember the three-decker as a shabby place, much worn and painted a dirty white. It was set back from the street, which gave it a lawn, but the grass was never mowed while we lived there, and there was a steel-wire fence between it and the sidewalk. And it had two tall trees, between which I strung an antenna for the crystal radio set I'd built in Concord. I remember the antenna as seventy-five feet long, but when I look at the place on Bing Maps (I avoid Google when I can, because it already knows far too much about me), I realize the lawn is no wider than the house, so my antenna couldn't have been more than fifty feet. Further, the grass today is nicely mowed, with no fence and no trees. Apparently the three-decker has been much refurbished since we lived there.

An elderly couple lived on the ground floor, and in the gambrel-roofed top floor were a young policeman, his wife Agatha, and their baby son. Apparently Monsignor Creagh had a lease on the thriftier-to-heat middle floor, as a home for the parish janitor. This arrangement would cause us trouble when Dad decided to move on again, as of course he did. For several months he'd mail Monsignor Creagh a check for the rent, and the Monsignor forwarded it unopened to Mom, because he wanted us out of there.

The three-decker was on the north side of Freeman Street, with St. Aidan's Church to the east and a driveway and another house to the west. The driveway led to an odd dwelling behind us that in 1945 had no electricity. We could see the pretty glow of its kerosene lamps at night.

A side door let us into a hallway and the stairs to the upper floors. I don't remember ever meeting the downstairs couple, though I must have done, but Mom became good friends with Agatha Berghaus, the policeman's wife, who was Irish-American like Joe and me. Our hall door opened into the kitchen, which in turn had a door to a porch that we never used – nor was any other porch used, as I remember. Perhaps the floors weren't safe. Each apartment had its own short porch, the same width as the kitchen. The rooms to either side had a fine bow window. On the left, facing the church, was a bedroom for Mom and Dad; and on the right was Joe's and mine, with a tiny room behind it that we used for storage. Our front window was easiest to see from the street, so it was there that we put the placard announcing that we needed a block of ice, with the amount – I think it was twenty-five pounds in the summer, fifteen in the winter – on the top. The iceman came by every week, his wagon drawn by a horse with rubber-coated shoes. He wore a waterproof cape; he'd hook a block of ice with his tongs, sling it over his back, and climb the stairs while keeping fairly dry. The Hood's delivery van was much the same, though the milkman didn't need a rubber cape, and he left our bottles in the hallway.

~ ~ ~ ~

Food rationing was still in effect that summer and into the fall. Mom was sick much of the time, and Dad had gotten rid of the old Chevy when we left Concord, so Joe and I did the shopping. Butter was almost always unavailable, even with the necessary coupons, so mostly we bought oleomargarine in a soft plastic bag with a bubble of orange coloring; when we got home, we'd take the bag in both hands, break the bubble, and work the coloring more or less evenly into the margarine. Sugar was another rarity. Most of the time we put Karo corn syrup on our Cheerios at breakfast and even in our Red Rose tea. And meat too could be hard to find. If we complained that the pot roast was tough, Dad would say, "You'll be glad to eat it when all we have is Spam!" But in fact we loved Spam, sliced and fried and eaten with a fork.

One time as I was walking home from Coolidge Corner, I saw a sign in a convenience-store window: BUTTER! I ran home, woke Mom from her nap, took a fistful of coins and a twenty-point meat and dairy coupon from her purse, and ran back to the store. The Jewish shopkeeper refused to sell me a pound, figuring I suppose that I'd been sent by an earlier customer hoping to double her supply of butter. I begged and begged, choking with the terrible injustice of it, and finally he gave in. He took my money – I don't remember what it cost – and gave me four red tokens in change for my twenty-point coupon. A pound of butter took sixteen points, which was an adult's week's ration for meat, cheese, and butter, whereas oleo needed only four points.

That hard-won butter must have come straight from the farm, because it was wrapped in waxed paper, without a label, and when we put it on our toast next morning, it proved to be "fresh," tasting very strange without the salt that Land O'Lakes Creameries had accustomed us to.

And now I've done it, haven't I? I've broken the Eleventh Commandment: *Thou shalt not stereotype*. But I must! In 1945, the Jews owned the shops, the Irish worked for the city, the Italians built the roads, the Chinese did the laundry, and the Negroes – we'd never heard of an African-American, and to call someone *black* was considered an insult – took out the rubbish. The Yankees ran everything else.

I don't think cigarettes were rationed, but they were hard to find. Dad by this time had switched from Camels to mentholated Kools, but he had to take what was available. So when I went shopping, I always tried to pick up a packet of Wings, with an airplane card to add to my collection.

~ ~ ~ ~

In addition to the church on Freeman Street and the rectory behind it, Dad took care of the parochial school, a block away and a right turn onto Pleasant Street. For the first time in our young lives, we'd made the move during our summer vacation! There was a downside to this, however: we had time to worry about it. Whenever I met a youngster on the sidewalk, I'd look him up and down, wondering if he would be an eighth-grader at St. Aidan's School, and if so, a possible threat.

Years later, when I was lecturing at a Rotary Club luncheon and recalled that I'd once been a pupil at St. Aidan's, I was told that Jack Kennedy was also an alumnus. Alas, however, the future president actually went to a nearby public school for his first four years, and to private schools thereafter, until the family moved to New York in 1927.

The convent and school occupied most of the half-block between Pleasant and Still Street. On the left as we walked through the gate was a two-story brick building. The high school, where Joe was a sophomore, was on the second floor, and there was an old State Guard armory from the First World War in the cellar. It was filled with rows of stacked Springfield 1865 black-powder rifles, last used by the U.S. Army during the Spanish-American War, and issued to State Guard units during the First World

War. I loved to run my hands over those guns, and apparently Dad did, too, because when we moved to Wolfeboro in the fall of 1946, I found that one of those rifles had moved with us, with its bayonet and cleaning rod attached.

The sisters of St. Joseph wore a full-length black habit, with a wimple – wonderful name! – to hide their hair, forehead, and ears. The nuns were so modest, indeed, that supposedly they bathed while wearing a garment covering them from shoulders to ankles, not to be tempted to look upon their bodies. It's odd that I don't remember what occupied the ground floor of the high school, but perhaps there were administrative offices, including for Sister Maria, the principal, who taught English and Latin to the high schoolers and also made occasional appearances in the elementary school that fronted on Still Street. She disciplined us with her ruler, flat on the palm for a girl, edge-down on the knuckles for a boy.

My eighth-grade teacher was Sister Mary Agnes, who was young and fairly pretty, though a pale shadow of Miss Agrafiotis. I don't think she ever disciplined us, but then she didn't have to. She could always call Sister Maria over if we got out of hand.

Sister Mary Agnes taught us the Catechism, of course, by rote. We had to memorize such bits of wisdom as this: "Why did God make me?" And the response, which seventy-six years later I can still rattle off: "God made me to know Him, to love and serve Him in this world, and to be happy with Him forever in the next." I didn't mind this at all, because I was rather religious at this time, believing indeed that I had a Vocation, as it was called, and might study for the priesthood. One of my classmates did just that, in fact, only announcing after he graduated from Boston College that he didn't seem to have a Vocation, after all, but thanks for the scholarship he'd enjoyed for the past four years.

Sister Mary Agnes taught geography much the same way, from a catechism: "For what is Syracuse, New York, noted?" And we would reply: "Syracuse, New York, is noted for its large production of salt." I find that this had been true enough during the nineteenth century, but by 1945 Sister Mary Agnes's geography was seriously out of date.

She did a better job in English, and thanks to her I discovered that I had a talent for writing fiction. She asked us one morning to write a one-page essay on a subject of our choosing. I looked out the window at the oak trees in the narrow park on the other side of Still Street, which was our playground, and I wrote: "The sight of autumn foliage brings to mind the memory of leaf-gathering expeditions I used to make." There wasn't a word of truth in this, but I enjoyed writing about it. When our time was up, Sister Mary Agnes asked us in turn to read our essays aloud, and when I read that first sentence, she asked me to read it again. She was impressed! She marked the story down to a B, however, because of my awful handwriting. The nuns taught Palmer Penmanship, the same graceful script Mom had learned at Ballygarvan National School; and in that subject I got an F. So did Billy Flanagan, who was left-handed.

I seldom wrote the truth for Sister Mary Agnes, which should have made me wonder about the depth of my Vocation. We were invited one time to compete for a prize by writing an essay about Bishop John Ireland. I gave the bishop the full treatment, with the green fields of County Kilkenny and all, and I did win the prize, which sadly turned out to be a copy of his biography! (His funeral was attended by seven hundred priests and twelve monsignors, and I wish I'd had the courage to name Monsignor Creagh as one of them.) Michael Tobin and I took the book into Boston and sold it for a quarter at the second-hand store on Newspaper Row. The owner penciled $1 on the flyleaf and placed it in his bin of recent hardcover books, which free-lance critics for the *Globe* or *Herald* had received as payment for their reviews.

Oh, and Latin! At St. Aidan's we started Latin in the eighth grade, no doubt to give us a head start for the seminary. Church Latin was modernized a bit, so I learned to pronounce *veni, vidi, vici* as the words are spelled, rather than sounding the first letter as a *w* as the Romans had, and as I later had to do.

~ ~ ~ ~

I palled around with Michael Tobin that fall, and we managed to stay out of trouble, though we'd occasionally shy a stone at an inviting window, thrilling at the smash of glass and our subsequent dash to safety. After one such escapade, a motorist stopped and glared at us, and Michael gave him what we knew as the Italian salute. Whereupon he drove slowly, keeping pace with us and speaking into a microphone. He was a plainclothes cop! (Or wanted us to think so.) We took to the alleys, where a car couldn't follow. But we broke no more windows after that.

We often went to the movies on Saturday afternoon. We'd stand in front of the S.S. Pierce Building at Coolidge Corner, and when an old lady came out, we'd chirp, "Carry your bags for a nickel, Lady?" If she shopped at S.S. Pierce, she had to be wealthy, and if she was old, she had to live nearby. When we got to her front door, we'd both hold out our hands, and often enough she'd give a nickel to *each* of us, though that hadn't been the contract. After a few of these, we had enough to to buy two fifteen-cent tickets for the matinee, plus a nickel or two for a candy bar. It was always a double feature, usually a War movie at which we delighted in spotting the identical footage of Japanese soldiers sneaking through the jungle, or a treacherous German playing dead, who then tried to shoot the American in the back. If there was a Western, we looked for a candy-bar wrapper in the dust, or a wristwatch on a cowboy, and we'd count the shots from his Colt revolver, which almost always came out to eight or ten without having to reload.

Sister Mary Agnes tried to steer us toward a sweet movie, like *The Bells of St. Mary's*, probably because she would have liked to see it herself. But sweetness wasn't on offer at the Saturday matinee, which was populated almost entirely by boys like us.

There was a house on Pleasant Street, almost to Coolidge Corner, with a sign over its front door: BROOKLINE PUBLIC LIBRARY. I spent hours in its stacks, and one day I discovered an astonishing album of female nudes. I had never seen one of these before, except for the unappealing tropical women in the *National Geographic*. These ladies quite took my breath away, and I found myself longing for Maryanne and her tree-house on Old River Road. Exploring these marvelous photos, and my own crotch, I soon felt a tickle, which I did my best to encourage, with increasingly intense results, which grew and grew until I wondered whether I might die, though it all ended quite happily.

I went back a week later, and the week after that, and after recovering my breath, my heartbeat, and my posture, I'd find a book that was safe to check out at the desk. Zane Grey was an easy choice, and I must have read a dozen of his novels that fall. I especially liked the three about the Zane family of Ohio, and the murderous Indians who attacked their homes, and best of all, the exploits of the Death Wind, Lew Wetzel, who avenged them by himself fighting like an Indian. I also read War books like *The Flying Tigers* and *God Is My Co-Pilot*, which forty years later inspired me to become something of a historian . . . and something of a pilot as well.

Halloween fell on a Wednesday in 1945, and a gang of us met up in the narrow park between Still Street and St. Paul Street that served as our playground. Some of the girls from our class were there, too, so we tumbled them and pulled up their skirts while they shrieked. "It's a *school night!*" "We've just been to *Confession!*" We ran off again, to smash pumpkins and chalk rude messages on driveways. When we got down to Commonwealth Ave, we were stopped by two policemen in uniform. "What've you been up to, then?" one of them asked.

"We've just been to Confession," Danny Kane told them.

"You're an altar boy, I suppose?"

"Yes!" said Danny. So the cop recited some Latin from the Mass, and Danny immediately and wonderfully gave the ritual response, and the cops sent us on our way. I was greatly impressed with Danny.

That Friday, I turned fourteen years old. And since November was a new month, I had a problem: I must go to Confession. I stalled as long as I could, and then I hung around St. Aidan's one Saturday night until I was sure it was the curate in the confessional, and not Monsignor Creagh. Danny Kane, who knew all about this stuff, had coached me on the process: "Bless me, Father," I began, "for I have sinned. It has been eight weeks since my last Confession," after which, on Danny's advice, I listed a few venial sins, like being angry with Dad or swearing at somebody at recess. Then came the hard part: "And I committed the sin of impurity."

Just as Danny had promised, the young priest asked: "With yourself or another person?"

"With myself, Father."

"How many times, my son?"

Now we were on fairly safe ground, though I took the precaution of halving the number of my encounters with the ladies in that wonderful book at 31 Pleasant Street. I came out of the darkened confessional, sweating, with my head down to lessen my chances of being recognized by the curate.

~ ~ ~ ~

In December, Danny Kane had a proposition. He had lined up a job at the Kiddie Kamp office in Boston, sending out its Christmas appeal for money to support a summer camp for poor city kids. (It never occurred to me that I was a poor city kid.) We'd each earn a dollar for two hours' work after school, stuffing envelopes, sealing them, and putting a three-cent stamp on each. Sister Mary Agnes was an easy mark, and she readily signed the form identifying me as a student commuter, so like Danny I could buy ten trolley tickets for twenty-five cents. That would give each of us a net of $4.75 a week if we didn't spend anything in Boston, and we didn't spend much. We might buy a nickel hotdog at Joe & Nemo's on Washington Street, or spend a quarter for a horror movie at the Trans-Lux, also on Washington, and once we splurged fifty cents at the Old Howard Burlesque in Scollay Square. (Here too I was treading on Jack Kennedy's heels. He was a devotee of the Old Howard as a Harvard student before the War.) I was amazed by the women on stage, miming intercourse with the curtain, by the housewives in the audience, and by the Military Police and the Shore Patrol in uniform, standing at the back and pretending to watch the soldiers and sailors in the audience.

And the vaudeville act between the strip shows! At intermission, the master of ceremonies stepped out and announced: "On Saturday night, Rose La Rose will dance the Dance of the Forgotten Bride." A drunk leaned out from a box to the left of the stage and shouted: "Rose La Rose is a whore!" "*Nevertheless*," the MC told us, "Rose La Rose will dance the Dance of the Forgotten Bride on Saturday night."

Only now, seventy-six years on, do I realize that the master of ceremonies and the drunk were both part of the act.

We also prowled through the Iver Johnson firearms store in Scollay Square, and the Radio Shack nearby, where I might buy something for the superheterodyne radio I was building to replace my crystal radio set.

But mostly, if we wanted something, we stole it, or anyhow Danny did. He was a great one for shoplifting, as much for fun as for profit. Once he led me into Shrafft's Restaurant and ordered two plates of apple pie, which we ate, though I felt unhappy in such a fancy place. When we finished, Danny picked up the check and walked toward the cash register, but before he got there he scooped a salt cellar off a table, tossed it to me, and shouted, "*Run!*" Which we did, sprinting through the door and down the sidewalk, shaking with laughter and with the salt cellar still in my fist. When we stopped to catch our breath, I threw the thing into the alley.

Our boss at Kiddie Kamp was a big man whose last name was Gordon, so naturally he told us to call him Flash, after the space voyager in the comic strip. Flash liked us and we liked him. Toward the end of our stint in the upstairs office of Kiddie Kamp, Danny decided that we must get a Christmas present for him, so we went to Filene's Department Store and he shoplifted a tie, which we took back to the office and presented to Flash, still unwrapped. "Merry Christmas," Danny said.

"Well, aren't you a pair of pretty good monkeys!" Flash said. He reached into his pocket and pulled out a dollar for each of us. So that doubled our day's pay.

I should also admit that when we crowded onto the Alston subway car at Park Street station, we liked to bump the women on the breast or bottom, meanwhile staring sternly ahead to show that it was entirely accidental. This was, I'm afraid, the best part of our daily adventure in Boston, except for the time we went to the Old Howard.

We finished at Kiddie Kamp a week before Christmas. I suppose we were feeling a bit nostalgic, because Danny got off with me at the Babcock Street stop, instead of continuing to Alston as he usually did. We crossed to the south side of Commonwealth Ave, and he jerked his head to the right, to walk past the fine apartment buildings, in one of which, on the third floor, Michael Tobin lived with his mother, his father absent I don't know where. He might have been serving with the military overseas, or he might have been dead, for all I knew. Young people aren't very curious about one another.

"Let's get some mail!" Danny said. I wasn't so sure about that, but I followed him into the lobby of a building. Since there was no mail scattered about, all we did was press the call buttons for the upstairs apartments, to stir up the occupants before we moved on. I think it was in the third lobby that

Danny found a mail slot with envelopes sticking out of it and more envelopes on the floor. He began to stuff them into his jacket. I took fright at this and left the building, walked down to Babcock Street, and turned for home, where oddly I found myself alone. I have no idea where the rest of the family was – at church, perhaps, though it wasn't a First Friday or another occasion for Mass-going.

I wasn't long in the kitchen before there was a knock on the door. I opened it, and in the dim hall light stood two men in suits who told me to come along with them.

"Where?"

"To the station."

"Are you police?"

"Yes."

"Can I see your papers?"

"What?"

"If you're police, you must have papers." I don't know where I'd picked up this wisdom, probably from Jimmy Cagney in some tough-guy movie.

With a sigh, the cop pulled out his wallet, flipped it open, and showed me his badge. So I followed him down the stairs, the other cop following me, and out to a plain sedan with Danny Kane sitting in back and avoiding my eye. We rode to the station in silence. I was told to sit on a bench while they took Danny to an interview room. I sat there for a very long time, it seemed, while uniformed cops came and went, once in a while giving me a look of contempt. "Can't stay out of trouble, can you?" one of them said.

"I didn't *do* anything," I said, but at least I didn't snivel. Voicing it actually helped a bit, since I knew I could protest my innocence without crying.

Eventually it was my turn in the interview room. The two cops had followed us along Commonwealth

Ave in their car, watched us through the outside glass doors, and watched me leave. They followed Danny a bit farther, until he took an envelope from inside his jacket, tore it open, looked inside, and dropped it on the sidewalk. Then they collared him and the evidence. They didn't explain the half-hour delay before they turned up on Freeman Street, but perhaps Danny had loyally tried to claim that he didn't know where I lived. But loyalty didn't seem to be high on his priorities, for the cops told me that Danny had pointed the finger at me as the one who first said, "Let's get some mail!"

I was outraged at that, and perhaps I convinced them, but I think the real reason they turned us loose was that Danny's father was a policeman in Alston, and of course we were all Irish together in Brookline, populated mostly by Protestants and a scattering of Jews. They drove me home first. Mom knew what had happened to me, because Agatha Berghaus upstairs had listened to the arrest, if you could call it that, when the two plainclothes policemen took me away.

~ ~ ~ ~

Not much was said at home about my brush with the Concord Reformatory. I suppose Mom and Dad and Joe regarded my fright as punishment enough. At school on Monday, Danny Kane and I avoided one another, and then it was Christmas vacation and I palled once again with Michael Tobin. When it snowed, we did a variation of Carry Your Bags by finding a short walkway, knocking on the door, and saying, "Shovel your walk for a quarter, Lady?" If she had no shovel, or if she tried to bargain us down, we moved along.

Still, I often wonder what would have happened to me if Dad hadn't tired of working for Monsignor Creagh. I'm pretty sure that no one in our class went beyond twelfth grade, save the lad who graduated from Boston College with his scholarship and his phony Vocation.

I finished eighth grade and got through the summer of 1946 without getting into further trouble, though God knows I had plenty of opportunity. I didn't pal around with Danny Kane any more, and indeed perhaps his father the Alston policeman had pulled him out of St. Aidan's. (No doubt I was considered a bad influence.) I should have gotten a job as Joe had done, washing dishes at Longwood Towers a mile away past Beacon Street, but instead Michael Tobin and I made a roving pair, carrying bags from the S.S. Pierce store and watching War films and westerns at the movie hall. I best remember *Passage to Marseille*, in which Humphrey Bogart escapes from Devil's Island and makes his way to North Africa to join the Free French forces. He becomes a gunner on an American B-17 Flying Fortress in order to make a symbolic return to his homeland. *Wait*, I thought, *we bombed France*? For all the newsreels I'd seen in Concord and at Coolidge Corner, and all the War stories I'd read in the *Boston Record*, it had never occurred to me that before invading "Nazi-occupied Europe" in 1944, we had bombed the hell out of France.

Once in a while that summer, Michael and I went down to Braves Field on Commonwealth Ave and looked for a ticket taker who had nobody managing the turnstile for him. "Turnstile, Mister?" we'd say, and he'd let us take control of the style until the first inning was well underway, and then we could go in and find empty seats in the bleachers. So we saw the Braves play the Giants and the Phillies. Alas, the Braves in 1946 didn't come close to winning the pennant, so there was no hope we'd see them play the Red Sox in the fall. Naturally we were Red Sox fans, but they were way off at Fenway Park.

I did most of the shopping that summer, and some nursing of both my parents. Mom was in bed much of the time with her mysterious ailments, and at least once I had to slide the hypodermic needle into Dad's soft white forearm as he shook with asthma and sang his customary hymn: "*Oh God, oh God. . . .*" I got a scolding if I didn't find the vein at the first try.

Dad decided that the city air had worsened his asthma, so in August he took the bus to Wolfeboro, a pretty lakeside town to the north of Alton, and found a job at a dollar an hour from a contractor named Andy Doe. This began his ballet with Monsignor Creagh, mailing a monthly rental check to the rectory and having it returned to us at 200 Freeman Street, as the Monsignor strove to get us out of there.

We even started the school year at St. Aidan's, Joe as a junior and I as a freshman in the second-story high school next to the gate on Pleasant Street. My homeroom teacher was now Sister Maria herself, so the easy times with Sister Mary Agnes were over. We had to stand when we recited, which caused great consternation to Michael Tobin one time. Perhaps he was daydreaming about Mary Jo Quigly or another of the girls, because he had a fine erection, which he tried to conceal by bending over his desk and pretending to refer to his textbook. "*Straighten up, Michael!*" Sister Maria raged at him. "What's the matter with you?" We boys had a great snicker over this, but I don't think Sister Maria had any notion of what was going on, nor how little control Michael had over the situation.

With Dad working in Wolfeboro, I was free to

explore the little storeroom over the side hallway, where I found great treasures in what was called a steamer trunk (because it held your worldly goods on the passage to America). It stood on end and opened wide, with drawers on the left and clothes hangers on the right, and it must have cost Dad a pound or two in 1927. There was a wide leather belt from his days in the IRA, and best of all his Colt automatic and a box of .32-caliber cartridges. I delighted in racking the slide and dry-firing the Colt at imaginary targets, but I wasn't so stupid as to carry it outside the apartment. It was otherwise with the bullets. Michael Tobin was entranced by them, and when we were standing on a bridge over the railroad tracks one day, he mimed throwing one into the smokestack of a locomotive passing beneath us. My heart nearly stopped, until he opened his hand and displayed it still in his palm.

All this came to a stop in October, when Dad drove down from Wolfeboro in his latest car, a nice-looking 1936 Plymouth sedan, followed by a stake truck with two men who took apart our furniture and loaded it onto their truck. For one piece, I remember, they had to remove our side window and lower the thing – icebox, highboy, steamer trunk, bureau? – down to the driveway with ropes. Small stuff went into the Plymouth, and they drove away.

I think we spent the night with Jere O'Brien and his family in Boston's South End. In the morning we walked to the bus station on St. James Street, and Breda Sexton met us there. After the three of us boarded the bus, she kept chatting with Mom through the open door. Finally the driver said, "Are you coming or not?"

"Yerra no, for the love of God!" Breda shouted at him. "You'll not get me up to that cold place!"

4 – *The Academy*

I DON'T KNOW what would have become of me, if not for Brewster Academy. I suppose I should be grateful to Dad for that – another bit of good luck, akin to his decree that I wait a year before starting first grade. They weren't meant as favors, of course. Indeed, nothing was further from Pat Ford's mind than his sons' schooling.

Brewster was one of those hermaphrodite institutions, privately endowed but serving also as a local high school. They were fairly common in northern New England in the 1940s, but they've since disappeared – they weren't able to keep up with all the mandates from the state and federal governments. Most became taxpayer-funded high schools, while a few, like Brewster, went the other way and became prep schools for those who could afford them. When I arrived in the fall of 1946, Brewster didn't charge tuition; in fact, its full and formal name was Brewster *Free* Academy. But a lot was going on, that first year of peace. Nearly ten million men had been released from military service, and in part to keep them from flooding the job market, they could get their college expenses paid and $50 a month for living expenses if they went back to school. And if they needed remedial courses to get into college, the "GI Bill" covered that as well.

So when Brewster opened in September 1946, eighty War veterans joined its two hundred townies and a handful of boarding students. Its endowment couldn't handle the strain. To keep the school afloat, the trustees voted to charge tuition of $150 a year, with the first half due in January 1947. Dad of course refused to pay, and I doubt that he was the only one. Mister Rogers, the principal, was kind enough not to expel the holdouts, and at the annual Town Meeting in March, the voters agreed to pick up the tab for the local kids. It must have come as quite a shock to Wolfeboro and neighboring towns, after sixty years of freeloading on John Brewster's bequest.

The colleges, meanwhile, were deluged with veterans. It actually worked out quite well for them: all they had to do was add beds, and the government paid for everything. (The University of New Hampshire took over the women's gym, filled it with bunks, and filled the bunks with ex-GIs until another dormitory could be built. And since the checks came from Washington, UNH could charge the much higher out-of-state tuition.) By 1947, nearly half the students in American colleges and universities would be ex-GIs.

There were no veterans among the fifty kids in my freshman class, and none when I was a sophomore. Joe did have some ex-GIs in his junior-level classes, but the big bulge was among the seniors, and this was still the case when I graduated. The ex-GIs gave us a considerable advantage in sports, since they were older and mostly taller, stronger, and heavier than the kids at Phillips Exeter and the other prep schools we competed against. Exeter had long used Brewster as its football opener, to give its team an easy victory to psych the boys for the season. That worked brilliantly until my own senior year, when our veterans got it all together and whipped Exeter. The preppies consoled themselves by chanting: "That's all right, that's okay; you'll work for us some day!" But I don't believe they ever played Brewster again.

My sport was track. I plodded up and down Pine Hill Road for two or three miles every afternoon in a pair of flat-soled Converse sneakers, and in the spring I tried out for the hundred-yard dash. Alas, I fell flat every time I sprang off the blocks. The coach – Mister Masters, a Spanish teacher – moved me up to the two hundred, then the quarter-mile, and half-mile. I was actually rather good at the longer distances. At a pentagonal meet, Mister Masters came running over to me with the news that just four boys had signed up for the one-mile race. "Get in there," he said, "and you can pick up a point for us!" So I came fifth, and I got better every year. By the time I was a senior, I was second only to a lad named Alan Carlsen, from New Hampton School, who in our final matchup ran the mile in four minutes, twenty-eight seconds, not bad at all. He later became a standby of the University of New Hampshire track team.

The same was true of Ed Roy, a big ex-GI who came to Brewster in my junior year. Mister Genowich, the science teacher who coached the field events, introduced Ed to the shot put, and sure enough, he flung it halfway across campus, or so it seemed to our astonished eyes. At our next track meet, Ed saw the discus and asked, "What's that?" and proceeded to win that event, too, and he did it again with his first throw of the javelin. "Brewster always does well in the field events," I heard one opposing coach say to another. Ed Roy did well at UNH, too.

Oh, and I boxed! This wasn't a school sport, but in my sophomore year two of our ex-GIs competed in the state Golden Gloves. They didn't advance to the national level, but in the meantime they outfitted the boys' basement as a gym, with a regulation-sized pad though without ropes around it. They happily coached us younger boys, with three-minute rounds and proper weight classes. I boxed as a lightweight and fancied myself very good at it. But I grew a bit that summer and as a junior I moved up to welter-weight, which at the time ran to 147 pounds. That may seem slim in today's culture, but believe me, a welterweight can *hit*. In the very first round, I took a punch so hard that I had to sit down on a bench to recover my wits. That was the end of my career as a welterweight.

~ ~ ~ ~

In addition to the ex-GIs, there were some boarding students of high school age, including two girls who became the queens of the school – the Heathers, as a future generation would know them. Most of these kids had been parked at Brewster while their parents got divorced, and this was true of Harry Nash, who eventually became my best friend, another Gordon Olsen or Michael Tobin. We didn't hang out as fresh-men, though, since he was a boarder and I was a townie. Not long after I turned up, the freshman boys had to settle a matter of protocol. As a little guy, Harry had been called Peewee at his previous school; but our class had a local Peewee, so we needed to negotiate these competing claims. The local boy naturally got more votes, and that was a good thing, because Harry grew a foot that year and became one of the taller lads at Brewster.

The Academy building stood two stories above a man-made hillock, which made a natural theater stage, with steps leading up on either side, and in June the seniors would climb one set, receive their diplomas from Mister Rogers, and descend on the other side to return to their seats, applauded by classmates, family, and townspeople. I remember the exterior as brick of a golden tan. The entry was magnificent, as if to a Greek temple, the door flanked by double columns that rose the full two stories, to be topped by a triangular gable with a clock at its center, as if to remind us that Chapel started at eight-thirty precisely, with Mister Rogers no doubt taking the names of those who were late.

As a townie, though, I entered at the back, by way of the boys' basement that also served to store our stuff, eat lunch, and fight a few rounds if we were so inclined. The back wasn't built up like the front, and it served as a parking lot for the upperclassmen lucky enough to own cars.

The ground floor had offices and science labs at the front, with the four home rooms ranged along the back wall. So the first thing we saw each morning as we entered our classroom was that splendid view Wolfeboro Bay, Barndoor Island, and Lake Winnipesaukee stretching off to the southwest.

We freshmen of course were a rowdy bunch, and our lady teacher kept the door open so that Mister Vaughn, whose classroom was across the hall, would come to her rescue when we got raucous. All Mister Vaughan had to do was appear at the door and gaze at us with his eyebrows raised and his remarkably expressive ears attuned, and we shut up and settled down. This tall, aristocratic man soon became my favorite teacher. The principal had looked at our grades from St. Aidan's, and without asking put Joe and me in the college-prep curriculum. So I marched across the hall twice a day, for first-year Latin at nine o'clock and college-prep English at eleven. I had a fairly easy time in Latin, save for pronouncing the V's, thanks to my year's head start with Sister Mary Agnes. English, however, was a far cry from St. Aidan's, for Mister Vaughan taught *The Odyssey* that fall. It was a week or two before I caught up, and more weeks before I realized that the men courting

Penelope and drinking Odysseus's wine and eating his food were *wooers*. I'd heard Mister Vaughan as saying "Woors," whom I pictured as a race of men like the Moors. (Modern translations say "suitors," so that today's freshmen, in the unlikely event that they read Homer, are spared this confusion.)

Homer was a whole new world to me, and he and Mister Vaughan changed my life. *"Sing to me of the man, Muse, the man of twists and turns / driven time and again off course, once he had plundered / the hallowed heights of Troy!"* God, how I love it! Twenty-eight centuries have passed, yet who today can sing as beautifully as Homer, whoever he might have been?

Mister Vaughan later became Brewster's principal, and I'm sure he was a splendid one. I never warmed to Mister Rogers, though Harry Nash liked him. Each morning at eight-thirty we climbed to the second floor to attend Chapel – girls on the left, boys on the right, freshmen in back, seniors in front – to hear Mister Rogers hold forth from the podium at center stage. First he led us in a Protestant hymn. "Number two hundred twenty-two," he might say, and we scrambled to find it in the red-cloth hymnal, in a rack on the next seat forward. There was a flourish from the piano on the left of the stage, and we roared in unison: *"Holy, holy, holy, Lord God almighty! / Early in the morning our songs shall rise to Thee. / Holy, holy, holy, merciful and mighty, / God in three persons, blessed Trinity!"*

Like *The Odyssey*, this was entirely new to me, and I enjoyed it. (So did Harry: "Best part of the day," as he remembers our morning hymn.) Catholics in those years didn't sing in church; like the Latin Mass and the Bible, the hymnal was reserved for our betters.

Mister Rogers followed with a bit of scripture, school announcements, perhaps a scolding, and sometimes we even had an inspirational lecture by a visitor more or less imposing. If Chapel ran overtime, it was up to our nine o'clock teachers to make up the difference.

~ ~ ~ ~

For the first time since 1933, we owned the roof over our heads. Perhaps Dad took out a mortgage to buy the house on Pine Hill Road, but the Depression had seared him, as it seared most Americans, and I wouldn't be at all surprised if he had first saved up the $2,500, determined that never again would a bank throw him out on the street. Joe and I both imbibed his caution. I only once took out a mortgage, which I soon paid off, while Joe avoided debt by never buying a house. Indeed, he never married, but lived with the ex-wife of a friend of ours, and when Joe died, she was able to claim his account at the Laconia Savings Bank that he'd opened as a fifth-grader at Mechanic Street School.

The house was an undistinguished bit of country architecture, one and one-half stories tall, about twenty-five feet square on a fieldstone foundation. The ground floor provided us with a kitchen, bath, and living room, with an attached shed that served as our entry and mud room. We had a front door, but it was a New Hampshire custom that a house wasn't finished until the front steps were in place, so the previous owner had cannily neglected to provide them, to save on taxes, and Dad of course did the same.

The attic was cramped, since there were no dormers. Joe and I slept in the double bed as before, and Mom in a smaller room that led off from ours. She seemed in better health than in Brookline, though she still took a long nap in the afternoon. Dad slept on the day bed in the living room. This was convenient because he made sure the fire in the coal stove didn't go out during the winter nights. The kitchen had the usual black-iron Glenwood range, but it had been converted to kerosene burners, fed by an inverted bottle that went *glug-glug* at intervals. We filled the bottle from a fifty-five-gallon drum in the back shed. There was a storage shed and workshop on the lot, and the coal for the living-room stove was stored there.

Following another New Hampshire tradition, the toilet flushed to a cesspool under the lawn. It proved to be dying when we moved in, so in the spring we dug a new one. We covered it with planks Dad brought home from whatever house he was working on, and we covered those with earth. Then we filled the old cesspool with rocks and more earth. It was days before I got the stink out of my nostrils.

We lived two miles from Wolfeboro, but the real Pine Hill was on a dirt road, beyond the neighboring property, which was a cemetery. Along that road lived the Kenney family, Scots-Irish who had gotten their politics from Andy Jackson, the Donald Trump of his day, who created the Democratic party on his roundabout route to the White House in 1829. These people weren't Irish at all, as Dad pointed out to anyone who'd listen. They'd been "planted" in the northeast province of Ulster during the seventeenth century, to tie Ireland more securely to Britain. They later emigrated to America in great numbers, mostly settling in the Appalachian Mountains, from Tennessee to Maine.

Though in Ireland the Kenneys would have been Presbyterians, they were now Baptists like most of Wolfeboro's poor people. The upper class went to the Congregational Church, next door to Brewster Academy, while the French-Canadians attended St. Cecilia's with us. However, the French speakers by now were all middle-aged or older, so the priest no longer delivered two sermons, once in English and again in French, as had been the case when we lived in Alton and went to Mass in Farmington.

Billy Kenney was a freshman, and we became pals riding the school bus morning and afternoon. The bus was intended for the elementary school, and some drivers charged Brewster students fifty cents a week for transportation, but Mister Tuttle let us ride free. As was customary, he was a farmer who lived toward the end of the bus route, so the bus spent the night in his driveway. Harvey Tuttle was in my class but usually caught a ride to school with his older brother. One afternoon, though, he waited with us at the back of the town hall, where we sheltered from the elements while we waited for Carpenter School to shut down for the day. We had about half an hour to ogle the eighth-grade girls before Mister Tuttle showed up. Harvey jerked his head at the driver when it drove in. "I'd like to shoot that son of a bitch," he said.

"Why? What's he done?"

"He's my father," Harvey said, as if no further explanation was required.

Billy Kenney's best friend was Lyle Crommett from Cotton Valley, off to the east of Wolfeboro, so I fell in with the Crommett brothers too. They came to school in a gorgeous 1934 Ford roadster with clamshell fenders, a rumble seat, V-8 engine, and knobby tires for better traction in Mud Season. Even at fifteen – like me, Lyle was a year older than most freshmen — he was a considerable beer drinker. "Oh, I got *hot* last night," he'd say, and prove it by blowing a stupendous fart. So it was quite a balancing act, Latin declensions and *The Odyssey* on one hand, Pine Hill and Cotton Valley on the other. Lyle got through Brewster because the state of New Hampshire obliged it to have a General Course for kids who weren't interested in college prep. Instead of Homer and Shakespeare, he read Owen Wister and Edgar Allan Poe, usually with the help of the Classic Comics edition; instead of physics, he took general science. Similarly, for the hillbilly girls, there were Jane Austen, shorthand, and typing.

Actually, as sophomores, Harry Nash and I took typing, taught by Mister Genowich's pretty wife. For an hour each morning we'd bang away at one of the big olive-green typewriters that Brewster had acquired as War surplus in 1946. I got a 70 in the first term, so I dropped out before Christmas, not to spoil my grade-point average – no way could I keep up with those girls! As a result of that bit of cowardice, I hadn't been introduced to the fourth row of keys, the one that contained the numbers.

Because of the Cotton Valley connection, I sometimes got drafted into playing hooky with the Crommetts, Lyle riding with his brother in the roadster's front seat, Billy Kenney and I in back. "Grab hold, you knobbies!" Henry Crommett would cry as the Ford slewed on the back roads. Summer and winter, he kept the top down. There was a gasoline-fueled South Wind heater in front, but that did nothing for Billy and me in the rumble seat. One time we planted Christmas trees in the rain, as a result of which I got a fierce bout of bronchitis. Another time we fought a forest fire in the back of beyond, near Province Lake on the Maine-New Hampshire border. Oh, that was an adventure! A state Forest Department truck drove us to the site, past homes that made Pine Hill Road look upper class, the people standing outside their shacks and staring at us with their mouths open.

We'd been sent to fight a back-fire, which was supposed to be small and controlled, downwind of the main fire, which would die out when it reached the charred area. Unfortunately, the wind changed direction and the back-fire was now making things worse. We each got a five-gallon pack-pump, which we carried by way of shoulder straps, and from it we sprayed a pathetic stream of water onto flames that roared like the MGM lion. "Like pissing into a volcano!" I complained. The crew thought that was a wonderful insight, and repeated it down the line.

We'd been promised thirty-five cents an hour from the state and another thirty-five cents from the town. But it turned out that we were in an unincorporated township, with no local government and therefore no budget, so all we got for ten hours' work was three dollars and fifty cents.

~ ~ ~ ~

The lads in the General Curriculum were puzzled by me, one day reading Homer and Julius Caesar with the preppies, the next day playing hooky with Lyle Crommett. "Hey Ford," said one lad in study hall, the big room on the upper floor that also served as a library. "What you gonna be when you grow up, a *preacher*?" I don't think this was an insult; he just couldn't figure out what I was good for. Some years later, when I was a freelance writer and he a welder at Portsmouth Navy Yard, we met again at La Cantina in Dover, and had a reunion. It was Thanksgiving Day, and Horace Lyndes and I were having draft beer and spaghetti for our holiday dinner. Probably the Brewster alumnus had been called in for an emergency on a nuclear submarine, which was the Navy Yard's specialty.

And that reminds me: I'd changed my name at Brewster! All through my boyhood, as Joe and I moved from school to school – Alton to Gilford to Laconia to Rochester to Concord to Brookline – my first name had haunted me. The teacher, trying to make the new kid feel at home, would ask me in front of the class whether I wanted to be called *Dan* or *Danny*, and I was obliged to say, "Frank." And everyone laughed! Then of course I'd have to explain that I was known by my middle name, which was *Francis*, which I didn't care for, so. . . . I was sick of this routine, and besides there was a judge in Massachusetts named Francis Ford, who regularly appeared in the news as he dispatched offenders to Charlestown State Prison and the Concord Reformatory. I'd already decided to become famous, and I didn't want to be confused with Judge Ford. So with the most wonderful twinge of joy, when I introduced myself to Mister Rogers that October morning, and he asked the invariable question, I answered: "Dan!" That evening I wrote to my namesake uncle in Australia and told him what I had done.

I would have liked to become a Forde while I was at it, but alas that was beyond my power. It wasn't as easy in 1946 to change one's surname as it had been for Dad in 1927.

By our sophomore year, Harry Nash too had become a townie! His mother, a nurse, went to work at Huggins Hospital, just down the road from Brewster, and they rented an apartment across the street from the Academy building. They had a few rooms downstairs at the back, but Harry's bedroom was at the upstairs front, very private unless his kid brother was eavesdropping through the heating ducts.

Now that Harry and I were friends, I had a pied-à-terre in the village. For my sixteenth birthday that

November, I ordered a J.C. Higgins bicycle from the Sears catalog, and I biked to town when the weather permitted. We became even more mobile when Harry turned sixteen in April and could borrow his mother's 1938 Ford sedan for the occasional outing. The first of these was driving to the Carroll County courthouse at Ossipee and taking the test for our driver's licenses. If the examiner wondered how we got there without someone to drive us, he was kind enough not to mention it. We both aced the written test – test-taking is a talent like any other – and we both cheated on the eye exam. Harry was color blind and I had no useful vision in my left eye, having been born with a lazy eye. This defect is easily cured today, but in the 1930s my brain simply instructed the inward-turning eye to quit sending images that overlapped with the information from the right eye. My peripheral vision was okay – nobody could sneak up on me – but my left eye had a blind spot at the point of vision. When the examiner told me to cover my right eye and read the letters on the chart, I just peeked between the fingers. I don't know how Harry got through the test. Maybe I whispered the colors to him.

The practical test was a different matter, for me anyhow. Harry had no problem, but when I brought the examiner back to the courthouse, he shook his head and said: "Well, stick around town for a while until you get the hang of it." No matter! We both had our licenses. I'm afraid the first thing I did with mine was erase the numeral 1 and type a zero in its place, so I could pass as eighteen and buy beer at Mister Lampron's convenience store in Wolfeboro Falls. (New Hampshire trusted us to drink at eighteen but not to vote until we were twenty-one, which strikes me as a lot more sensible than the reverse.)

Henceforth, when there was a storm brewing, Harry would drive up Pine Hill Road to collect me, and off we'd go to a trailhead on State Road 109, running along the shore of Lake Winnipesaukee and more or less paralleling Pine Hill Road. We parked, ran to the height of land, and climbed the Abenaki Tower to watch black clouds roll in across the lake. It was a magnificent scene. Supposedly some Indian trails had gone through here, but more likely it was just a handy name, just as the Abenaki were blamed for the notion that Winnipesaukee meant Smile of the Great Spirit. In any event, the lake wasn't smiling now, with those gorgeous thunderheads and jagged bolts of lightning spearing the horizon. I don't suppose there was much danger to Harry and me, since Abenaki Tower was built of wood.

We thought of the tower as located in Melvin Village, but like Cotton Valley it was actually part of another town, Tuftonboro in this case. Confusingly, though, there *was* an actual village, which was sad and lonely now, in the spring of our junior year. But during the summer it boasted a store that offered fat ice cream cones for a dime, and also a hall where barn dances were held on Saturday nights. Employing my altered driver's license, Harry and I would buy a quart of Pickwick Ale to drink before we braved the dance-hall and the Boston girls who summered at the Lake. I liked to open the bottle with the Ford's bumper, as the Crommett brothers did, catching the cap on the edge of the bumper and giving it a good smack with my free hand, which sent the cap flying into the night. One time, I misjudged and broke the rim of the bottle. It wasn't until we were back in the hot and noisy hall that Harry noticed the blood on the front of my shirt. He got me out of there and drove me home, by which time my mouth had stopped bleeding.

We also ventured to Alton Bay, where there was a roller skating rink, and we'd hustle the Boston girls who frequented that place.

And we went hunting! I answered an advertisement in *Guns & Ammo* magazine and ordered a box of 45/70 ammunition by railway express. (The caliber was .45 inch, and though it contained smokeless powder, the power was the same as those seventy-five grains of the black powder that had betrayed the location of American soldiers to the Spanish in 1898. The Spaniards were armed with the smokeless Mauser repeating rifle, whose supersonic bullet the Americans called "the Spanish Hornet.") Dad by this time was working summers in Arizona, so Harry and I took the Springfield to the town dump, not far from our house on Pine Hill Road, and shot the rats. We then invested in a hunting license – just one, for me, since we had only the one rifle – and went looking for a deer. We got a good laugh from the hunters we met, but alas we never saw a deer. Then Joe borrowed the license for a hunting expedition of his own; his car was stopped, or he had some other encounter with the police, and my license was confiscated.

Our most distant adventure was to Worcester, Massachusetts. In our senior year, Brewster was visited by a recruiter from Wesleyan College in Connecticut. Mister Rogers hooked him up with Harry, who duly applied for a scholarship, and in time he was invited to an interview by a Wesleyan alumnus in Worcester. This was a considerable trek on the roads then existing, in Missus Nash's 1938 Ford with dim lights and brake cables that had a tendency to stretch. (Like all American lads, we loved Detroit automobiles and their power, but it is terrifying in retrospect to understand how truly primitive they were. This not a reflection on Detroit! British cars were more adorable than ours, and even less reliable.) I don't remember the drive down to Worcester, nor what I did while Harry sat for his interview at the law office, but I do remember the drive home. Night came on, the headlamps flickered, and the brakes didn't seem to work at all. Finally Harry pulled to the side of the road, and we crawled under the car, he with a pliers and I with a flashlight as dim as the headlamps. I'd shake it and get another moment of illumination, while Harry grunted and squirmed and did his best to tighten the cables.

Our best adventure, though, was the time he decided he would seduce one of our less respectable classmates while I crouched in the trunk with a pencil, notepad, and that same flashlight. Brewster had several such girls – townies, of course, enrolled in the General Curriculum, and tending to live on Railroad Avenue near Wolfeboro's only beer hall. Most of us had only a shaky idea of *how* disreputable they were, because our classmates never boasted about their conquests, if indeed they had any. Only if a girl came up pregnant did we know for sure that she was sexually active. This had happened only once since I'd come to Wolfeboro, to one of the dormitory girls, who was sent home in disgrace. The boy responsible was never identified.

We chose a French-Canadian girl named Ethel. She was a junior like us, in the General Curriculum, living on Railroad Ave, and though pretty she was rather fat, so we figured she was the girl most likely to fall for Harry's charms. He made the date, I climbed into the trunk, and Harry drove to her house just beyond the railroad station. I couldn't hear what they were saying, but we drove off to some lover's lane, where Harry coaxed her into the back seat. I switched on the dodgy flashlight and wrote down such of the conversation as I could hear. I'm afraid it amounted to very little, and all I got out of it was a rather bad cold.

~ ~ ~ ~

Who cares, really, about the sexual fantasies of adolescents? I went to Confession and Communion every month, though my fancied Vocation had long since faded. There was no curate at St. Cecilia's, to whom I could confess my sins as I had done at St. Aidan's, so I had to face the elderly and bilingual Father Poirier. "Bless me, Father, for I have sinned. It has been five weeks since my last Confession. I committed the sin of anger against my father. And I . . . I committed the sin of impurity."

The priest had to pretend he didn't know who was kneeling on the other side of the screen, so he asked, "With yourself or another person?"

"With myself, Father." And so it went, every month of my young life.

Yet I feel I must say *something* about our romantic lives. Harry was a good-looking guy, and by our junior year he was taller than anyone else at Brewster except an ex-GI who was Mister Genowich's prize contender for the high jump, pole vault, and broad jump. (Like Al Carlsen the miler and Ed Roy who threw things, he too would go to UNH and star on the track team.) In the fall of our senior year, Harry paired up with a pretty girl from Wolfeboro's upper class, the doctors and lawyers, insurance brokers, and owners of automobile dealerships who lived in fine homes on Sewall Road, which signaled status just as Railroad Ave signaled the lack of it. She and Harry made a virginal twosome until she ditched him in the spring for a lad from Grosse

Pointe, Michigan. Many years later, I met them at a Brewster reunion, and we talked about skiing. "The children *love* Kitzbühel!" she told me.

I didn't know how to dance; and it was Joe who inherited Dad's good looks, while I had my mother's wide forehead and narrow jaw; and that forehead, alas, was now peppered with acne. I regularly fell in love, of course. There was Suzie, for example, a pretty little girl from out of town who broke my heart by getting a Model A Ford roadster for *her* sixteenth birthday. Fat chance I'd have of dating her on my bicycle! Then there was a darling eighth-grader whom I admired while waiting for Mister Tuttle's bus. I took her out a few times, and I actually put my arm around her while we watched an awful Hollywood musical at the cinema which, like so much else in Wolfeboro, was located in the town hall and named for the Brewster family. And I took her to a party one time. But of course I ran into the insuperable problem that one must *talk* to the girl, and I hadn't a clue what to say.

In our senior year, a girl named Helene turned up. She was the niece of our Spanish teacher, and I think she lived with Mister Masters' family on campus. She was stunning. Really. She had a lovely face, an impressive figure, and a great line of chatter, and best of all she was exotic, since she came from Bermuda, which she talked about all the time. She sat in front of me in the senior home room and I think in English class, and we flirted shamelessly – no problem with talking to Helene! But I didn't date her. I don't think anyone else did, either. Helene was too glamorous for the Class of 1950, even the ex-GIs among us.

I should have dated Joan Githens. As Harry Nash emailed me, many years later, "Joanie was a lovely girl, only we were too stupid to know it." She and I were pals, and we worked together a lot, in the school play and such. But I never thought to ask her out. Like Helene, she wasn't in the dating circle at Brewster. She turned out well, however. She married and lived somewhere along the New Hampshire seacoast, where she developed and ran an abortion clinic. Horace Lyndes lived in the same town as Joanie's clinic, and sometimes when I drove down to visit him, the pro-lifers would be picketing the clinic, and I'd give them the finger. When I mentioned this to Horace, he gave a great laugh and said: "So do I!" He's dead now, so I no longer have any occasion to salute the pro-lifers. But I do send a hundred dollars to the clinic every Christmas.

And that reminds me: Ethel came up pregnant in our senior year! This created quite a sensation, especially when Gene Edgerly quit his job and joined the Army, the traditional refuge of a father-to-be who wasn't interested in marriage.

~ ~ ~ ~

There was no volume of nudes in the town library, and of course not in the Academy's study hall, which also served as its library. The latter was strong on Rudyard Kipling, and I devoured a dozen of those compact green volumes before I was done. The town library was strong on Leslie Charteris, and I read about the same number of his stories about the Saint, the Robin Hood of Modern Crime, whom I admired for his flair and his joy in skirting the law, and who was a considerable step up from Zane Grey westerns. There were novels by Louis Bromfield and Kenneth Roberts, and there were also, I'm sorry to say, *Reader's Digest Condensed Books* that I could read in an evening or a rainy afternoon.

I'm surprised that none of the English teachers

at Brewster took any interest in my reading, which was only marginally above the rubbish I'd read at St. Aidan's. The closest to guidance was a discussion with Missus Zulauf in my senior year, when she tried to persuade me that Rafael Sabatini's historical fiction was better than Kenneth Roberts's. We read a Shakespeare play each year – *Romeo and Juliet*, *The Merchant of Venice*, *Hamlet*, *Macbeth* – and at some point we read Dickens's *A Tale of Two Cities*. But that was it, apart from the awful poetry in our English textbooks: *"The snow had begun in the gloaming / And busily all the night / Had been heaping field and highway / With a silence deep and white,"* stuff so dreadful that it burrowed into my brain and never left, like that jingle from Chiquita Banana.

Actually, my brother contributed more to my reading habit than the Brewster faculty did. When he graduated from high school in 1948, he too became a great reader, and he'd borrow books from the town library like Viktor Kravchenko's *I Chose Freedom*, Mikhail Sholokhov's *And Quiet Flows the Don*, George Orwell's *Nineteen Eighty-Four*, and Arthur Koestler's *Darkness at Noon*, all of which I read. I think Joe was also responsible for introducing me to Frank Harris's *My Life and Loves*, smuggled home from Paris by some veteran of the War.

~ ~ ~ ~

Summertimes, of course, we worked. I was fifteen that first summer in Wolfeboro, 1947, and the best job I could find was washing dishes at the Colonial Arms, a tourist hotel and restaurant on the outskirts of town. I earned eighteen dollars for a seven-day week, but I didn't come in until ten o'clock, to wash the breakfast dishes, and I had three hours off after lunch and before I returned to wash up from dinner.

(The black chef slipped me a plate for both meals.) I spent the hours between three o'clock and six at Brewster Beach, owned by the Academy but in the ecumenical manner of the time serving also as a public beach. I got a fine tan and learned to swim what we called the Australian Crawl, a great advance over the dog-paddle that had served me up till now. I also got a plantar's wart, which Doctor Bovaird burned away with a pen-like electrical device that made an awful smell. I thought of Howard Long, and how he would fared if New Hampshire had owned a modern electric chair instead of bringing that hangman down from Canada. Doctor Bovaird charged me five dollars. I also paid Mom five dollars a week toward my room and board, so I didn't have a lot to show for that week's work.

The next summer, I was cashier and sometime soda jerk at Dockside, a casual restaurant on the Wolfeboro dock and town parking lot. Harry worked at the hardware store on Main Street, so we could eat our sandwiches together at lunchtime. Dockside was seven days a week also, alternating between daytime and evening shifts; it paid fifty cents an hour, so I earned twenty-eight dollars a week and saved quite a bit of money. (Knowing this, Dad had decreed that I should contribute ten dollars toward my room and board, as Joe was doing.) I even got the occasional tip, when I was on the night shift and had to wait on tables when the movie let out and the restaurant filled up. The waitresses carried a glass of water in each hand when they went to a booth. Applying my mind to the challenge, I realized I could do twice as well if I held two upright glasses on each palm and used my elbow to nudge the water tap on and off. Ah, but when I reached to the table, I had no way to set the glasses down and had to ask the boys to help me out. They enjoyed that, and perhaps were showing off to their dates, and they left me a twenty-five-cent tip, my best of the summer.

That summer was a tipping point. Henry Crommett and Joe Ford were both in the Class of 1948 at Brewster, and Henry had joined the Navy, which meant that Lyle would inherit that darling 1934 Ford roadster. And the day after Joe got his diploma, Dad gave him the keys to the Plymouth and himself boarded the bus to Boston, New York, Richmond, Dallas, and Tucson – three days and five drivers, on the way to the Wild West he'd dreamed about as a boy in Ireland. It's not everyone who can achieve his life's goal at the age of forty-eight!

Why didn't Joe go to college? Well, nobody in our family ever had, and probably Dad didn't trust me to manage the Plymouth, Mom, and the house on Pine Hill Road. I was nowhere near as responsible as my brother.

Joe worked at the First National store, at the produce stand under an old bachelor named Mike. The pay was an astounding ninety-seven and a half cents an hour – about $11 today – so I begged him to get me in there the following summer, and he did, and Billy Kenney coasted in as well. The First National was another of those "combination" stores, with separate cash registers for groceries, meat and fish, and produce. It was closed on Sunday, and we got a day off, so Joe or I would take a turn at the meat counter, to make the shifts come out right. The hours were long, especially on Friday when the store was open until eight and the meat counter had to be scoured after all the fish we'd sold that day. Joe and I did this work, too, and we supplied the lemons for everyone at the meat counter, to get the fish smell off our hands. We weren't paid for overtime, nor for opening up in the morning, which took half an hour.

Once a week, the meat truck would double-park on Main Street, and we'd each go out and have a half of beef deposited on our shoulders. When it was my turn, and the two hundred pounds settled down on me, I felt I'd lost an inch in height. I staggered into the store, down the aisle, and into the walk-in refrigerator at the back, where Delmar Tutt swung a hook from the ceiling, impaled the side of beef, and I bent my knees and walked away from it.

Dad came back in September, burned as brown as an Indian and full of tales about the dude ranch where he'd worked, and which apparently was populated mostly by divorcees and saguaro cactus. Summer of course was the off season in Arizona, while autumn was the start of Wolfeboro's off season, but as usual Dad had a job with Andy Doe a few days after getting off the bus. He even got a raise to a dollar and a quarter an hour, with Saturday afternoon off.

We got only a half-hour break at noon for lunch, though Billy Kenney and the others would go out back and enjoy a cigarette on the dock. So I became a smoker too, for the sake of that hourly eight minutes in the sun. The dock wasn't there for our relaxation, but as a lure for the occasional motor boat from one of the islands, whose residents therefore became our customers. It didn't take long for Joe to become a smoker too.

~ ~ ~ ~

Mister Gunn, an English teacher who sadly got fired for giving himself a loan from the student activity fund – I'm sure he meant to pay it back, but Mister Rogers was as tough on his teachers as on us – told me that in my final year I'd been the subject of great discussion among the faculty. Except for that one quarter in typing with Missus Genowich, I not only had good grades, but actually once got a perfect one, for geometry. Mister Hurst called me into the teacher's room to explain the impossibility of this. "Nobody's perfect," he apologized, and gave me a 98 instead of the 100 I had earned.

On the other hand, there were my friends from Pine Hill and Cotton Valley. I was especially fond of Lyle Crommett; I loved his jagged mind and hillbilly humor. After that spell of planting Christmas trees in the rain, I developed a cold and a hacking cough – probably the first example of the asthma that would sometimes bother me when I was older. "Goddamned mucus," I complained after a hacking bout in the boys' basement. Lyle thought that the funniest thing he'd ever heard. He began to call me Mucus Membrane, soon shortened to Muck.

We sat together in chapel as seniors, in the third row. One morning during Mister Rogers's spiel, Lyle blew one of his stupendous beer farts, and we both began to giggle. Mister Rogers turned red. "Leave the room, boys!" he said, and as we reached the door he added, "And don't come back until you can behave like gentlemen." Like a good Scots-Irishman, Lyle wheeled about and raised his fist, but I grabbed his arm and hustled him down the stairs.

I enjoyed this sort of tumult, but it soured Mister Rogers on me. So it was that, when the Wesleyan recruiter showed up, it was Harry Nash whom the principal thought he should meet. I'm sure it also helped that Harry had started out at Brewster as a boarding student.

The Irish National Schools provided a six-year education, so the notion of high school was new to Mom and Dad, while college was a mad leap into a world inhabited by the likes of Professor Damon and

Mister Laughlin. Joe had now gone to work at the First National's rival at the other end of Main Street, the A&P supermarket with grocery carts and aisles instead of clerks who waited on customers. He bought a green 1941 Ford sedan for an outrageous nine hundred dollars – $10,000 today – but a new car cost twice as much, and none were built during the War. So the family was not at all supportive when I said I might apply to the University of New Hampshire. Why in the world would I do that, and how could I possibly afford it?

Mister Hurst doubled as the college counselor, and he gave me a vocational aptitude test, which showed that I had an affinity for things horticultural. "Having an aptitude for something doesn't mean you have an *interest* in it," Mister Hurst pointed out, but I knew there were county extension agents who advised New Hampshire farmers on best practices, and that seemed a career I might aspire to. Getting into UNH was no problem; it accepted anyone graduating in the top two-fifths of a New Hampshire high school, with a "tuition grant" for anyone who needed it. I reckoned that I could squeeze through freshman year for four hundred dollars, and I had that much in the bank, from summer earnings and those ten-cent loans that helped win the War. For a bit of a cushion, I went to work for Mister White, the Brewster janitor, sweeping the floors after school. I even helped set out the bleacher chairs for my own graduation.

I had a rifle, which I sold to a teacher for ten dollars, and I sold my bicycle to a boy on Pine Hill Road for fifteen dollars. Fred White, the janitor's son, was also raising money for UNH, and I bought his Smith Corona portable for twenty-five dollars. So I didn't come out ahead on these transactions.

Harry Nash had another scheme going. If he didn't get into Wesleyan, he too would go to UNH, and he'd seen an old camping trailer for sale. We could live in it and feed ourselves more cheaply than renting a dormitory room and eating meals at Freshman Commons. It was a good thing that this idea was quelled, because where would we have parked the trailer? Anyhow, it came to nothing when Harry got his acceptance letter from Wesleyan. It was brought to him in chemistry lab; perhaps Wesleyan assumed he was a boarding student, or perhaps Missus Nash had delivered it to the principal's office. Harry was holding a test tube at the time, and when he realized he'd been accepted to this rather tony institution, the glass shattered in his hand, and Mister Rogers's secretary had to apply first aid to the future doctor.

Mister Rogers, fortunately, did not control all decisions at Brewster. I was the obvious choice for class valedictorian, since that was done entirely by grades, and against all logic the faculty also voted to add my name to the plaque in the front hall, the first thing a visitor saw when entering the academic building. It saluted that person in the graduating class who'd contributed most "to the honor and good name of Brewster Academy." I'm sure there were some dissenting votes, and I didn't have Mister Gunn to speak for me, because he'd been fired, so I felt this was quite a triumph for Pine Hill Road.

Mister Gunn kept his family afloat that spring by peddling the *Lincoln Library of Essential Information*, our generation's version of Wikipedia. Harry Nash was loyal enough to buy a copy.

I had my first hangover the day I graduated. We'd had a considerable party the night before, which wound up on Sewall Road, where lived Wolfeboro's upper class. I only remember the end of it, when I kissed a girl with remarkably soft lips. "Oh, that's *good*," she said, and we kissed again. That was the only time in high school that I kissed a girl. I don't know who she was, and I had no chance to pursue our acquaintance, because suddenly I was arguing with a plump townie named Gassett – her date, perhaps! We went from shoving each other to punches, and I aimed a classic roundhouse at his chin, only to miss and fall flat on the warm asphalt of Sewall Road.

Honor and good name, indeed.

Winters in Wolfeboro could be fierce. I was home for Christmas in 1951, when I took this photo, and Joe (second from left) had become assistant manager at the A&P supermarket on Main Street. He wrote poetry, was elected to the state legislature, and in due time followed me to the University of New Hampshire.

5 – The University

IT'S AMAZING WHAT YOU CAN LEARN in college, especially when you come from Pine Hill Road and nobody in your family ever ventured beyond high school. The freshman dining hall – the Commons – occupied the first two floors of what otherwise was a dormitory. It was one of three similar brick buildings – Commons Row – on the south side of Main Street. They were designed by a University architect named Huddleston and who was later honored by having another but less handsome building named after him. We were told that Commons Row was of "Georgian Colonial design," and it did make a grand display the first time I saw it, when Joe drove me down to Durham, the day after Labor Day in September 1950. UNH was only fifty miles from Wolfeboro, and the bus that brought us up from Boston had taken us through downtown Durham four years before, but this was the first time I'd actually seen the campus.

When I went into Commons that first evening, I was amazed to see a girl shaking vinegar and oil onto a salad. She was the first person I'd ever seen, flavoring lettuce with something other than mayonnaise. The main course – a green pepper stuffed with rice – was likewise new to me. Over the next four years I would learn to prize American cuisine, especially pizza, spaghetti with tomato sauce (and beer!), submarine sandwiches, and hot dogs – two for a quarter at the Wildcat lunch counter, very popular with the ex-GIs at the end of the month as they waited for that check from the Veterans Administration.

There was a jukebox in Commons. I was familiar

with the Hit Parade from my summer at Dockside, but those jukebox songs embedded themselves into my bewildering first year at UNH. *"I was dancing with my darling to the Tennessee Waltz / When an old friend I happened to see"* . . . *"There's a tree in the meadow / With a stream drifting by"* . . . *"Sometimes I take a great notion / To jump in the river and drown."* (I wonder if Harry Nash at Wesleyan was listening to Patti Page sing "The Tennessee Waltz" in the fall of 1950? *And my friend stole my sweetheart from me* . . . and off his darling went, to Grosse Point and Kitzbühel!)

Weirdly, a year or two later, the jukebox gave us Rachmanioff's "Rhapsody on a Theme of Paganini," after it became the background music for *The Story of Three Loves*, starring Kirk Douglas, Leslie Caron, and other Hollywood notables. Not long ago, as I was driving with the radio tuned to WCRB in Boston, I had to stop by the side of the road when the "Rhapsody" came on, sweeping me with the smells and sounds of Commons dining hall in the 1950s.

I roomed in East Hall for all four years, arguably the longest stretch I'd ever lived in one place. Like its twin to the West – they were connected with a washroom annex – it was built by officer cadets in 1917 as a barrack, later divided into cramped doubles and triples. All the financially strapped students opted for it, as did the worldly-wise ex-GIs. What did one need but a bunk, a desk, and a gooseneck reading lamp? The low rent was as good as a scholarship, but in time the University decided that East-West was beneath its dignity, and the barracks were demolished and replaced by a parking lot and loads of student debt.

The washroom connector between the two buildings was another revelation: for the first time in my life, I could take a shower. Somewhere along the line, Joe and I had given up our sponge baths in the kitchen, but we still only bathed on Saturday night, given the bother and expense of heating kettles of water for the tub. At UNH I could shower whenever I liked! Laundry wasn't an issue: I mailed it to Mom every second week, in a brown fiberboard carton with a two-sided label, her address on one side, mine on the other. I also put in a typed letter, thus saving the three cents for a first-class stamp, and sometimes she tucked homemade cookies into the return package.

East-West had a community shower, and I was surprised at how many of my fellow students were circumcised. I knew about the Jewish practice, and indeed my brother had to be circumcised as a teenager, but there couldn't have been *that* many Jews and tight foreskins in the U.S. population! Quite a few Americans, it seemed, had been able to afford a nonessential surgery during the Depression.

One day, coming out of East Hall and looking over at Commons, I saw the Bone Man. He had been a regular visitor to the First National, picking up bones and the fat trimmings we hadn't mixed in with the hamburger stock, and apparently he did similar duty at the University of New Hampshire. I hurried over to say hello, as if seeing a long-ago friend from home. He promised to deliver my good wishes to the staff at the First National meat counter.

I was *so* lonely, those first few weeks in Durham! But East-West was populated with wild men, so I fit right in – Pine Hill Road and Cotton Valley gone to college! Our house mother was Maw Bailey, a fat lady of considerable years. The women who oversaw the dormitories, fraternities, and sororities at UNH were all roughly the same age and proportions, and all, I think, were widows who'd fallen on hard times during the Depression. As they died or retired, they were replaced by graduate students called Resident Counselors, a warning of the great bureaucratization that would come to higher education – indeed to most areas of American life – as it expanded to accommodate the Baby Boom. Those who were deans in the 1950s are now vice-presidents, with deans reporting to them, and assistant deans beneath those, to administer such passions as diversity, inclusivity, equity, and sustainability.

My favorites among the residents included Norman Stevens, a tall lad who seemed to spend all his spare time in the library, and to have read everything worthwhile – no Louis Bromfield or Leslie Charteris for Norman! At the other end of the scale was Ted Alexopoulos from Worcester, recruited as a football player though he never went out for the freshman team. Norman dubbed him Ted the Greek, after Nikos Kazantzakis's novel about the rogue named Zorba.

Ted the Greek was as slow as Norman Stevens was smart, but he had his ways, which I'm afraid I sometimes abetted. When we were rising juniors, the faculty became suspicious of Ted's ways, and Mr. Medesy, the Dean of Men, made him take an IQ test, on which he fared badly. It was impossible, the Dean declared, for anyone with an 80 IQ to slide through four semesters of college without cheating, so he sent Ted back to Massachusetts.

Not that I swept through my first month or so at UNH. In Freshman English with Mr. Goff, I got a C on my first "piece." UNH had a famous writing program, headed by Carroll Towle, whose *Complete College Reader* was our textbook, and who taught Advanced Composition and Writing as an Art, heavy on what he called "pieces" and on individual conferences. Mr. Goff followed this model in English 1-2. He asked us to write a list of the books we'd read that summer, and at our first conference, I realized he was not much impressed by mine. So I set out to read what I understood to be the three great writers of the past fifty years: Ernest Hemingway, F. Scott Fitzgerald, and John Dos Passos. I especially liked *This Side of Paradise*, which gave me a twinge of regret that I hadn't applied to Princeton.

I liked Mr. Goff. I liked all my courses – English 1, Spanish 3 with Professor Bergunza, Botany with an elderly woman who like Mr. Goff had no doctorate, and World History with a funny iconoclast who had been crippled by polio

I even liked Chemistry 1 with a young instructor who at ten o'clock Monday, Wednesday, and Friday chalked an outline of his lecture on the blackboard in James Hall. I learned more about note-taking than about chemistry in that class. I copied his outline into my notebook with a space between each item, then filled in the blanks as he lectured. Thank you, sir, and I'm sorry I've forgotten your name! For an assistant, he had an elderly gnome who turned out to be Professor Fogg, one of the greats who'd made the UNH Chemistry Department rather famous in the 1920s and 1930s. Professor Fogg had apparently exhausted his brain in the process, and now puttered around James Hall, setting up displays for the young instructors. (Professor James had been another of the greats.) There was also a learning opportunity when the class ended, and the perky girls – the Heathers! – flocked to the instructor's desk and engaged him in flirtatious conversation, so he would remember their charms when he handed out the grades. Alas, I didn't learn the lesson, believing as I did that merit trumped charm. Not that it mattered much, since I didn't have a lot of charm.

We earned three credits per lecture course, plus one for chemistry lab on Tuesday afternoon, for a total of sixteen each semester. That left us Aggies two credits short of what we needed to graduate in four years (the same was true of the College of Engineering), and those were provided by Phys Ed and Military Science, both mandatory for boys. I didn't much care for gym, which involved a lot of mindless running about the dusty Field House. So I joined the rifle team, firing .22-caliber bullets at a bulls-eye fifty feet away and slightly smaller in diameter than the bullet. This was the bolt-action Springfield that the U.S. Army still used as a sniper's rifle, though with a different barrel. I was rather good at this, regularly scoring a 98 in practice. But the coach soon learned not to take me to an actual meet. When I fired in competition, my heart would pound, and the throb traveled through my arm and along the leather sling, causing the muzzle to jump with each heartbeat. The top shooter on the freshman team was an arrogant lad named Eddie Antz, who never doubted that he would win every match, so he did. He also had incredible eyesight. When he spotted for me in practice, he made a big thing of pushing the scope aside, since he could actually *see* where the bullet hit.

It was in Military Science – the Reserve Officers Training Corps – that I got my edge over Norman Stevens. For our first two years, we boys had to spend our Thursday afternoons on the drill field, otherwise belonging to women's field hockey, and Norman couldn't keep cadence. When we bobbed up, he sank down, which was okay, but it followed that when we sank down, Norman's head bobbed up, to the fury of our officers, juniors and seniors whose tuition was paid by the Department of Defense. They took drill very seriously.

It was also in Mil Sci that Ted the Greek struck his fatal blow against academia. Usually he survived by signing up for the less popular section on Tuesday, Thursday, and Saturday, so he could cadge the questions from someone who'd taken the hour exam the day before. This didn't work in Mil Sci, which had only the one section, and he was close to failing. So he and another lad broke into Pettee Hall one night and stole a copy of the final exam. Faced with the questions, though, they had trouble figuring out the answers. Ted called others into the ring, and in the end they sent for me. (Ted called me "Ford." I suppose he looked upon me much as Mrs. Damon regarded Dad, as someone whose curious talents came in handy around the place.) He lived on the second floor of West Hall, and his room that night was redolent of sweat. Ted used it as his gym, with a barbell and a full set of weights. I pitied the boys who lived beneath him, who had to suffer the noise of those weights hitting the floor, and who wouldn't dare to complain.

The Mil Sci final was a fifty-question, multiple-choice test, and by the time I finished drilling the gang, I knew the answers by heart. During the test, I took the precaution of marking two of them wrong, so that I came out with a 96. But Ted– oh, Ted! – got a perfect score. That was the second semester of our sophomore year, and the mistake that led to his downfall. The Mil Sci instructors may not have been the brightest bulbs on the faculty, but even they knew something was wrong when Ted the Greek got a perfect score.

~ ~ ~ ~

Perhaps the most important thing I did as a freshman was what I *didn't* do, to wit: I didn't go to Mass. There was a pretty Catholic church in downtown Durham, improbably located on Madbury Road, also known as Fraternity Row, site of drunken parties and probably the occasional rape, though that was something never discussed in those years. The priest was a genial man named O'Connor, so he was known as Father Okie. I didn't check in with him upon arrival, and that first Sunday in East Hall, I was very conscious that the eight o'clock and then the eleven o'clock Mass were happening without me, as I sat there at my desk and by the light of my gooseneck lamp read the opening selections in the *Complete College Reader*. This was the textbook for English 1, and I had already determined that I would do the bulk of my studying on the weekends. UNH was a "suitcase college," with half or more of the students going home on Friday afternoon and not returning until Sunday night. There were no distractions on Saturday and Sunday, and I could hit the books without getting a reputation as a bookworm. It was a great time for the likes of Norman Stevens and me, though I'm afraid that Norman kept up the pace all week long.

If you came from a non-Catholic household, or grew up in a home with no religion at all, you can't appreciate what a momentous day that was, my first Sunday morning in Durham. Five years earlier, I had thought of becoming a priest, yet here I was, avoiding Father Okie altogether. Harry Nash and I had discussed our increasing doubts before we'd set off for college. I should have phoned him at Wesleyan, to find out how he was doing, but long-distance calls were for the affluent. I let the morning pass while I pondered "The Death of the Ball Turret Gunner,"

Randall Jarrell's bleak poem, unlike any I'd read at Brewster, and the first that didn't celebrate America's contribution to winning the War: "When I died they washed me out of the turret with a hose."

What would I say about *that* in Mr. Goff's class on Monday morning?

~ ~ ~ ~

The going wage on campus was forty-five cents an hour, about $5.00 today, but I managed to earn a nickel more at Dunfey's coffee shop on Main Street. (Durham did have a tiny First National, but it was a one-man operation, and he didn't need student help. That was a pity, because under union rules I'd have earned the same ninety-seven and a half cents as in Wolfeboro.) Dunfey's was one of several small restaurants and clam bars owned by an Irish-American family from Massachusetts. They'd opened the one in Durham so the sons could take turns running it as they made their way through the University of New Hampshire. (They were all, I think, ex-GIs, and more mature than the usual undergraduate.) I was a dishwasher during the day but became a short-order cook as well when I was on the evening shift. Before the cook went home at seven o'clock, he would teach me how to make the dinner specialty, so I could feed any late eaters.

That job turned out to be a bit of luck. Fred White, the Brewster janitor's son, lined up a carpool when we went home for Christmas. I had worked the afternoon shift that Friday, so our driver – a well-off businessman's daughter who had her own car – waited outside Dunfey's while I shucked my apron and put on my coat. I suppose I reeked of dishwater, fried clams, and onion rings. On the ninety-minute ride by way of the Governor's Road, a now-disused route to Wolfeboro, Fred and another freshman got to fussing about the two weeks of final exams that loomed before us in the New Year. Since I hadn't complained about any of my courses, he turned to me and said: "What about you? All A's, I guess?"

"Well. . . ."

The car was struck silent. *Nobody* got straight A's in college in those years, but I didn't see how I could miss. Even Mr. Goff had come around. One day he'd asked the class why Oscar Wilde was sent to Reading Gaol, and I dutifully gave him the answer. As with the pronunciation of José in fifth grade, I have no idea where this information came from, but it was there when I needed it: "gross indecency with other male persons." That's the virtue of reading widely and without discretion. I'd read anything, at any time. I would read the backs of cereal boxes and the labels on cans, if nothing else was available at mealtime.

Anyhow, back in East Hall for second semester, I got a letter from Wolfeboro, and inside was a check for two hundred dollars. That equates to $2,284 in our much-debauched currency, and it more than covered my second semester's tuition. Evidently our carpool driver, flush with the Christmas spirit, had told her father about the straight-A dishwasher. I think her name was Katherine Avery, whose dad ran the town insurance brokerage. In any event, he also had the running of a charitable trust – another bequest from John Brewster, perhaps – and for the next three years, I would get a similar check in the mail. Dean Medesy just about matched it, so with my summer and part-time jobs, and my extreme frugality, I made it through UNH just fine.

Sophomore year, I did get back to that union wage at the First National. I signed up for five classes in a row, starting at 8 a.m. That gave me fifteen credits, plus the two for Phys Ed and Military Science. So at one o'clock on Friday afternoon I could grab a sandwich and hitchhike to Dover, five miles away, to work a six-hour shift at the self-service meat counter at the supermarket on Central Ave. And on Saturday I did the standard eight-hour day. The schedule was awful, but I earned almost fourteen dollars a week, which more than paid for my meals, especially with the small steak I might slide into my jacket on Saturday night. That provided Sunday dinner for my roommate and me.

My job was to prowl the self-service meat counter. I wore a starched jacket-apron, restocked the refrigerated bins, chatted up the customers, and filled any special requests. The actual work was done in the back room, where the butcher and six or seven Dover girls packaged the hamburger, filleted the fish, and did the other messy stuff that Delmar Tutt, Billy Kenny, Joe, and I did when we worked on the meat counter in Wolfeboro.

Those girls were every bit as much of an education as the one I was getting in Durham. "What's that smell?" Doris asked, and the answer came in a snap: "Ah, you're walking too fast, dearie!" I couldn't keep up with their banter. They wore me out. When I left in June, they gave me a sweet going-away present, a collage of a flower, each petal a rolled condom.

~ ~ ~ ~

I wasn't long at UNH before I realized that Mr. Hurst was right when he said, "Having an aptitude for something doesn't mean you have an interest in it." I still liked my courses, except for Trigonometry in the second semester of my freshman year. But I was increasingly skeptical of my classmates and some of the teachers, especially the Trig instructor. Then I got “rushed” by the Aggie fraternity, Alpha Gamma Rho, known on campus as Alpha Grab a Hoe, and realized I didn’t want to cast my lot with them. And one day I went for a conference with Mr. Goff about my latest “piece,” and found his office empty. I checked the hall and found him hurrying toward me. “Have you ever thought of majoring in English?” he said. “I’ve been to the Registrar to look at your transcript, and I wondered. . . .”

And then there was Trig, a required course for Aggies. I’d taken trigonometry at Brewster, so I snoozed through the first month or two, then awoke (like the ball turret gunner in Randall Jarrell’s poem) to find myself in trouble. So was everyone else. “Nobody is getting anything higher than a C!” one of the Aggies protested. To which the instructor replied, “That’s because there are no A or B students among you.” I saw nothing but trouble ahead, so I dropped the course and transferred to the College of Liberal Arts.

Now what? I could major in English, sure, but what did that prepare me for? I thought of college as an elevated vocational school. I didn’t want to be a high-school teacher, and the notion of teaching on the college level never occurred to me. I was only beginning to learn; how could I presume to replace Professor Damon at Brown, or even Mr. Goff at UNH? In addition, the English Department had a multitude of requirements, and Dr. Towle’s writing classes didn’t count toward the major.

For a while I thought I might major in Spanish. I fancied I was rather good at it; I could get a job at the United Nations, perhaps, translating for the high and mighty. (A more preposterous notion, actually, than replacing Mr. Goff.) But several of the gang in East-West had opted for Government, which at some schools was dignified as Political Science. (Government as a science – what a fantastic idea!)

Bob Sampson had signed up as a Government major. A refugee from the College of Technology, where he too was done in by Trig, he praised Jack Holden as the best teacher he'd ever encountered. Then there was Carleton Eldredge, who had joined the peacetime Army to get the GI Bill, after which he he joined our class: he planned to be a lawyer, and pre-law was offered by the Government Department. And Norman Stevens! For whatever reason – in the end, he became a librarian – Norman too was a Gov major.

What the hell! It was a bit vague, but there were lots of jobs in Washington that paid fairly well, and they came with a pension. Dad by this time had settled in Arizona and worked at Davis-Monthan Air Force Base in Tucson. It was the perfect job for him, cannibalizing old warplanes for parts, designing a crate, building it, and shipping the parts wherever in the world they were needed. He thought it a great idea for me to be a GS-5 with a starting salary of $3,500 a year.

So at the last possible moment, toward the end of my sophomore year, with Gov 1 and most of Gov 2 under my belt, both under the tutelage of the golden-voiced Jack Holden, I registered as a Government major. You cannot begin to imagine the amount of worry and soul-searching that decision cost. I didn't regard college as a way to produce educated fools, as Dad did, but like him I believed it ought to lead to a satisfactory career, whether as county agricultural agent, United Nations translator, or GS-5 in the State Department, maybe even the Foreign Service. Education for the joy of it wasn't something that came easily to a child of the Great Depression.

It would be none of the above, of course, but I didn't know that in 1952. A whole year of worry for nothing! I only recently read a line that captures my angst of that year: "The migrant has no ground to stand on until he invents it." At UNH I was just sixty miles from the hospital in which I had been born, but I'd never been rooted anywhere, and I hadn't yet invented a ground on which I could safely stand.

I did sign up for Advanced Composition. I enjoyed Dr. Towle's sometimes-weird lectures, but the value came in our weekly conferences, when he would draw a circle upon my latest offering, then put a dot in the middle of the circle and say: "What is the *itness* of this piece?" That was a great question, as valuable for journalism as for what he refused to label Creative Writing. ("*All* writing is creative," he told us.) I once submitted a story about a newspaper reporter just turning thirty, playing off the notion that he was accustomed to type *-30-* at the bottom of his stories, newspaper shorthand for "the end." Dr. Towle was in his fifties and seemed older, but he was kind enough not to find this laughable. Indeed, he told me the sequence might have come from a novel, which left me puffed with pride.

Government too had some interesting teachers, above all Jack Holden himself. And he had recently hired a young Harvard graduate named Allan Kuusisto, whose specialty was international relations. For a textbook, Dr. Kuusisto assigned us Hans Morgenthau's *Politics Among Nations*, an amazingly hard-nosed view of the world. Not for Morgenthau – hence not for our teacher and not for us – was the sweetness and optimism of Woodrow Wilson, the League of Nations, or the UN in its new and vainglorious headquarters in New York. "The struggle for power is universal in time and space," Morgenthau wrote. "The desire to dominate . . . is a constituent element of all human association." This equipped us very well, I think, for the world we'd live in for the rest of our lives.

~ ~ ~ ~

I had signed up for the student newspaper when I arrived on campus, dropped out when I went to work at Dunfey's, and rejoined when I got that boost from Mr. Avery in Wolfeboro and could cut back my hours in the kitchen. The newspaper staff rolled over in January, so the outgoing editors could train their replacements. (That was theory, anyhow. In reality, the new guys didn't want to have their predecessors looking over their shoulders.) I became news editor in my sophomore year and editor in chief when I was a junior. The *New Hampshire* was a trivial paper by Ivy League standards, an eight-page tabloid that came out every Thursday, but as far as we were concerned it was the *New York Times*. We pounded out our stories on a manual typewriter – twin of the War surplus machines in Mrs. Genowich's class – on the third floor of Ballard Hall. Our words were set in type by clamorous Linotype machines in the basement of Hewitt Hall, to be printed four pages to a sheet on an even noisier flat-bed press, later to be flipped over and printed on the other side. In our Ballard Hall newsroom and editorial offices, we laid out pages two, three, five, and six on Sunday night. We finished the work on Monday night, important news on the front page and editorials and such on page four. The sports editor took care of pages seven and eight in his own office.

Like Brewster, the *New Hampshire* changed my life. I loved the writing and the mechanics of putting it together, though not so much the interviews and schmoozing that went with gathering the news; and I loved the people who worked on the paper over me, alongside me, and eventually for me. I especially enjoyed the small tempests we created in the teapot of the University of New Hampshire – the editorial-page photo of empty beer bottles in front of T-Hall, the Victorian administration building; the fire extinguishers we found to be empty because some ex-GI had used the contents to dry-clean his trousers; the impossible pranks that students played, like luring a cow into a music classroom and leaving her there for the professor to find in the morning. We phoned the Russian embassy in Washington and told the night duty officer we were about to come out in favor of a Marxist government, and what did he think of that? If nothing else was going on, we'd get Bob Sampson to drive us to Dover so we could buy a case of beer at the Teach Your Dollars More Cents store and drink it on the way back to Ballard Hall.

Sam charged fifty cents for the taxi service. Of course he paid it back as his contribution to the beer. One time someone spotted a tear in his flannel shirt, fingered it, and somehow ripped it further, which led to everyone piling on, until we left our driver nearly shirtless. We were high, not on the beer but on the joy of being young. Sometimes I didn't get to sleep until two o'clock in the morning, still laughing from our merrymaking in Ballard Hall. My roommate, an accounting major, was peeved when I'd come came banging into Room 215 in the middle of the night, but we put up with one another because that is what young people do. Ray was his name. I can't remember his last name, but he was the best sort of roommate: we had nothing whatever to do with one another's lives.

The newspaper staff split the profits from advertising and the student activity fee according to a long-established formula. The business manager worried about that. I don't really know how it worked, but I came away with roughly $200 from my stint as news editor, and $500 as editor-in-chief. All in all, I would graduate from UNH with more money in the bank than when Joe drove me down to Durham in the fall of 1950.

~ ~ ~ ~

My brother was a slow starter, and rather frail, but nothing could stop him once he got moving. In the fall of my sophomore year, as I was being introduced the study of government, Wolfeboro's longtime representative to the General Court breathed his last. His designated successor filed for the vacancy – and so did Joe. What effrontery! Twenty-two years old and not "from around here," yet he presumed to join the state legislature to represent the interests of Wolfeboro? (In his quiet way, Joe was indeed rather presumptuous. He had taken to writing poetry, too, and he sent some poems to a newly established magazine. The editor turned them down because they didn't rhyme. Joe responded with a stern letter, explaining that poems didn't *have* to rhyme – "The Death of the Ball Turret Gunner" didn't! – and sure enough, he then became a regular contributor to the magazine.)

He knew everybody in Wolfeboro from his years at the First National and the A&P. He easily won the Republican primary, which in rural New Hampshire was tantamount to victory, and he would take his seat in the next session of the legislature.

And he applied to UNH. He wrote Dean Medesy and asked for permission to keep his 1941 Ford sedan on campus, a privilege never extended to freshmen. The Dean of course complied – Joe would be another friend of the University in the General Court! Durham had a representative of its own, who conveniently was the director of the UNH News Bureau. And another student-legislator was coming along, Barney Robinson, a Korean War veteran from the North Country. The three of them would carpool to Concord, each pocketing the ten-cents-a-mile travel allowance that supplemented his constitutionally mandated salary of $200 every two years.

Joe lived in West Hall, also on the second floor. He roomed with a black kid, one of two African-Americans at UNH at mid-century. Perhaps Dean Medesy realized that, unlike most of our classmates, Joe and I had known minorities for years, going all the way back to Alton, where the Damons had a black cook named Jack, with whom Mom and Dad had exchanged Christmas cards for many years; and Brookline, where Missus Berghaus upstairs had an unmarried sister named Margaret McGinty, who became great friends with Mom and often visited us in Wolfeboro, accompanied by the Filipino butler in the home where she was the housekeeper. And of course there were the "colored" cooks who shopped at the First National and the A&P in Wolfeboro. (One of them had a side arrangement with Mike on the produce stand, whereby Mike padded the bill and the cook kept the overage.) Joe didn't have the slightest bit of racial prejudice, nor did I until I found myself in the 272nd Infantry Regiment, 69th Infantry Division at Fort Dix, New Jersey. There's nothing like real life to disabuse us of the ideals of youth.

Joe would be a Gov major, too. I suspect he had a hard time of it at first, following two years behind his kid brother. I noticed that, once in a while, Jack Holden would slip and refer to Joe as "Danny," his pet name for me.

~ ~ ~ ~

I was, by this time, editor of the *New Hampshire*, and in the summer of 1953 I parleyed that into a job at the *Winnipesaukee Times*, a throwaway tabloid. I was editor, sole reporter, delivery boy, and advertising salesman. I had an office in the basement of the ballroom at Weirs Beach, a few miles from the Manning Place, and I had my first car, an unreliable 1935 Chevrolet I'd bought from Bob Sampson for seventy-five dollars. I roomed with Clarence and Amy Dame in Gilford (Clarence had helped Dad build the caretaker's cottage in 1940) and in exchange I drove them to Laconia every Saturday to shop for groceries. Otherwise they would have paid for taxis, going and returning.

That was a fun summer, except for the part about selling ads. I wasn't very good at that, and I wasn't invited back the following summer. In my spare moments, both at my basement office and in my bedroom at the Dame farm, I started my first novel, about a tough Irish-American lad with perhaps too many similarities to Studs Lonigan, hero of a 1930s trilogy by James Farrell. (My hero was Bart O'Meara, and he lived in rural New Hampshire, not Chicago.) I had signed up for Carroll Towle's advanced class, Writing as an Art, and I meant to give myself an easy fall semester by turning in a chapter a week.

I also spent a lot of time on the beach, where one day I met a darling girl in a UNH sweatshirt. "That's quite a compliment to the University of New Hampshire," I told her, and got her to pose for my huge Speed Graphic press camera. She wore a white Jantzen swimsuit, with no straps and a tantalizing glimpse of her cleavage. Her name – I needed it for the caption, I explained – was Betsy Warwick. I used the best of the set for a bit of cheesecake in the

Winnipesaukee Times, and when I next saw her on the beach, I gave her a few copies for herself.

Alas, she then disappeared from The Weirs, nor was she at UNH in the fall. It seemed that Betsy had come up pregnant and, according to the custom of the time, had taken the year off to have the baby and give it up for adoption. Not my doing! I was still a virgin that summer.

~ ~ ~ ~

Betsy's name will turn up again. In the meantime, you should meet my college girlfriend. For my first three years I'd had the traditional crush on one or another girl, but in September 1953 I fell properly in love. When we turned up on campus – the newspaper staff came back early, to prepare an introductory issue for the freshmen – my managing editor and likely successor, Tommy Bennett, showed me a photo of a friend from home. It was one of those wallet-sized pictures that came out of a vending machine at a railroad station or some such place. I fell in love with it, a plump face under an astonishing fall of black hair. "Who's she?" I asked, scarcely trusting my voice.

"Rosalie Labranch. Friend from high school."

She was transferring to UNH from the University of Vermont, where she'd had the bad luck to fall in love with the girl who lived in the dorm room beneath hers. (Tommy didn't tell me this; Rosie did, after we became a couple.) I suppose that homosexual yearnings were as common at mid-century as they are today, but they were usually quashed or concealed. We did have one declared homosexual in East Hall, but such honesty was rare. The queer lad – called Tookie, of all the nicknames in the world – was tolerated by the residents of East-West, just like Joe's black roommate. But we didn't use the weasel word "gay," and to be honest I never noticed much gaiety among those of my friends who later came out of the closet. Those included Tommy Bennett himself, as it turned out. Like Rosie, he was a junior that fall, and hadn't yet gone to bat for the other team. Indeed, he had a girlfriend in Emma, my assistant editor and a great friend.

An English major, Emma had persuaded me to read James Joyce, though I stopped with *Dubliners* and *Portrait of the Artist as a Young Man*. She wanted me to read Edith Wharton and Henry James, too, but after glancing through their books at the University library, I let them go for another day. I preferred to read about people whose lives I might emulate – Stephen Dedalus the young writer, Lieutenant Henry the ambulance driver, Amory Blaine the Princeton student. I had no time for wealthy New Yorkers of the nineteenth century, or indeed for Leopold Bloom of Joyce's *Ulysses*, though Emma assured me that the book was an Irish version of *The Odyssey*, which I had so loved in high school.

I was sometimes led astray by this habit of modeling myself on fictional heroes. When I read, in *Tender Is the Night*, that the wealthy doctor Dick Diver hung the day's shirt on a hanger so it would be neat for tomorrow, I began to do the same, not realizing that Fitzgerald had meant this as a flaw in his hero's character.

Well! When Rosie Labranch turned up on campus – Tommy brought her to Ballard Hall and introduced her around – I broke precedent and asked her out. To the movies, I suppose it was. There wasn't much else to do in Durham, save a cup of coffee at Dunfey's or tea at the Notch, a lobster-shaped building on a hill overlooking West Hall. A onetime U.S. Army club for enlisted men, the Notch had been donated at the end of the War to serve as a student recreation center. It got its name from a nearby cut through a granite ledge. There was a large hall in back and a smaller wing to either side, like the lobster's claws. Rosie and I would spend a lot of time in the Notch, where tea was only a nickel, compared to ten cents for coffee downtown.

I kissed her when I delivered her to her dorm before ten o'clock curfew. This was another unusual step for me. I'd done the usual fumbling, starting with Maryanne in her tree-house, but I'd never actually *dated* a girl and sealed the evening with a kiss. In Morrill Hall next day, instead of taking notes on what Jack Holden was saying about Plato's *Republic* – political philosophy turned out to be my favorite course at UNH – I sketched a calendar in my notebook and listed the number of times I could ask Rosie out without making a fool of myself. Once a week, I think it was, while occasionally skipping a week. I soon abandoned the schedule, whatever it was. At some time in the fall – I was wearing my Sears, Roebuck winter jacket, plaid with a faux-fur collar, so likely it was November – we went into College Woods, I put my jacket on the ground for a mattress, and lost my virginity. As for Rosie, it wasn't her first time; to test her sexual orientation after the University of Vermont experience, she'd seduced one of the local lads. "It didn't *prove* anything," she told me.

That first romp was okay but awkward, what with the condom and all, and I was terrified, to be honest. But I soon got the hang of it, and we made love in every nook and cranny of the UNH campus: in College Woods, beneath the Thompson Hall entryway as the night watchman passed by, in the press box overlooking the football field, in the editor's office at Ballard Hall, and once in the shadows beneath West Hall. We also made a study of what the Catholic Church oddly called the Rhythm Method, counting the days of the month, so we could dispense with the condom for a few nights before and after her period. (I was still using the petals of my going-away collage from the girls at the First National.) The resulting sensation was something I'd never imagined, the – forgive me for this, but it was a great moment in my life – the way her honey pot *clung* to my dongle once we got going. Nothing had prepared me for this endearing outcome. The lads from Pine Hill and Cotton Valley had their own rough ways with women; the books I had studied in high school – *My Life and Loves,* by Frank Harris, smuggled in from Paris, and *Ideal Marriage: Its Physiology and Technique,* by the wonderfully named Dr. Theodoor Hendrik van de Velde – were silent on the matter; and if Harry Nash or another of my friends knew more about sex than I did, he hadn't shared it with me. Curiously, I never asked Rosie if she knew what her innards could do to me.

One time, the condom broke. Rosie didn't notice, but like a gentleman I asked her to marry me, just in case she came up pregnant. "Ask me again when you come home," she said, "and I will." So this was toward the end of my senior year, and I was already bound for graduate study in England. I shudder when I read this now. A proposal made in post-coital languor might have changed my life, and not, I suspect, for the better.

Maw Bailey had retired by this time, and a grad student named Dick Gagne occupied her suite as our Resident Counselor. When I got the news of my Fulbright Fellowship, he called me into the office and poured a glass of whiskey to celebrate. He too had won a Fulbright in his senior year, but turned it down because he was in love. "That was stupid," he told me. "We broke up before Christmas, so I'd have been as well off in Europe." I congratulated myself on my own superior wisdom. Rosie would be waiting when I came home, and if she wasn't, well, that was okay too.

~ ~ ~ ~

In my last week at UNH, I enlisted Bob Sampson as advisor and went searching for a car. We decided on (and it was a bad decision) a 1940 Hudson sedan we bargained down to one hundred dollars. Among other shortcomings, it turned out to have a hole in the muffler. Sam helped me mend the flaw by splitting a large tomato can from the Commons trash and clamping it over the hole. I drove back to the salesman in Newmarket who'd unloaded the Hudson on me; he made a show of listening to the sound, approved it, and gave me the necessary inspection sticker.

Next I discovered that the Hudson burned motor oil at such a rate that I had to buy the stuff in a two-gallon can, stopping every hundred miles or so to add another quart to the engine. I put a lot of miles on the Hudson that summer, driving across the state to see Rosie. (She lived on the wrong side of the tracks – really. After three years in academia, I had learned to scorn the petty bourgeois lifestyle, so I found this admirable.) And I'd drive north to Colebrook to visit Sam at the Balsams Hotel, where he helped his father maintain the hydroelectric plant and did other chores around the place. Sometimes Rosie came with me. We slept on a mattress in the power plant, with the turbines roaring; we made love in the night, and nobody the wiser.

Joe also owned a Hudson by this time, though a

postwar model. (He would have done better to keep his 1941 Ford. Those Hudsons were awful pieces of machinery.) Now that Dad lived all year in Tucson, he had sold the house on Pine Hill Road and Mom had rented an apartment in downtown Wolfeboro. We boarded with her that summer, each paying ten dollars a week, which covered our food and her rent as well. Dad wouldn't send her any money, arguing that she should come out to Arizona with him, so all she had to live on was her pension from the Irish government.

Joe worked for the Republican State Committee in Concord, and I for the State Park Division, writing press releases and such. We took his Hudson to Concord one day and mine the next. On one of these commutes, we spotted Dodier's Camp – the first place I can remember living in – as a heap of ruins by the side of the road. In September I sold my car for forty dollars and a ride home. (It was so low on gas that the salesman had to put a dollar's worth in the tank. I didn't mention that it would soon need a fill-up of motor oil as well.)

The Fulbright people had sent me a ticket to Boston, another for a Pullman berth on the overnight train to New York, and a third for the *SS United States* at Pier 96 on the Hudson River. I may have slept a bit on this journey, but I doubt it. This was, after all, the first time I'd ever been south of Boston. And I was on my way to Europe! Not to Paris in the 1920s, it's true, but to London a generation later. But surely I could mine the experience for a novel, just as Ernest Hemingway, Scott Fitzgerald, and James Joyce had done?

This was, I think, a rump meeting of the Young Republican Club in my junior year. Joe the freshman has a glass at left, I have a quart of Pickwick Ale at right. We're sitting on an East Hall bed that could be mine or perhaps Billy Bryant's, seated behind me with Carleton Eldredge raising a glass beside him. The other two lads are Dave Scully and Charlie Radcliffe.

6 – *The Polish Girl*

DAD MUST HAVE BEEN PUZZLED why, when I graduated from college, I didn't head straight for that GS-5 job in Washington, but instead took myself to yet another university. And not just any university, either, but one in *England* – an England, what's more, presided over by Winston Bloody Churchill! One of my enduring memories of my boyhood is Dad's face becoming red and his voice tremulous as he told us how the Bloody Damned English had lashed rebellious Sepoys to the mouths of cannon and blown them into the next world. And you may be sure that Winston Churchill would have done the same with Michael Collins, Éamon de Valera, Pat Forde, and every other troublesome Irishman, if not for fear of annoying America, which might then decline to rescue England from the next war it stumbled into. In his orations, Dad seemed to grow wider of shoulder and bigger of head. Fortunately, in 1954, we were separated by 2,700 miles of mostly two-lane highway. Phone calls were for the rich, so we wrote letters, and those not very often.

I have no explanation for my fascination with the land of Winston Churchill. "There is a forgotten, nay almost forbidden word, which means more to me than any other," the great man is supposed to have said. "That word is *England*." Though an American, whose parents had gone to war against the Crown, I felt the same way.

Dad no doubt blamed my treachery on the propaganda we were fed as boys, those wonderful photos in *Life* magazine and those static-filled, sonorous broadcasts from Edward R. Murrow: "*This* . . . is

London!" (And in the background, at least in my memory, the crash of bombs and the roar of airplane engines.) There was no question where I wanted to go after I collected my surprisingly small diploma from UNH, redeemed somewhat by the words *summa cum laude*. Norman Stevens got *summa*, too, but four B's in Military Science dropped him to second place in the Class of 1954 with a grade-point average of 3.99. So I became the class marshal, and Rosalie decorated my baton with alternating bands of blue and white. By that point, I confess, I was a bit sorry I hadn't tried my luck at Harvard instead of what Harry Nash called Cow Hampshire. But I might have been a B student in the Ivy League, hence no longer a prime candidate for a fellowship. (Harry, meanwhile, had dropped out of Wesleyan and was now in Korea with the U.S. Army. Fortunately the shooting stopped before he got there.)

I had applied for anything that might get me to England: Rhodes Scholar, Marshall Scholar, Fulbright Fellow, the first two without success. But there were dozens of Fulbrights every year, and UNH almost always got one or two. They were a device to let Europeans pay off some of their War debt and postwar reconstruction in their own currency, since they had no dollars to spare. So Prime Minister Churchill could use British pounds to pay my tuition, send me a monthly stipend, and enroll me in the National Health Service while I furthered my education in his cold, straitened, and bomb-damaged country, with the cost credited against his dollar debt. (Between 1942 and 1955, the U.S. gave the equivalent of more than a trillion dollars in military equipment, food, and reconstruction grants and loans to other countries. The loans were at two percent interest, and inflation eventually stole away most of the cost. Britain didn't finish paying off its debts until 2006, by which time they had lost 95% of their wartime value.)

I had applied to LSE, the fabled London School of Economics and Political Science, but it eluded me. "We had the devil's own time, finding a spot for you," the Fulbright greeter told me in London. "Journalism isn't an academic subject in England, you see. It's something for English concentrators to do after they graduate, if they don't want to settle for a teaching position. But the University of Manchester took you! It's a splendid place, really, one of the older redbrick universities." As it turned out, like a befuddled English major, Manchester didn't seem to know what to do with me. Probably it only wanted the tuition money that I would bring.

No matter! For the first time in my life, I was the most affluent person in my immediate society. I got fifty pounds a month in "blocked sterling," which couldn't be taken outside the country. British students got forty pounds. Indeed, some got less, including the Polish girl I fell in love with. Basia wasn't a British citizen, so she had a "travel document" instead of a passport, and her stipend came from the Polish government in exile, which had fled to London in 1939 to escape the Germans, and had remained there after the War for fear of the Russians who had occupied it. I think Basia got twenty quid a month – fifty-six dollars at the then-current rate of exchange. It was possible to live in Europe on two dollars a day, as I would later prove, but you wouldn't gain weight on the diet.

About the first thing I bought with my stipend was a gray Harris Tweed jacket. I paid five guineas for it, a guinea being an imaginary coin valued at twenty-one shillings (three dollars exactly) and used to price clothing and upscale rentals. I wore the jacket in all weather, because it would shed a light English rain and, when cold, button to my throat.

An American visiting England today can't begin to grasp the devastation left behind by the Second World War. It wasn't just the "bomb sites," as the gaping cellars were called, but *everything*. The War was nine years over when I arrived, but it might have ended the day before yesterday. The rubble had been cleared away, but few of the buildings replaced. (As I would find in my travels with Basia in the spring, France had fared better, though it had been bombed just as vigorously, and by both sides.) Even the British weather seemed ruined: gray skies, cold and constant rain . . . and the rain was filthy. The University of Manchester buildings were black, bathed as if by coal miners' tears, the soot coming down with the rain. In London, Parliament and Big Ben were black as well, not the golden hue a tourist sees today.

Most of the students had dark streaks on their teeth, from lack of dental care when they were children. I noticed the decay especially on the girls, in part because they smiled more than the boys, but mostly because they were girls. There wasn't much orthodontia, either, but that was true at home as well.

Food wasn't scarce, but there was no variety, and the last ration card had been phased out just a year before. Cafeteria meals were dreary. No doubt there were some upscale restaurants in Manchester, but I never ventured into them; my culinary adventures were limited to an Indian restaurant uptown. I fell in love with curry, just about the only spice I encountered in England. Apparently Indians did not much dine at noon, so the meals were half-price then and the place nearly empty. And the waiter was overly polite, never bringing the bill until signaled. Once I discovered this, I'd take a red Penguin paperback – two shillings, Not For Sale in USA – with me, so I could read for half an hour in what for me were opulent surroundings.

As always, I read a lot in Manchester, and indiscriminately: Evelyn Waugh, P. G. Wodehouse, Virginia Woolf, my old favorites Fitzgerald and Hemingway (I bought a hardcover novel called *Fiesta*, which turned out to be *The Sun Also Rises* in disguise), and a dozen or so apocalyptic Pan paperbacks about life after nuclear holocaust, a popular obsession in England at the time. I had an allowance for textbooks, and that's what paid for *Fiesta*. I also bought the six volumes of Winston Churchill's *The Second World War* and plowed through them, a feat I didn't mention in letters to Dad, though he might have been interested to know that Henry Laughlin had encouraged the project and written a big check to start it off.

As I'd done earlier with Scott Fitzgerald, I sometimes missed the point of a book. I acquired a copy of Goethe's *Faust* and was intoxicated by the hero's pact with the devil, promising him all the experience that life can offer, in exchange for Faust's soul when they met on "the other side." To which Faust stoutly replies: "*The other side weighs little on my mind. If once to the fleeting hour I say, 'Remain, so fair thou art, remain!, then bind me with your fatal chain, for I will perish in that day.*'" Yes! I thought this a noble sentiment, the bravest possible challenge to fate. I didn't realize that Goethe meant that, without God, life had no meaning, and that Faust's bargain must bring tragedy to him and his beloved Gretchen.

Perhaps I should have read Sartre instead of Goethe. As I later discovered, the Frenchman really did believe that we should embrace everything possible. Like Faust, Sartre seems to have applied the maxim mostly to women. We were all guys together, weren't we?

~ ~ ~ ~

At Manchester, I was known as the Half-bright Fellow. (There were two of us, actually. The other Half-bright was a chemistry PhD from the Midwest. We roomed together for the Michaelmass term, before we each found his own digs.) Right away I reported for duty at the *Mancunian*, the student paper. The editor asked about my previous newspaper experience, and when I admitted I'd been the editor-in-chief, the room fell silent. "But I'm only interested in reporting," I hurried to say. That settled things down, and Frank, the editor, who had a beard and was a veteran of the Korean War, became an enthusiast. It would be a fine idea and indeed amusing, he thought, if I used American spelling, grammar, and such in the articles I wrote. To celebrate the arrangement, I invited them to join me for beer at the pub across the street from the Men's Union, where the newspaper office was located. Women could enter the Union to work on the *Mancunian* and to attend the Thursday-afternoon debates, though only men could put on an academic gown and take the stage.

Over a pint of bitter, I found that English ale wasn't bitter at all, and that a pint went down very easily. I bonded especially with a lad named Malcolm Hopson. He had an amazing mop of black hair, and like Frank had completed his National Service, so he was more nearly my age than most of the students. He came from Liverpool; he had a girlfriend named Sheila; and he was fascinated with things Welsh, including Dylan Thomas's poetry and the town named Llanfairpwllgwyngyllgogerychwyrn-drobwllllantysiliogogogoch. Over the second pint of bitter, he drilled me on the name, and I can still rattle it off today, after a fashion.

So I'd made my first friends in Bloody Damn England. Basia wasn't among them; she came later. I've already written a book about her, so I'll try not to repeat myself here, and I'll try especially hard not to contradict anything I wrote in *Poland's Daughter*, which I regard as the best thing of mine in print.

I'm a bit vague about how we met. I had long believed that it was an encounter in Caf, over a cup of that strange English coffee, adulterated I think with chicory, and that it happened soon after the Christmas long vacation, which I'd spent in Ireland with two aunts and their families. Mom had arranged my schedule. I took a train to Holyhead and the ferry to Dún Laoghaire – O'Leary's Fort, now isn't that grand? – which the English still called Kingstown, but anyhow the port of Dublin. From there I took the train south to the County Cork. I knew somehow that Henry Laughlin now owned a home on the Blackwater River called Castle Hyde. My cousin Seamus Butler drove me past it, but we didn't venture to knock on the door. Though grander than the Concord mansion, the layout was actually rather similar, including the river behind it – famous for the salmon fishing, Seamus told me.

Basia remembered things somewhat differently: we'd met at the annual Rag Ball, she thought, a more or less formal dance that ended Rag Week, in which students raised hell while raising money for charity. That would place it in February 1955.

Apparently we were both wrong. When my brother died in 2011, I inherited the footlocker in which he'd kept his memorabilia, including his typewritten diary from UNH. (Only Joe would spin a half-sheet of paper into his typewriter and dutifully peck out an account of his day, supplemented with a carbon of any letter he'd written.) To my astonishment, I found that he had ventured where I had not, dating the shapely Betsy Warwick whom I had photographed for the *Winnipesaukee Times*. After taking a year off for her adventure in maternity, Betsy was back at UNH in the fall of 1954 while her mother took care of the meadowlark. She caught Joe's eye, among others', and they were close enough that she gave him a copy of that cheesecake photo, which I had given her, and which fifty-seven years later I would inherit along with his diary.

Joe and I had quite a correspondence that fall, I telling him about England, he telling me about UNH, and both talking about our romantic lives. I gave him wise advice about Betsy Warwick. And toward the end of November, I confessed that I was courting "a veritable Saint" in Manchester. Who could that have been, if not the Catholic girl from Lvow in eastern Poland, later annexed by Stalin to western Ukraine?

Whatever the chronology, we were something of a couple in the Lenten term in the late winter and early spring of 1955. I suppose this was very bad of me, because I was still pursuing my airmail affair with Rosalie Labranche, now a senior at UNH. Joe had seen her at Follansbee's restaurant, waiting on tables. "She is a very charming waitress," he wrote me. "I still wish she'd cut her hair though."

But Basia swept it all away! She was a crush on steroids, and my bright spot in that dreary year. I bought the *Manchester Guardian* every day for the thesis I was writing about the coverage of American news in British papers, as compared to the coverage of Britain in America. (Joe mailed me the needful copies of the *Boston Globe*, which I figured was the equivalent of the *Guardian*, just as Boston and Manchester were about the same size and significance.) While I did this, I also noted the previous day's weather, which for rain was usually "trace," and for sunshine "nil." We also had one of England's infamous pea soupers, during which, while walking down to Withington village for a packet of Player's Navy Cut, I fell off the sidewalk because I couldn't see the concrete beneath my feet. Basia meanwhile was riding the bus from Piccadilly Gardens to the far side of Manchester, where she lived with her aunt and uncle. The bus driver similarly lost his way, and a Bobbie had to be dispatched to lead the bus with a lantern.

It has been terrifying, as the father and grandfather of girls, to remember how driven I was by my gonads in my twenties. In November I had browsed a jewelry store near Piccadilly Gardens, which was the center of Manchester, complete with a statue of the obese Queen Victoria holding the globe in her right hand. I'd found the perfect engagement ring for Rosie, both pretty and within my newly expanded budget, though I hadn't gone so far as to buy it. But all that flew out of my mind when I sat across from Basia in Caf and looked into her impossibly blue eyes. My own eyes were blue, as were those of everyone in my family, and indeed those of almost every student at the University of Manchester. But Basia's eyes were so *dark*! Forgive me for gushing, but I felt I could dive into them and be lost forever in their depths. I scrambled to name their color. They were like . . . lapis lazuli. No! Like *cornflowers*!

Yes, they were the color of cornflowers. When I was back in my digs on Mauldeth Road West, in the urban village of Withington, I grabbed paper and fountain pen and wrote my adoration into poetry:

I think the fields of Eastern Europe
Are small. Stone walls surround them, and
The women wear kerchiefs against the sun.
They're gathering cornflowers for the market,
And the color is a blue beyond blue.
Your eyes, Basia, your eyes!
I have never seen eyes so lovely.
I have never seen eyes so blue.

I kept the poem to myself, though I suppose my roommate at Mauldeth Road West had seen it on my desk. But I did tell Basia that her eyes made me think of cornflowers. Whereupon they blurred with tears! It seemed that her father – a colonel in the Polish Army, murdered by the Russians in one of the massacres that are grouped under the name of Katyń – had a pet name for his younger daughter. He called her *Chabrus*, which meant . . . cornflower! I felt very close to the old soldier that afternoon, and I wished I could kiss away his daughter's tears. Alas, Basia had made it clear that kisses weren't welcome, and that I must keep my lips and hands to myself.

~ ~ ~ ~

It was a courtship conducted in Caf over cups of that dreadful English coffee, at the foreign-movie cinema uptown (*La Strada*, *Le Salaire de la peur*), in the pub across Oxford Street, and on the upper deck of the Number 2 bus when I was allowed to accompany her halfway home. I couldn't bed her; I couldn't even kiss her, because she turned her face away. Unlike me, Basia hadn't shed her Catholicism as a first-year University student – indeed, that probably wasn't a possibility, since she lodged with her Uncle Jan and his wife and her mother, and they no doubt whisked her off to Mass on Sunday and ensured she went to

Confession and took Communion every month.

So Basia followed what, at Brewster, Harry Nash and I had dubbed the St. Joseph's Aspirin approach to birth control, more reliable than the Rhythm Method. ("How does that work?" the listener was supposed to ask. "Does she swallow it or . . ." No, no, she holds the tablet between her knees!) The Poles, no less than the Irish, were very firm about the sin of impurity with others. For my high-school misdeeds, Father Poirier had let me off with a few recitations of the rosary. It would have been quite another matter if I'd brought a girl into the game.

I had, by this time, pretty much given up the pretense that I was working toward a master's degree. (I did eventually obtain an MA, and from King's College London at that, but not until 2010. It was an online "programme" in War in the Modern World, and King's mailed me a truly impressive diploma with a crest at the top and the words "*With Distinction.*" I was immensely pleased that, at the age of seventy-eight, I still had the knack.) First I gave up the suggested reading, then I stopped going to class, and by March I stopped visiting my tutor. I don't think he was at all sorry to see the last of me and my thesis. Journalism, as the Fulbright greeter had warned me, was not an academic subject in Britain.

One day in Caf, at the table reserved for the newspaper staff and our friends, Basia announced that she planned to spend the Easter term at the University for Foreigners in Perugia, to polish her knowledge of Italian language and culture. "I will visit Paris on the way," she said, "and Florence of course. I would love to have company! Won't one of you go with me?"

"Yes," I said, as I later learned she meant for me to do. "I will!"

~ ~ ~ ~

I am pleased to see that, like King's College London, the *Universitá per Stranieri* now offers online courses. Its website boasts that it "is the oldest and most prestigious Italian institution involved in teaching and research activities as well as in the diffusion of the Italian language and civilization in all expressions." But you may instead know Perugia as the place where a British girl was bizarrely murdered twelve years ago. Her roommate, Amanda Knox of Seattle, was convicted and sentenced to twenty-six years in prison, and she served nearly four of them before the sentence was annulled by the Italian high court.

That 2007 sensation of sex, drugs, and bloody footprints was a world away from the Perugia of 1955. Nevertheless, Uncle Jan was scandalized that Basia intended to travel through Paris – sinful Paris! – and much of France, Switzerland, and Italy on her way to her studies. He wrote a fiery letter to the University of Manchester, and he didn't settle down until Mama Deszberg decreed that Basia must find a travel companion, whom Mama would vet before the young people boarded the boat train to Dover and the ferry to Calais.

I had a beard by this time, and worse, I was an American and no doubt as louche as the rest of my countrymen. I'd seen enough plays and vaudeville skits to understand that, to theater-going Englishmen, Americans were figures of fun. We walked about with our hands in our pockets and drawling "I guess I reckon," which was always good for a laugh. (English movies were much more discreet, since they needed the U.S. market to make a profit. I notice the same diffidence today when it comes to Chinese characters in American movies.) But it seemed that I had an asset, too. During the family's hegira out of Russia, Mama had worked as a waitress in the American officers' club in Tehran. The men called her "Susie" – her given name was Zuzanna – and perhaps one or two of them ventured to pat her *pupka*, or fanny. She had married Colonel Deszberg at eighteen, and was only thirty-two when the family escaped from exile and found comparative safety in Iran. I've seen photos of those years, and she was a beautiful woman.

One of the Americans actively courted Mama, and in the process sometimes treated Basia and her sister to an ice-cream cone. Apparently I came under the umbrella of this fond memory. To prepare me for meeting Mama, Basia gave me lessons in the Eastern European custom of kissing a lady's hand. As an American, I ought to have recoiled from this decadent practice, but if I couldn't kiss the sweet bow of Basia's lips, I was happy enough to kiss her hand. Indeed, I once turned it over and kissed the palm.

I didn't have a word of Polish, though I picked up a few later; and Mama's English was restricted to what she needed for shopping: "How much is that? Five shillings? Too much!" But we got along all right, and I passed the test I didn't know I was taking. I slept in the spare room, which was also the laundry room, so I washed my shirt, dried it in front of the electric fire, and ironed it before breakfast. "I will see Basia safe to Perugia," I assured Mama in the morning, though I'm not sure she understood me.

I wore the Harris Tweed jacket that was my all-season garment in Manchester, Basia wore her tan duffel coat, and we carried our rucksacks upon our shoulders. Did Mama watch us from the window as we walked down the street to North Ealing Underground? I'm sure she did, and I'm equally sure that neither of us looked back. Basia was twenty-one and I was twenty-three, and we were off on the adventure of our young lives.

~ ~ ~ ~

I think we'd already decided to hitchhike to Italy – hence our rucksacks. I'd done some backpacking in England, to the Lake District in a snowstorm with Frank, the editor of the *Mancunian*, and by myself to Land's End in Cornwall, so I was equipped with the necessary stuff: pack, sleeping bag, and a copy of the little red *Youth Hostel Guide*, which not only listed the hostels in each country, but its major attractions as well. In the bottom of the sleeping bag, I had tied a nylon sack containing thirty one-pound notes. They were from my blocked sterling account, but it would be a brave customs officer who unrolled that sleeping bag and found the contraband. The English, as I recall, could take only ten pounds out of the country. No doubt Basia had a special allowance, since she'd been given permission to spend the Easter term abroad.

We had tickets as far as Paris – train to Dover, ferry to Calais, and train again to Gare du Nord, in an open carriage on the American style, much cleaner, brighter, and faster than the English version. And it was electrified! Even on my first day on the Continent, I could see that Britain had come out of the War in sadder shape than the countries invaded first by Germany and then by the Western Allies.

We took the Metro to Place d'Italie on the south side of the city and checked in at the youth hostel – one hundred francs each, or twenty-five cents at the then-rate of exchange. That, plus our Metro tickets, a liter of wine, a loaf of bread, half a kilo of cheese, and a pack of thick, heady Gauloises cigarettes, brought the cost of our first day in Paris to one pound sterling for each of us. We'd purchased our London-Paris tickets at Victoria Station, so that didn't count against Basia's overseas allowance.

It was the first week of April, and we were warmer than we'd ever been in Manchester. The sun shone every day, or anyhow I remember Paris that way. We walked to the second level of the Eiffel Tower, climbed the steps to the Sacré Coeur, shared a beer at Les Deux Magots, and even went to Mass at Notre Dame. I was in heaven, or as near to it as I could imagine. April in Paris, and I was there with the girl I loved and, what's more, could interpret for me. . . . Ah, but why had I wasted so many hours at Brewster and UNH, struggling with Spanish, when I could have learned this enchanting language that rippled off Basia's tongue? And she had never actually *studied* French! She'd picked it up in Beirut, on one stage of her eight-year journey from Poland to Russia, Iran, Lebanon, Egypt, and finally England.

And I met Gordon Olson! The youth hostel, a concrete-block structure rather like a jail, had a trampled back yard with a few tents in it, and in one of them slept my pal from fifth, sixth, and seventh grade. Like me, Gordon had graduated from his state university in June and set out for Europe. He'd visited relatives in Norway, gone skiing in Austria, then shipped his skis home and made for Paris, where a sly hand in the Metro stole his wallet and passport. The hostel concierge let him pitch his tent in the yard and use the kitchen and common room while he waited for a new passport. His father had sent him a check for fifty dollars but American Express wouldn't cash it. "Look me up in Manchester at the end of April," I told him, "and I'll cash it for you!"

~ ~ ~ ~

Basia, I'm afraid, is unhappy with me, because she wants to walk on instead of standing still at a choice spot for hitchhiking. The rides were few and far between on Easter Monday, when I took this photo outside Chambéry. That's my rucksack in the foreground, with a length of French bread beneath the flap.

Our first day on the Route d'Italie was a triumph. We walked from the hostel to Place d'Italie and I held up my open palm, having been warned by Gordon that raising my thumb in the American fashion was considered a rude gesture by Europeans. A farmer in a squat Citroën Deux Chavaux stopped for us, and we were away! Basia sat in front and chatted him up, while I was fascinated to see that the gear-shifter was in the dashboard. Again, it must be difficult for people in the twenty-first century to grasp how *different* countries were in those years, each with its own currency, automobiles, cigarettes, wine, bread, cheese, coffee – and language, as it seemed to me. I would later find that Switzerland, as if unable to make up its mind, used variants of three of them, and a mixture of its neighbors' automobiles. The road signs, at least, were uniform throughout the Continent. And to see the occasional Route d'Itali*e* sign posted beside the endless, straight, two-lane highway, close-bordered by tall, identically shaped Lombardy poplars . . . oh, that was very heaven.

We were in Lyon by nightfall, walking up the east bank of the Rhone and ignoring the tram that would have taken us to the door of the youth hostel. We'd covered five hundred kilometers, three hundred miles, not a bad day's work even by American standards. And the night was absolutely balmy, like sailing in the Caribbean!

That was Saturday, April 9. We'd planned to cross the Alps next day, triumphant like Hannibal in Italy; we hadn't allowed for the fact that in April the Col du Mont Cenis would still be buried in snow. Or that it was Easter! That had never entered my mind, though it may have troubled the Catholic girl beside me. Bad enough to skip Mass, but to miss one's Easter duty of Confession and Communion, that was a sin indeed.

Certainly everyone else was at Mass or at home that Sunday, and in all that long day we got no farther than the town of Les Abrets. I have great affection for Les Abrets, because we were obliged to put up at the town's only *auberge*, and for economy to share a room. Basia asked for a room with two beds, but apparently she'd decided to explore that business with the lips that I'd so often attempted, only to be foisted off with the back of her hand (and once the palm). After sharing our bottle of wine, she slid to the floor and blessed me with a smile. I slid down beside her; we kissed; we embraced; we rolled about on the floor and even on her bed. But I didn't manage to dislodge that metaphorical aspirin tablet between Basia's knees.

No matter! I was happy.

Easter Monday was another hard day. An avalanche had cut the Route d'Italie, and we had to go around it on a railroad bridge, and when we reached the border town of Modane, we learned that the only open route to Italy was a tunnel that had no automobile traffic. (We'd been following, for the most part, the old Route Nationale 6, since eclipsed by a divided highway. And Modane is now a destination on the TGV bullet train!) For a few hundred francs we bought tickets to the next stop, which turned out to be the tunnel exit some distance above the village of Bardonecchia, which had no youth hostel but did have the great virtue of being in Italy. The truck driver who took us down into the village offered to put us up for the night, and when Basia took the only bedroom, he first tried to join her in bed and then, rebuffed, tried his luck with me. Uncle Jan, I realized, was fully justified in his suspicion of Continental travel, while underestimating his niece's ability to foist off men with a lift of her perfect eyebrows and a smile on the sweet bow of her lips.

Well, we finally reached Perugia, sleeping Tuesday night in the long-distance truck that had taken us to Alessandria, I on the bench seat, Basia on the bunk behind it; and on Wednesday, happily for me, in a hotel in Pontedera, home of the Piaggio company and its Vespa motorscooter, named for the wasp whose shape it had borrowed. (These hotels cost each of us the equivalent of a dollar, so we were still within our budget of a pound a day.) We were in the pretty hilltop town of Perugia by Thursday afternoon, where Basia registered for the Universitá per Stranieri and rented a room in the apartment of an American couple, the husband also a student. For my part, I unrolled my sleeping bag in a nearby apple orchard.

~ ~ ~ ~

After a few days I moved on to Rome, then Venice, then Milan, and by the end of April I was back at Mauldeth Road West. Easter term seemed to take no time at all. Gordon Olson turned up and I cashed his check. This was a good deal for both of us, because I gave him eighteen pounds, a better rate than American Express would have provided, while depositing Mr. Olson's fifty-dollar check in my U.S. dollar account at the National Westminster bank on Oxford Street. I could now afford ten ten-dollar traveler's checks to cushion my return to the United States. The Fulbright people were kind enough to exchange my June return ticket for one toward the end of August. I wrote an article about youth hostels and vagabonding for the *Christian Science Monitor*; I assume they published it, because they sent me a check for ten dollars, which on my next trip to London I exchanged for sterling from a nice woman at the newspaper's European office.

I wrote Rosalie and my draft board that I would be somewhat delayed in returning to New Hampshire. As perhaps I'd hoped, this ended my quasi-engagement. "I won't be staying home anymore," Rosie warned by return mail. Well, of course not!

I got my last fifty pounds from the Fulbright people on May 31, closed out my accounts at Nat West, and put my U.S. dollar traveler's checks in my footlocker along with the best of my Penguin paperbacks, a few hardcovers (*Fiesta, The Last Tycoon and The Great Gatsby*, and Churchill's wartime memoirs in what the British frankly labeled the Cheap Edition), and such of my belongings that seemed worth taking home. It was very emotional, saying goodbye to my friends at Caf, at the *Mancunian* office, at Mauldeth Road West. I checked the footlocker at Euston Station in London and was back in Perugia by the second week of June. Basia wasn't there! She'd fluttered off to Capri with a French vagabond named Laetitia. That would have delighted Rosie, had she known!

~ ~ ~ ~

After a detour to the Adriatic and the republic of San Marino, I did have my reunion with Basia in Perugia. The plan, it seemed, was that the four of us – our number now augmented by Laetitia and a charming homosexual named Giorgio, who identified himself as a *marchese* and who gave me a business card to prove it – would hitchhike to the Mediterranean and the fabled youth hostel at Lerici. This was fine with me. Anything was fine with me, as long as Basia and I made a pair: we had to divide our force, since the invariable Italian automobile was the tiny Fiat called *Topolino*, meaning Mickey Mouse, which couldn't fit more than three people in addition to the driver. The

Topolino had a 1930s look. I was told that the post-war models boasted a more powerful engine – sixteen horsepower! – but I couldn't tell the difference.

I wish I had kept Giorgio's card! It made no impression on me at the time: if he claimed to be a noble, who was I to doubt him? It seemed all in the nature of things that I should be hitchhiking with Basia to Florence, La Spezia, and the Gulf of Poets, with a plump French vagabond and a delicate Italian marchese following along behind. By mid-afternoon we were a foursome again, sitting on the battlements of a fourteenth century Pisan castle, high above the fishing village of Lerici and the blue water stretching to the westward. (The Mediterranean wasn't a wine-dark sea, as Homer and Mr. Vaughan had assured me at Brewster Academy. But neither was it blue, come to think of it. We see what we expect to see.) As I understood matters at the time, the gulf got its name from Byron, who drowned there, and from Shelley, who danced around his funeral pyre and snatched his heart out of the flames. Or perhaps it was the other way around. I'd picked up that bit of lore from Emma, my associate editor on the *New Hampshire*, and hadn't given it the attention it deserved. Who knows what will prove useful in the years ahead?

The hostel was run with a firm but forgiving hand by a sprite of a woman named Madi. The Youth Hostel Association supposedly limited the clientele to people no older than twenty-eight, traveling by foot or bicycle, and staying no longer than three nights in any given place. In England and perhaps other countries, the rules were enforced though nobody fussed about hitchhiking. But in France and Italy at least, there were no rules. On the Adriatic I'd met a German family who drove up in a Volkswagen of recent vintage – *Muti*, *Vati*, and two kids – and were welcomed with the rest of us. The hostel managers did what they liked, and Madi liked us, so we stayed, and stayed.

I am trying here not to repeat myself from what I wrote in *Poland's Daughter*, but there are a few paragraphs worth repeating, about the remarkable solipsism of the young:

~ ~ ~ ~

But most of all, we were happy! The sky is always blue in my memory of Lerici – the sunset is always glorious – the moon is always full – and the tide is always high. Sunrise or sunset, Lerici was *nostro pezzo del cielo caduto in terra*, our piece of heaven fallen to earth.

What a distance Basia and I had traveled, from Piccadilly Gardens in the March rain! At Lerici, we lived in an eternal Now, suspended in time and space. Our castle was the center of the universe – and not just our universe, either, but the center of the entire, star-spangled, infinitely expanding cosmos. The sun rose each morning for a single purpose – to light the castle's ancient stones, to bronze our shoulders, and to warm the sand beneath our feet.

Like the sun, and like the castle, this month of July in the year 1955 was the moment toward which evolution had been trending since the earth had cooled. History had reached stasis, with us as its intended end. In some remote corner of our minds, I suppose we understood that this wasn't really the case – that Madi hadn't been put on earth to mind the Castello di Lerici, nor Enrico to row us to the *Grotta Azzurra*. Perhaps Basia, with her history of war and exile, understood that better than most of us – understood that the earth had a crust as thin as an eggshell, which might crack at any moment and plunge us into the abyss. A first-hand brush against catastrophe is a great asset when it comes to understanding the precariousness of human existence.

And perhaps I – the American unmarked by the War, who actually had profited from it – understood this less than the others, even the Australian lads and the Irish girls, for whom the War had come almost close enough to touch. But all of us, I think, believed that the world was created for our enjoyment. Even Basia believed that! The whole point of being twenty or twenty-one or twenty-three years old is to ride the cusp of history, with children and old people as bit players in the drama of our lives.

~ ~ ~ ~

That's a bit overheated, but it was the way I thought at the time. And that raises the obvious question: if Lerici was so wonderful, why did I move on? Well, Basia was little more forthcoming in July than she had been in April. We were chums! Was there ever a more humiliating role for a young man with a libido? I liked Giorgio, liked Laetitia, adored Basia, and enjoyed Madi and the *vagabondi* who ebbed and flowed through our castle, but I had a date with *RMS Brittanic* at the end of August, and I wanted to experience more of Europe before going home. Toward this end, I'd picked up a few essential German phrases (where are you going? where is the youth hostel? how much does that cost?) from *Vati* at the youth hostel on the Adriatic, and other phrases (straight ahead, to the left, to the right, sausage with potato salad, a beer please) from the German bicyclists who swan-dived from the battlements into the Gulf of Poets.

Indeed, one of the bicyclists went with me to the Autostrada toll gate and chatted up the drivers until he found one who'd take me all the way to Milano.

After gaping at Leonardo's "The Last Supper" in its dark setting at the convent of Santa Maria delle Grazie, I pressed on to Menagio, which the wise travelers at Lerici had assured me was much more "authentic" than the more famous Como. From there I walked – walked! – to Switzerland, where I had a great encounter with one of the lads from Caf, who was doing the Grand Tour with two others. They made room for me in their little Ford Anglia, and they dropped me off in Luzerne, because I had a yen to walk across its famous covered bridge. (Why? What did I care about historic bridges when Basia's soft lips remained in Italy?) From there I made my way to Lichtenstein, since I was still collecting small countries; to Innsbruck in Austria; to Munich and its *Hofbräuhaus*; to Wiesbaden and the Rhine steamer that took me past castles and such to Koblenz; to Brussels and its *Manneken Pis*; to Ostend and a ferry back to England, which after all this foreignness now seemed like home.

I had fine reunions in London. Malcolm Hopson came down from Manchester, where, having failed his year-end exams, he'd been hired to teach the incoming freshers! Tommy and Emma, formerly of the student paper staff at UNH, now married and setting out on a European tour of their own, also turned up. We got very drunk, and we ended with Tommy passed out in one room with the door locked, and Emma and I in bed together in the other, to our shame and to no great pleasure, at least not on my part.

I sold another travel piece to the *Christian Science Monitor,* which edited out my references to hitchhiking and put me on a bicycle instead. I visited the Elgin Marbles at the British Museum and Karl Marx's grave in Highgate Cemetery. I saw *Tales of*

Hoffmann at the Royal Opera House and *Hamlet* at the Old Vic, and in time I boarded *RMS Brittanic* and went home. It was all wonderful, educational, mind-expanding. . . .

Well, no, it was ashes and sackcloth, to have left those cornflower-blue eyes behind.

Climbing to the St. Gotthard Pass, the engine on Anthony's little Ford Anglia suffered a vapor lock. We got out, turned the car around, jumped in, rolled downhill, and popped the clutch to force the poor thing to start again. On his second try, Anthony made it to the height-of-land, where he took this photo of me, appropriately serious on top of the world.

7 – *The Army*

BACK FROM EUROPE IN THE fall of 1955, I lodged with Mom in Wolfeboro long enough to shave my beard and buy a nice 1948 Ford coupe for $275. I drove to Durham, which by now felt more like home than my home town did, and rented a room for five dollars a week. The student newspaper had no photographer, so I offered to provide photos for five dollars each and the use of their darkroom. The editor (a girl!) told me that an advertising agency in Manchester was looking for a copywriter, so I drove over there, and we agreed on fifteen dollars a day, three days a week, leaving me time to write a novel if I could think of one. My boss was a delightful little Jewish guy. One day when we encountered a pretty schoolgirl, he elbowed me and said, "Now, that's *eating* stuff." I understood the concept, more or less, but was startled to hear it from a middle-aged man. Later he wanted me to write a Christmas letter to his clients without using the actual word. So I rhapsodized about the "holiday season," only to have that blue-penciled as well, since it suggested that the season was *holy*. I think we compromised on Winter Holidays. We were ahead of our time! My granddaughters are now in college, and they aren't given a week or so off for Christmas and Easter, but for Winter and Spring Break, and Thanksgiving is known as November Break.

The Selective Service System – not so selective, as it turned out! – caught up with me in December. I had an induction date of Tuesday, January 3, 1956, which I suppose was designed to give me Christmas at home and a day to recover from New Year's Eve.

So I packed up, rejoined Mom at her second-floor apartment on Lake Street in Wolfeboro, found a lad to buy my beloved Ford coupe, and had a great time skating with Harry Nash and his girlfriend. Harry was back at Wesleyan and bound for medical school, and he teased me about my date with the Army: "Kind of wondering what it's all about, aren't you?"

I was certain that I'd be scorned as 4-F, unfit for service. After all, I was effectively blind in my left eye, and I had flat feet! So it was with a fair amount of confidence that I packed an overnight bag and took a taxi to the county courthouse in Ossipee – where Harry and I had acquired our driver's licenses in 1948 – and with another lad was given a bus ticket to Manchester by way of Exeter. In Exeter we were told that the Manchester bus had ceased to operate as of January 1, and we were given a complimentary taxi ride and an overnight in a rather stolid Manchester hotel. When all this was done, one doctor said to the other, "Well, they don't march them as much as they used to." I was passed 1-A for service, which happened to few other of my classmates.

I survived basic training thanks to Seymour Major, a friend from UNH who unwisely told the truth when asked: "Are you now or have you ever been a member of the Communist Party USA?" I'd said No to that question, and would have given the same answer even if I'd had a CPUSA card in my pocket. In the 1950s, there was no way to cross-check such things. If the FBI had done a security check on every draftee, it would never had had the time to catch criminals or tap Martin Luther King's telephone.

As a security risk, Si would never be promoted beyond buck private, nor could he travel beyond the orderly room of Golf Company, 272nd Infantry Regiment, 69th Infantry Division at Fort Dix, New Jersey.

(We merrily called ourselves "the Cocksuckers.") The training cadre – the officers all white, the sergeants mostly black – thought it hilarious that our company clerk was Private Major. Bless his too-honest soul, Seymour was good at his job, so he was allowed to do pretty much what he wanted, and he'd call me over to the orderly room for a typing detail whenever a speed march or some other impossible task was on the schedule.

My traveling companion from Center Ossipee was also in the orderly room from time to time; he was forever wandering off from training and being told to report to the First Sergeant. I don't remember his name; I'll call him Bradley. The First Sergeant (who was white) would employ Brad as a courier for the rest of the morning or afternoon, sending him here and there with some paperwork or other. When he didn't return, the First Sergeant dispatched me to find him, and always he was sitting in the tiny Post Exchange or whatever it was, a cafeteria with soft drinks and a jukebox playing "Little Band of Gold," "The Great Pretender," and "Blue Suede Shoes." A jukebox of the time held only twenty-four records, so as with my summer at Dockside and the dining hall at UNH, I heard the same songs so often they bored into my brain. I had a glass of orangeade with Brad, we talked about classical music (he knew a lot more than I did), and after awhile I took him back to the orderly room.

The First Sergeant went into outrage mode: "Where have you been? Why didn't you come back from Battalion?"

"You didn't *tell* me to come back," Brad said – which was true – and he began to cry.

"Stop that crying! *Why* are you crying?"

"Because I'm afraid of you, First Sergeant."

The sergeant sent him into the Captain's office, where Brad fainted. We heard him hit the floor.

"Faking," the First Sergeant said to Si and me. "I *know* he's faking." But if Brad were faking, he was good at it, and early in February he got a Section Eight discharge – "mentally unfit for military service" – while I continued in the mud and snow of the New Jersey winter, pushed and prodded and cursed by black sergeants who'd fought in Korea and knew that when untrained men went into combat, they were apt to throw down their weapons and run.

This was the first time in my life that I was bossed around by blacks or spent much time working with them. I liked the cadre well enough, though their command of English was extraordinary, saying "casuals" for *casualties*, "they" for *there*, and "has" for *have*. Of the M-20 bazooka rocket launcher, a sergeant told us: "They is the AP or anti-personnel round, and then they is the armor-piercing or *AP round*" – really!

I was amazed by the stamina of the lads from Harlem, who after twelve hours of training would climb the fence and go carousing in Bordentown. My favorite was Private Porter, who either spent entire nights in Bordentown or else suffered from sleeping sickness. He'd fall asleep while marching, and one time he was dispensing potatoes in the chow line, and when I held out my tray, he just stood there with a ladle full of mashed potatoes, his eyes and mouth wide open, fast asleep. What with one thing and another, I'm afraid I didn't come out of Fort Dix as free of racial prejudice as when I arrived.

~ ~ ~ ~

If the U.S. Army had let me go on St. Patrick's Day 1956, when I graduated from Basic, I would have been a fairly useful member of the Army Reserve, because I accomplished everything it asked of me except the infamous speed march, and I even qualified as a Sharpshooter with the magnificent M-1 Garand. What a great rifle that was! Fortunately for me, and probably for the nation, I was never sent into combat, but if I had to do it, I'd want no better weapon than that never-jamming, rapid-firing (for its time), and happily-named M-1, the first in its field.

But that's not what happened. After a two-week furlough, which I divided between Wolfeboro and Boston (Emma and Tommy were now living on the back side of Beacon Hill, as were several other UNH graduates), I reported to the Special Warfare Center at Fort Bragg, North Carolina. Here I was to be trained as a radio broadcast specialist, and here we Psychological Warfare geeks served alongside the fabled Green Berets of U.S. Army Special Forces. And we shared a recreational center – a twin of the Notch building at UNH – with the equally fabled 82nd Airborne Division.

The Army that summer adopted a British-style tropical uniform of knee-length shorts and calf-high wool socks. Once, when entering the recreational building, I met two black Airborne troopers on their way out. They stared unbelieving at my shorts. Behind me, I heard one say to the other: "That PsyWar don't show me shit."

I think I know what I was doing that day. It seems that in June 1956, as Basia was graduating from the University of Manchester, a young man she'd met at the Polish Hearth Club in London proposed to her, and she accepted. I went to the enlisted men's club on Smoke Bomb Hill to use one of its coin-operated typewriters to compose a letter of good wishes. How that must have pained me! Enough that I banished it from my memory until we connected again in 2010.

That 82nd Airborne trooper was right, of course. Our uniform was absurd, Fort Bragg was beastly hot, and PsyWar was a waste of time. I did my best to make something out of it, escaping to New York City whenever I could cadge a pass from the company clerk and catch a ride with someone heading in the same direction. (We would rendezvous Sunday night at Grand Central, where I tried to sleep on a bench and MPs tried to keep me awake by whacking the sole of my shoe with a billy club.) I went to the ballet if I could find one, or to a play, and in this fashion saw Samuel Beckett's *Waiting for Godot* and Jean-Paul Sartre's *No Exit*. I loved them both, especially *Godot* and the character played by Bert Lahr, whom I had last seen as the Cowardly Lion in *The Wizard of Oz*. Since I was still in my Faustian period, I especially liked *Godot*'s takeaway line: "One day we were born, one day we shall die . . . is that not enough for you?" Alas, not everyone in the audience agreed with my judgment: the couple in front of me walked out, there were a few boos at the curtain call, and *Godot* closed a few weeks later.

In June I hitchhiked to Durham for Joe's graduation– 1,700 miles round trip – and got back to Smoke Bomb Hill at two or three o'clock Tuesday morning. (That was the weekend I met Horace Lyndes, who later became a great buddy.) Another time I caught a hop in a C-119 Flying Boxcar to Grenier Field in New Hampshire by way of the nation's capital, which gave me the opportunity to use the relief tube to piss on the Pentagon. From Grenier, I hitchhiked the rest of the way, serendipitously meeting Billy Kenney in Navy whites in Alton Bay, bound like me for Wolfeboro.

This was all very well, but not enough to reconcile me to Fort Bragg, so I wrote to Senator Styles Bridges.

If I *must* waste two years of my life, I pleaded, why couldn't I do it in Germany? A few weeks later I was called to Battalion headquarters. "So you want to go overseas?" the Major said.

"Yes, Sir."

That "overseas" had an ominous sound, as he no doubt intended. He folded his hands and looked at me. "Soldier," he said, "I've been in the Army for fifteen years. My dream assignment was always Japan, but the Army needed me elsewhere, so I never saw that country. Do you understand?"

"Yes, Sir."

"Well! I can put you on the next levy out of here, but it might not be Germany. It might be Greenland – cold weather and Eskimos. And mosquitoes in the spring, do you understand?"

"Yes, Sir."

"Do you still want to go?"

Was he serious about Greenland? I swallowed and said, "Yes, Sir."

I bought a red hardcover, *German Without Toil*, at the Post Exchange, and a few weeks later I was standing in line with my duffel bag – I think on the New Jersey side of the Hudson River – to board the troopship *General Darby*, bound for Bremerhaven. The man behind me was a small guy who introduced himself as George Araujo. "I'm not black," he told me. "I'm Portuguese." He was a boxer, it seemed, and a few years earlier had been a serious contender for the lightweight championship. I didn't bother telling him that I'd boxed for fun in high school. Looking at George, who had won fifty-eight fights, all but three by knockouts, I decided it was a good thing I hadn't tried out for the Golden Gloves. George had been New England champion in 1948, the year of my pretensions as a boxer.

We became good friends on the seven-day passage to Bremerhaven, and after all my study of German, he and I were directed to a sleeper carriage bound for Paris. When we woke up in the morning at Gare de l'Est, I was thrilled to be able to translate for my mates in the couchette – triple-decker bunks on either side of a narrow aisle, the top two folding against the wall during the day – who wanted to buy ham sandwiches and coffee, all that the vendors had on offer. With some others, George and I were sent to Gare d'Austerlitz and from there to the little city of Orléans. I was told to report to the orderly room of Headquarters and Headquarters Company, but George was put on a bus to another destination.

I soon discovered that we had just one black soldier among the four hundred men in "Head and Head," as it was called, the company that housed and fed and otherwise took care of the men who staffed the various offices in Coligny Caserne – the policemen, lawyers, musicians, the whole panoply of the American military overseas, to a total of thirteen thousand officers, enlisted men, wives, and children in Orléans. But Hamp was a college graduate, so he was allowed to stay at Coligny Caserne. George Araujo, however, was sent to the boondocks. Orléans was supported by half a dozen outlying posts, just as we supported the infantry and armored divisions in Germany that were supposed to stop the Russian tanks, when and if they poured through the Fulda Gap to conquer West Germany.

Yes, we really believed that could happen, and indeed I would be the man charged with driving that belief into the minds of the men at Coligny Caserne. And, unlike most educated Americans today, I still believe that if the U.S. Army hadn't been in West Germany, the Red Army would have been. There seems to be something in the Russian gene that impels it to expand into any country unlucky enough to border it. Didn't it do just that in 1939? And do it again in 1945? And doing much the same thing today, with Mr. Putin messing with every small country within reach?

I saw George from time to time thereafter, when he came in from wherever he was stationed, but he was surrounded by a gang of white guys – dodgy types, like race-track touts – so we just exchanged a wry hand-wave in passing, in memory of the week we'd shared on the *General Darby*. Once, on shipboard, George had apologized to a card game for leaving it to join me in a walk around the deck. "I like this guy," he explained. "He's *diff*-rent." I was learning that the Army wasn't the best place to make friends, though Fort Bragg had been something of an exception. I often missed the PsyWar lads in the year and a half I spent at Coligny Caserne: Ted, the Harvard graduate who stuttered, or pretended to, so he became the center of attention, and who claimed to have read *À la recherche du temps perdu* in the original, seven books, a million words; Glovsky, the artist, who made a running gag out of being the sensitive Jew ("*Jews?*" he would cry, if asked to pass the orange juice; "who's talking about *Jews?*"); and others of that ilk. There was even a kid from East Germany who'd slipped through the Iron Curtain and volunteered under the Lodge Act, five years in the U.S. Army and a fast track to citizenship.

~ ~ ~ ~

Because it was twice the size of a normal company, Head and Head was commanded by a major, with a captain as executive officer, each a grade above the custom. I spent my first day getting outfitted at the Supply Room and squared away at Personnel.

"You're in the orderly room," the supply clerk told me as he issued my field gear – olive-green wool trousers and shirt, many-pocketed battle overalls, combat pack, half a pup tent, one tent pole, entrenching tool, bayonet – all the stuff that would transform a bespectacled radio broadcast specialist into an infantryman if the Cold War turned hot. "We don't go to Training," he explained, "and you don't clean your weapon." He nodded at the armorer, who waved a carbine at me and put it back in the rack. I don't remember the serial number because I never cleaned it or otherwise cared for the thing.

What good, after all, was a Sharpshooter armed with the United States Carbine, Caliber .30, M-2? In basic training, we'd been shown the carbine but not asked to fire it. "I could stand over there on that fence," the cadre instructor told us, "and you could shoot at me all afternoon, and you won't hit me." At Fort Bragg, I'd found how useless a carbine was, or at least the weapon issued to me: serial number 1048803. The magazine held fifteen rounds. I was rarely able to fire more than five of them before the bolt jammed open and I needed the armorer to fix it. On the plus side, it didn't make much noise and it weighed only half what the Garand did. And supposedly I could use it as a machinegun, though in the case of 1048803 that would only hasten the moment when the bolt jammed open and I'd be standing there with a five-pound extension for my bayonet

Fully equipped, though without a weapon, I reported to the orderly room, where everyone I saw was white – the two clerks with Specialist badges on the sleeves of their Ike jackets, the five-striper Sergeant Brown who'd become my mentor and friend, and the six-striper Sergeant Smith. There were some Puerto Ricans in Head and Head, but no blacks except Hamp. (I assume his last name was Hampton, but if so I never learned it. We mostly used nicknames when addressing one another.) Even the cooks in the mess hall were white. They were French, as were the blue-uniformed women who served us in the cafeteria line and tidied up after us. I suppose this was a French equivalent of my Fulbright Fellowship: some portion of Marshall Plan money had been a loan rather than a gift, and it was now being recycled in the mess hall, pumping up the local economy while preserving France's horde of dollars.

Sergeant Smith paid me no attention. Sergeant Brown escorted me into the CO's office. I snapped to attention: "Private First Class Ford reporting as ordered, Sir!"

"Well, Soldier, we've been waiting for you for a long time."

"Sir?"

"Going to be a teacher, aren't you?"

"No, Sir."

He shook his head: this wasn't going according to plan. "Went to college, didn't you?" he said, as if playing his ace.

"Yes, Sir."

"Well, then, you're going to be a teacher! And we need a Troop Information and Education NCO."

He paused, so I gave him the expected answer: "Yes, Sir."

"Sergeant Brown will get you straightened away."

So now I knew about the Training that the Supply Room people wouldn't have to attend. Every Tuesday and Thursday afternoon, Sergeant Brown explained, I would deliver an hour-long lecture about current events and a topic of interest to the U.S. Army and presumably to the troops. Many of these were geographical – *Our NATO Ally: Greece, Our NATO Ally: West Germany*, and so on. Others were hortatory: the Code of Conduct and what we were permitted to tell the Russians if taken prisoner.

Most of the sergeants in Head and Head were veterans of the Second World War, and some indeed had been officers who afterward had preferred being reduced to the ranks to the challenge of making a life in the real world – a former chaplain included! Even Sergeant Brown, who was probably just my age, was a veteran. He'd served in Korea from the very first month. "I was an MP in Japan," he told me. "When I landed at Pusan, they looked at my armband and said, 'We don't need anyone directing traffic. Everybody's going the same way – south!' So they put me in a tank." His face was scarred with the pockmarks he'd acquired, driving a buttoned-down Chaffee that August, while I was getting ready for my freshman year at the University of New Hampshire. And he had a medical slip permitting him to wear street shoes with his field uniform: he couldn't wear combat boots because his feet had been ruined by frostbite in the November retreat from the Frozen Chosin, when I was washing dishes and cooking the occasional omelet at Dunfey's. "You can always take another step if you have to," he said. "I remember a guy with his left foot blown off, walking back from the Yalu. He just hopped along on his right foot and the stump of his left."

I learned more from Sergeant Brown than I ever taught my troops, two hundred men on Tuesday afternoons, two hundred more on Thursdays.

The Major, he also confided, was in much the same position as the former chaplain and many of the sergeants in Head and Head: he'd been promoted to the extent of his ability, or beyond it, and he'd served too many years at his present grade, so must either retire or accept a demotion to his highest non-commissioned rank. The Major was lucky in this respect, since he'd been a warrant officer before getting a field commission as a first lieutenant. A warrant officer was like a mule, neither one thing nor the other, rather like the Specialist Third Class I would soon become. A Spec Three had the pay and other privileges of a two-stripe corporal, but without any command authority. If the Russians did come through the Fulda Gap, and I found myself with my carbine defending Orléans, a real corporal could order me around as if I were still a private.

Anyhow, the Major outlasted me at Coligny Caserne, and his demotion was still pending when I left on January 3, 1958.

~ ~ ~ ~

The weird thing about life in the Caserne was how slowly it dragged through the day, and how swiftly the days – weeks, months! – sped by with nothing accomplished except the beer we drank in the NCO Club, the cigarettes we smoked, and the movies we saw, most often a Western, which we called a Shoot-'Em-Up. Some nights we cheered the cowboys or the 7th Cavalry, some nights we cheered the Indians. I should have been reading a book, or studying French, but somehow all ambition had leached away. There was a fairly good library at Coligny Caserne, but I couldn't interest myself even in the rubbish I'd formerly devoured, Lew Wetzel or the Robin Hood of Modern Crime or England after Armageddon.

My first lecture was a disaster. I got through current events okay, but when it came to *Our NATO Ally: Turkey*, about twenty minutes into the hour my mouth opened and my mind went blank. I had nothing to say. Nothing! I stared at my two hundred trainees, and they stared back. Believe me, four hundred is a great number of eyeballs to wake from a doze and begin staring at you. The silence went on, and on, until Sergeant Brown levered himself off the wall against which he was leaning, and roared, "'Ten HUT! Diss MISS!" The theater emptied in a rush, as much a relief to my trainees, I'm sure, as it was to me.

When he showed up on Wednesday morning, the Major gave me the eyeball, and I dutifully followed him into his office. "Sit down, Ford," he said, the first time an officer had ever invited me to sit in his presence. He gave me a little pep talk, which mainly consisted of providing me with a joke about Elvis Presley that I should use on Thursday afternoon to get the trainees relaxed and on my side. (It seems that Mrs. Presley was upset that her eldest boy was called Elvis the Pelvis, since he had a younger brother named Enos.) I did tell the joke, though I prefaced it by saying that it had come from an officer, so I knew it was funny, and that *did* get a laugh, and I got through *Our NATO Ally: Turkey* without my mind betraying me.

As a lecturer, it seemed, I was a slow starter, just as my brother was slow to catch on with academics. Though he didn't fail his first year at UNH as he'd done at Alton Central School, Joe had been a *C* student as a freshman, a *B* student as a sophomore, and was now a *magna cum laude* graduate with a $1,500 fellowship at Harvard. What's more, as he informed me in a letter, he'd lost his virginity, I suspect with my friend Emma from UNH, now separated from Tommy but still living in their apartment on the back side of Beacon Hill. I'd introduced her to Joe on furlough between Fort Bragg and *General Darby*, and she became a great admirer of his poetry.

Joe had started slow and ended well, and that's how matters turned out for me as Troop Information and Education NCO. Things went especially well after Sergeant Brown tipped me to the movie archive. The U.S. Army had captured many Russian training films during the Korean War, given them an English-language voiceover, and distributed them to bases around the world. I loved those films, which instructed Red Army recruits how to fight from house to house in a city, how to cross a river without a Bailey Bridge such as the British and Americans used, how to cross a minefield, how to go to ground as a sniper invisible to the enemy – great stuff! And the best part of those training films was that I could step down from the stage and take a seat in the front row (nobody sat in the front row where he could too easily be called upon) and watch the movie with everyone else.

The other days of the week, I was the third clerk in the orderly room, filling in when someone was on furlough or sick, pitching in when things got busy. Much of what went on in the Army had to do with a man's serial number (mine was US51330425, and I'll never forget it) and whenever I filled out the morning report or a three-day pass, I had to type one or several serial numbers. Most began with "US", because most of us were draftees and belonged to the Army of the United States. The sergeants of course were RA for Regular Army, and a few soldiers were ER for Enlisted Reserve. After a few months in the orderly room, I could touch-type the serial numbers as well as any of the girls in Mrs. Genowich's class. And a good thing too, because I later had to spend a week in an office with an Addressograph machine, normally used for punching out mailing labels. A soldier somewhere had sued the Army for putting a P on his dog tag when he wasn't a Protestant but some sect other than Catholic (C) or Jewish (J) or Indifferent (Y) or None (X). Muslim, perhaps? As a result, the order came down that all dog tags must show the religion *spelled out*. Since like eyeballs, each soldier had two dog tags, this took me some little time in my private office with the clanging Addressograph machine. For fun, I recorded myself as ATHEIST. I loved to see an officer's eyes widen when he saw that during a company inspection.

Once it was a lieutenant colonel from SHAPE – Supreme Headquarters, Allied Powers, Europe, a post reserved for people with connections. (When Harvard expelled Teddy Kennedy for cheating, he'd joined the Army and was assigned to the honor guard at SHAPE.) To punish me for my disregard for religion, the colonel took my carbine, inspected it, and finding it faultlessly clean he fired the last arrow in his quiver: "What's the serial number of this weapon, Soldier?"

I had no idea, since the only time I ever saw the carbine was when I borrowed it from the supply room before an inspection. So I drew myself up and rattled off the number I remembered from Fort Bragg: "Ten forty-eight, eight oh three, Sir!"

His eyes narrowed. "That's not the serial number of this weapon, Soldier."

"Then it can't be my weapon, Sir."

It's amazing what you can get away with if you take a positive attitude. The colonel held out the carbine and released his hold on it, hoping I'd drop it and could be punished for that, but I caught it before it fell, and he had to move on to the next man in line, no doubt wishing me dead. But what could he do? Demand an interview with the company armorer?

He had a schedule to keep, and probably he wanted to be done with the inspection as badly as I did.

~ ~ ~ ~

For my first year at Coligny Caserne, I lived in a six-man room on the second floor of a big mansard-roofed building, one of three such buildings in the compound. The orderly room was on the ground floor, and I suppose there were other offices there as well. This was to the left of the parade ground, after I entered the black iron gates immortalized by Marcel Proust in *The Guermantes Way*: "I waited at the barracks gate, in front of that huge hulk, booming with the November wind, out of which at every moment – for it was six in the evening – men emerged into the street in pairs, staggering unsteadily, as if they were coming ashore in some exotic port where they were temporarily stationed."

The street was the Faubourg Bannier, and the "huge hulk" would have been my barrack, or the four-story building on the far side of the parade ground, which in my time contained our mess hall, NCO Club, cafeteria, library, and Post Exchange. A third and similar building completed the layout on the right side of the parade ground and was, I believe, entirely given over to offices. There were some smaller buildings too, including a theater and some prefabricated metal buildings such as I'd never seen before, a straight-sided variant of the Quonset or Nissen Hut.

When we weren't wasting time at the NCO Club or a Shoot-'Em-Up, we talked. Of all the deep philosophical topics at our disposal, a favorite was the question of our servitude in the U.S. Army. Was there any value in it at all? I argued that if the Russians came through the Fulda Gap, I'd be a negative factor, getting in the way of the real soldiers, like Sergeant Brown. And if the *real* U.S. Army didn't spend so much time, money, and manpower training reluctant draftees and afterwards looking after them, it would have the resources to mount a more spirited defense in West Germany.

This being the case, if we had the option of going to sleep for two years instead of being conscripted, would we take the offer?

"Well, what about furloughs?" someone asked. Indeed! We got four weeks off each year, eight weeks altogether, almost two months! Surely they would be deducted from the Big Sleep?

"And a three-day pass once a month!" said someone else.

"And sick days."

"And Sundays and holidays!"

"And nobody serves the full two years, anyhow. Everybody gets out a week or two early."

In the end, we calculated that eighteen months of sleep should take care of our active-duty obligation. (We'd been drafted for eight years, with six to be served in the Army Reserve after we got out.)

"Sarge," I'd asked a cook at Fort Dix, while I scrubbed the mess-hall floor beneath his boots, "when are you going to get out of the Army?"

"When they start training civilians," he said.

No, the cadre at Fort Dix wouldn't have agreed to our scheme, nor would Sergeant Smith in the orderly room at Coligny Caserne. Nor would "Engine Charlie" Wilson, the Secretary of Defense, and perhaps not General Eisenhower, now enjoying his retirement years as President of the United States.

~ ~ ~ ~

But it's true that when I look back on Army service, it is the furloughs that I remember, and the weekend and three-day passes. There were a lot of passes, since I was in the orderly room and could type my own, then slip it in with other paperwork for the Major or the exec to sign. (Captain DeMarco was sharper than the CO. "Haven't you already had a three-day pass this month?" he asked one time, and I had to negotiate it down to a weekend.) We were seventy-five miles from Gare de l'Austerliz, an hour and a half by train, and among my earliest French phrases was "*Paris, s'il vous plaît, aller et retour, deuxième classe.*" I found a great little hotel on the Rue Monsieur le Prince for a thousand francs a night, or two dollars and a half. (It might have been an earlier version of Le Clos Medicis at number 56, which today offers a winter rate of $120 with breakfast. There are a few other hotels on Monsieur le Prince in the same price range.) If it were a weekend pass, I'd take the room for Saturday only, returning to Orléans Sunday evening or tiptoeing through Gare de l'Austerliz after midnight and catching a few hours' sleep in a second-class carriage on the early-morning train.

I went to *Le Contes d'Hoffmann* at the grand old Opéra, now called the Palais Garnier. What a hoot that was! I had no suit and tie, so I wore my Class A uniform, Ike jacket with my Spec 3 insignia on the sleeve, walking up the grand staircase and beneath the grand chandeliers and sitting on a sort of stool in a box high up on the left, trying to remember how *The Phantom of the Opera* had turned out. (Which chandelier had come crashing down?) *Hoffmann* was a bit of a challenge. I'd seen the movie at the Franklin Theater in Durham and the real thing at the Sadler's Wells in London (now the Royal Opera House), but in Paris the language was French! I wasn't prepared for that, nor for the tenor, who was middle-aged and had a great paunch. I don't remember the soprano at all, nor the mezzo who is Hoffmann's faithful companion and muse.

Foolishly, *Hoffmann* was my last opera for a quarter of a century, and I limited my Paris theater to ballet, where language was no obstacle and I could pick out the prettiest ballerina and concentrate on her for the evening. I acquired a tiny monocular at the PX – all I needed with my lazy left eye – and could see the very sweat above her upper lip. The Opéra Ballet had an evening to itself every now and then, and the New York City Ballet came over one time to give us a dose of modernity, and all in Charles Garnier's opulent theater, the most gorgeous in the world.

There were of course less elegant weekends. Larry Hoff, the Head and Head mailman and our resident black-marketeer, drove us to Paris one time. After selling his month's cigarette ration – four cartons of Lucky Strikes, somewhere near the grand old food market of Les Halles – he drove north along the Rue Saint-Denis and turned right on the Rue Bondel. The little Opel boasted a sun roof, and our resident photographer, a tall lad named Ted, was ready to capture the beauties as Larry drove slowly along the street. The daylight, I'm afraid, did no favors to most of the women, though there was one, younger than most, who caught my eye. I confess I called her "Odette" in my mind, and the next time I was in Paris (with Bob Sampson from UNH, as it happened) I went looking for her with no success. On this first afternoon, our eye contact was broken when Ted stood up to take his pictures. Apparently this had happened before, because half a dozen *poules* rushed the Opel and and rained spittle on it.

Larry drove us other places, too, to the cathedral at Chartres, to gape at its glorious rose window; to

Mont-Saint-Michel; and – on a three-day pass – to Switzerland. When Larry drove through a town that interested him, he'd toss his red Michelin guide to me in the back seat. "Here," he said, "see what that was all about!" In Geneva, we went into a workman's tavern where the proprietor served us a beer apiece and ignored us for the next hour or two, until we slunk away. I was delighted to discover that the Swiss postal service had a cheap rate for postcards if the message was short enough, so I bought five for a franc and mailed them to Mom, Joe, Emma, and a few others to tell them: "Swiss postcards are limited to seven words."

On another three-day pass, I went to London on the Friday-night ferry and back again Sunday morning. By the most amazing coincidence, I ran into Malcolm Hopson near Victoria Station, where we had the most glorious reunion. To think: I could have found Basia as easily! She was teaching Latin at a girls' school in some outer borough, but apparently I didn't care to open that old wound. Indeed, so thoroughly did I bury the fact of her marriage that, though I must have remembered it in 1957, it later slipped below the surface. When we met again in London, more than half a century later, Basia showed me the letter I'd typed that spring at Fort Bragg, and that she had pasted into her wedding book. I was touched by the pretty sentiment: "I hope you have many daughters, and I hope they bring as much happiness to the world as you have brought to me."

~ ~ ~ ~

France had been humiliated in Vietnam when I was a senior at UNH, and it had left the country to its own devices shortly after, split between a Communist regime at Hanoi and a Western-style government at Saigon. Now France was fighting its last colonial war in Algeria, a struggle commemorated on every railroad overpass from Orléans to Gare d'Austerlitz. These were U-shaped black steel structures like the bridge Basia and I had crossed in order to reach Modane in 1955. The messages were in bold white paint, and they alternated: ALGÉRIE FRANÇAISE! on this one, FLN on the next. That is: *Algeria is French!* to support the French army, and *Front for National Liberation* to support the rebels. This is all we Americans saw of the war. Technically, Algeria was part of metropolitan France, not a colony, but the Algerians didn't seem to agree. They began fighting for independence soon after France gave up the fight in Vietnam, and they kept it up for years. Arguably, it was the nation's worst convulsion since the revolution of 1796, and among its casualties would be the Fourth Republic that had governed France since the end of the Second World War.

On a lighter note, there was the occasional white message: AMI GO HOME! This was of course aimed at the GIs of Coligny Caserne. It didn't trouble us at all, since we understood *ami* to be the French word for "friend," when the French (and Germans too, as I would discover) intended it as an insulting shorthand for "American," much as we had used "Jap" during the War.

~ ~ ~ ~

I 'd had two weeks' furlough after Basic Training and another two weeks before sailing to Bremerhaven, so it was 1957 before I qualified for another. For the first, a lad named Ryan and I took the train to Cologne and got on a Douglas DC-3 for the flight into West Berlin. I felt that we were recapitulating the Berlin Airlift of 1948-1949, when a plane landed every few minutes at Tempelhof, every day and every night for fifteen months, to fuel and feed a city Stalin hoped to add to his dismal empire. Even now, in 1957, East Germany was wrapped in darkness. Only a single bulb was lit in each town, and that at the railway station. Then we saw West Berlin, an incandescent riot of light. I heard the passengers gasp and marvel, even over the roar of the Wright Cyclone engines.

Even in daylight, West Berlin was magical. The main street was the Ku'damm, as busy as Times Square though cleaner and brighter, with Beetles and Opels, Jeeps and Chevy Bel Airs competing for space, and sidewalk cafes that served a raspberry-flavored beer that I remember as *weiss mit himbeer*. (The name seems to differ now.) When the magic faded, we could pass through Checkpoint Charlie to find ourselves in desolate East Berlin, where a woman or two crouched over a pile of fallen bricks and tapped with a hammer to rid them of mortar. This seemed to be the major industry in the Communist capital. . . . I wonder if those bricks were later used to build the Wall that would imprison a generation of East Berliners?

In France, as American soldiers, Ryan and I were accustomed to being viewed with contempt, but in West Berlin we were heroes. How the world had turned around since 1945!

We flew back to Cologne and took the train to Copenhagen. On the overnight Gedser Ferry, we fell in with two Swedish nurses returning from an ingenious holiday in Italy: some American tourists had rented a car in Rome and driven north to take their flight back to the U.S. The car-rental agency then employed Ingrid and Kai to return it whence it had come, along with gas money and train tickets home.

Ryan fell in love with Ingrid on the overnight

passage, and when I awoke with a stiff neck he announced that we were going to drive the girls home. What, to Sweden? Yes. Well . . . why not? What was the point of being a GI in Europe if you couldn't drive two pretty nurses home to Sweden?

It worked out well for Ryan, and when he got another furlough a few months later, he headed back to Uppsala, where the girls worked at the University Hospital. He came back engaged to be married. For my part, I went to Frankfurt-Rhine Air Base and caught the first flight out, which happened to be a C-54 cargo plane for Madrid, which I was astonished to find in the throes of celebrating – Columbus Day! I had a hard time adjusting to Spanish hours, with breakfast at nine in the morning and dinner at nine in the evening. I bought a ticket for the bullfight but it was rained out. I took the train to Algeciras so I could admire the apes in Gibraltar and cross over to Tangiers on what I fancied was the *Captain's Paradise* ferry. Tangiers struck me as not very much of a paradise, with far too many flies, and I spent only the one night. Except when I was on a military aircraft, I did all this in civilian clothes and with my American passport. I loved to add stamps to the pages, and I confess that in Gibraltar I took an afternoon walk into Spain, just to collect an additional souvenir.

Back at Coligny Caserne, I found our barrack and office in the throes of being remodeled, with the orderly room moved to one of those metal buildings and the troops sleeping at Harbord Barracks several miles away. We were bussed back and forth, morning and evening, and we slept in a vast room meant to be a ward for the wounded from combat at the Fulda Gap. For a week or two, I was the last man of a hundred or so to fall asleep and the second to wake up, a horrific routine. Finally I borrowed a cot from the supply room and hid it and my sleeping bag in a locker in our new orderly room. This proved to be an excellent arrangement. The mess hall, NCO club, movies, and library functioned as before, and few of the gang spent their evenings out at the barrack-hospital, so there was plenty to do, and I slept better even than in our former six-man bunkroom. I just had to be sure to get up at five, stow my gear in a locker, and disappear for an hour.

In addition to the cooks and waitresses and other French civilians who tended to so many of our needs, security at the Caserne was provided by a company of Polish Guards, the younger men recruited from refugee camps in West Germany, though some of the older ones were veterans of the Polish army of 1939. They'd escaped to the West and served in the French or British army. One morning I chatted with a man who'd been captured by the Russians, put in a punishment battalion, captured anew by the Germans, who sent him to guard the French coast at Calais, where in June 1945 he happily surrendered to the English – so the Guards were his *fifth* army, counting a year or two in the Polish Brigade of the British Army. I loved talking to these men, and often in the evenings I met them again at their favored tavern on the Faubourg Bannier. It had a coin-operated turntable and a pile of records beneath a plastic lid with an arm-hole in it: you chose your record, put it on the turntable, put a ten-franc coin in the slot, and the turntable revolved, playing a polka or a patriotic song. As the evening wore on, the Poles got drunk; they danced with each other or the rare Frenchwoman who ventured in; they brawled; and always in the end they sat and wept for their lost homeland. They were wonderful. If I stayed too long and missed the midnight curfew at Coligny Caserne, they'd take me across the street and slip me through their own guardhouse.

So I was AWOL for the last few months of my Army career. Since I worked in the orderly room, this was no problem. When the Charge-of-Quarters came in with last night's bedcheck roster, I erased my name from the list of absentees. The CQs soon got used to it.

Looking back at November and December of 1957, I realize that my affection for these exiled Poles was likely a hangover from my love of Basia. And I now know that the rousing song they played so often was "Dabrowski's Mazurka," a hymn to the exiles who'd fought under Napoleon's banner at the end of the eighteenth century, after Poland had been partitioned and occupied by Russia, Germany, and Austria. What's more, Basia's name was actually mentioned, though I never caught it at the time:

Her father said to Basia, with tears in his eyes,
"Hear our soldiers, child, marching to their drums!"
March, march, Dabrowski, from Italy to Poland.
We will follow you, and win back our nation.

8 – The Overseas Weekly

OF MY SEVENTEEN THOUSAND hours as a soldier, the happiest were those I spent at Les Longchamps on the Champs-Élysées, sipping a *café au lait*, smoking a Gauloises, and reading my way through the *Sunday Times*, just arrived from London by the early-morning boat. Though one time it was the Paris edition of the New York *Herald-Trib*. I was with the gang from Coligny Caserne, and the vendor was a darling American girl, waving a *Trib* with one hand while clutching the rest of the bundle to her breasts.

"Buy me a paper!" I said to Larry Hoff, wealthy from selling his month's cigarette ration on the black market. She offered him the paper in her hand. "No," Larry said, "I want *that* one," and pointed to the copy nearest her breasts.

She gave it to him; Larry gave it to me; I kissed it and handed it back to her. She blushed – yes, pink as a cherry blossom! We coaxed her to sit down with us and tell us her life story – "which," as I wrote to my brother, "didn't take long, as she is only seventeen."

This sort of thing, I decided, was what life had meant for me to do, and Paris was where life wanted me to do it. So when I became "short" – that is, could count the days until my release – I filled out the paperwork to leave the Army at Coligny Caserne. It wasn't a discharge, alas: I'd been drafted for two years on active duty and another six in the Army Reserve. And that was another benefit of staying in Europe: I'd be assigned to a paper unit at the U.S. Embassy, with no summer camp or monthly meetings. I could even grow my beard again!

"You know," said the clerk at Personnel, "if you rotate back to CONUS, you'll be home for Christmas."

"I don't have a home." Which was true enough. While I was in France, Mom had given up the battle, joined Dad in Arizona, and added nearly two thousand miles to the distance separating her from the green land that *she* called home. I wasn't at all interested in Tucson, and Wolfeboro attracted me no more. It would have to be Boston or New York or Paris, and there was no question which city attracted me the most. I liked to brag that my tombstone would have to read: *Here lies Dan Ford / His first fixed address.*

"You'll need a passport."

"I already have one." Indeed, I had used that splendid green booklet on all my European travels except two hops on Air Force transports, Frankfurt to Madrid and back to Frankfurt. My collection of visas and entry and exit stamps was quite impressive by this time.

By all accounts, the time for Paris was the 1920s, with Ernest Hemingway, F. Scott Fitzgerald, Ezra Pound, Sylvia Beach, Gertrude Stein, and a dollar as strong as gold. Even Thomas Wolfe, not a particularly adventurous man, had come to Paris in the 1920s. If the city had a band of expatriate American writers in 1957, I couldn't see it from my sidewalk table at Les Longchamps. Never mind! The gnomes at Fort Knox had once again squirreled away most of the gold in the world, the exchange rate was favorable, and Paris was still Paris, so why not? The 1950s were a great time to be alive, a great time to be young, a great time to be an American, and an especially great time to be an American in Europe.

The next step was to get a job on the *Trib* – not

the struggling mother paper in New York but its international edition on Rue de Berri, a few blocks down from where I was sitting at Les Longchamps. I read the *Trib* every weekday morning at Coligny Caserne, starting with the impossibly funny column by Art Buchwald, who seemed to be my generation's substitute for the great writers of the 1920s. (James Baldwin had lived in France since 1950 but went home just when I arrived. Richard Wright was still here and still writing, but not for long, and even Art Buchwald would soon repatriate. Dozens of would-be writers had come to Paris on the GI Bill, ostensibly to study, but the living seemed grim to them, and they didn't stay long.)

I wrote and I phoned, but alas I couldn't get an interview. So I slipped a three-day pass into Captain DeMarco's pile – by this time, the Exec would sign anything I put in front of him – so I could present myself at Rue de Berri on a Friday afternoon. I was met with a shrug. Except for Art Buchwald's column and a bit of local gossip, it seemed, the *Trib* took its news from the Associated Press wire and its features from an airmailed copy of the *Herald Tribune* in New York. It didn't need any actual reporters.

So I got another pass and went to Germany. I did score an interview at *Stars and Stripes*, the stuffy military newspaper in its compound near Darmstadt. But – *compound?* I'd had my fill of military compounds, and being a Department of the Army civilian didn't seem a whole lot different than reenlisting. I didn't care for the notion of a GS-5 rating, either, as much as it would have pleased Dad in Tucson. What he liked about government work – the permanence, the job protection, the pension – was exactly what frightened me. On November 2 I had celebrated my twenty-sixth birthday, drinking with the Polish Guards at their tavern on the Faubourg Bannier, but I figured the Army years didn't count. I *felt* like twenty-four, and I wasn't ready to settle down.

So I took the train north to Frankfurt. Unlike Darmstadt, much bombed and rebuilt and flavored by the U.S. military, Frankfurt still seemed European. Ten or twenty thousand Americans faded into the background among six hundred thousand Germans. If I stayed away from the Hauptbahnhof, the vast iron-and-glass railway station that somehow had been missed by all those British and American bombs, and away from the lofty I.G. Farben building, occupied now by the U.S. Third Armored Division, I'd scarcely ever see an American soldier.

I made my way by tram and foot to the Overseas Press Club, its first floor given over to a tavern and dining room, patronized mostly by Americans and Brits who flew for Lufthansa while a new generation of German pilots went through their training. (The airline wasn't allowed to hire veterans of the wartime Luftwaffe.) The *Overseas Weekly* occupied the second floor, and I loved the place at first sight. It was the *New Hampshire* reborn, or the *Mancunian*! A lobby with desks and tables, a crowded newsroom, many Army-surplus typewriters, a few private offices, and the smell of cigarettes.

The editor, as I knew from my study of the *OW*'s masthead, was Marion von Rospach. I guessed that she was female, though that wasn't certain because of how she spelled the first name. I guessed also that she was an American, though *von* sounded awfully German. And this was the time before "Ms." came into the language: would I address her as Miss or Mrs.? I went into the newsroom.

"I'd like to talk to the editor," I said to the only

person there, a fierce German woman of fifty or so.

"*Ach*," she said, as if spitting in contempt. I would later learn that this was Johanna Prym, and that *ach* was her way of saying *oh*. "John is news editor, but he is out." She pronounced news much as Glovsky had done in his riffs on Jews, so it came out as *noose*. "You must talk to Marion in her office." She pointed to a door at the end of the hall. Well, now I had a Dornberg, a von Rospach, and an obviously German secretary, but at least I knew Marion's sex. And apparently the staff called her by her first name.

Life magazine had described Marion as "5 feet 3 inches, 31, and supercharged," and *Time* would later call her "a stocky, energetic divorcee with a tomboy bob." If you're not familiar with *Time*'s shorthand, you can translate *stocky* as "overweight" and *divorcée* as "tough broad." Both were fair enough, though Marion at her desk struck me as more muscular than fat. I confess I was a bit intimidated.

"What do *you* read for news?" she asked when I said I was looking for a job, and I had to confess that my newspaper was the Paris *Herald Trib*. "Then why do you want to write for *us*?" So I explained that I couldn't get an interview at the *Trib*, and that while I'd just talked to *Stars and Stripes*, I hadn't liked the atmosphere. That was apparently the right answer, because after glancing at one of my clips from the *Christian Science Monitor* she offered me a four-week trial at sixty dollars a week, with the use of an apartment for which the paper would deduct twenty-five or thirty dollars from my first week's pay, depending on whether I chose the top floor or the one below. "The top," I said. Twenty-five dollars a month seemed a lot, five dollars more than Mom's old apartment on Lake Street.

"When can you start?" We settled on Monday,

January 6. I could move into my apartment at 5 Quirinstrasse, across the river in Sachsenhausen, the Friday before. Splendid! That was the very day, January 3, when I'd be separated from the U.S. Army after what I regarded as two years and a day. (I was drafted in a Leap Year.) There was one hitch: Marion had spotted the bearded photo in my passport, and that was a deal breaker. "If the Army sees a beard," she said, "they think you're a Communist."

~ ~ ~ ~

I find that Marion was thirty-two years old in January 1958. She'd met her husband on the staff of the *Stanford Daily*, a more impressive student paper than either of mine; and by 1950 they'd married, divorced, and expatriated, or anyhow Marion had. She was then on the staff of *Stars and Stripes*. With two soon-to-be-discharged servicemen, she put together three thousand dollars to start the *Overseas Weekly*, which she produced from her home and "an elderly Volkswagen," as Wikipedia has it, though in truth no civilian Beetle was more than three years old in 1950.

Soon enough she was the paper's sole owner, because her partners had their military service extended when North Korean tanks rolled into Seoul, and she was in debt for ten thousand dollars. But she made a go of it, and in the process acquired the right to process color film for all the Post Exchanges in Germany. Since there were three hundred thousand American soldiers and airmen in the country, plus maybe a hundred thousand wives and children, that was a lot of film. The home slide show was the 1950s equivalent of Facebook.

By the time I turned up, the *OW* had a circulation of sixty thousand copies a week, or so it claimed. Like the other papers I'd worked on, it was a tabloid – half the size of the *Herald Trib* – and it came out on Thursday, though it didn't reach Coligny Caserne until Friday morning. The front page always showed a half-naked young woman, plus a large-type headline and a couple of smaller ones, each promising a thrilling story inside. There was a centerfold with more cheesecake – sometimes the same young woman, sometimes several. Six news pages before the centerfold were given over to courts martial, the doings of Play-for-Pay Girls, a scandal or two, and many advertisements. The six pages following the centerfold provided sports news, a travel or feature story, more ads, and – perhaps the main reason for the newspaper's success – a week's worth of "Beetle Bailey" comic strips, a full page of them. Enlisted men loved the "Oversexed Weekly," as they called it. Officers loathed it.

When I turned up that first Monday, John Dornberg seized upon me and introduced me around the newsroom, to Johanna Prym whom I'd encountered on my first visit, to a slow-moving guy named Ed Morris, and to the other reporter present, whose name I've forgotten because he was the man I would replace. "We're opening a Paris office," John said, "and he'll be it." I had a pang. That should have been my job! "He'll take you down to Stuttgart and show you the ropes. Meanwhile, here's a rewrite for you." He gave me a sheet of copy paper with MORRIS-1 typed at the upper left. "You can use that typewriter."

I went to the empty desk and rolled a fresh sheet into the typewriter. What now? Ed kindly came over and told me to type MORRIS-FORD-1, drop down a couple inches, and start the revision. He didn't seem at all insulted that the new guy was going to improve his work. Which I did, or so I thought. When I finished the first page, John Dornberg came over and pulled it out of my typewriter. "You guys can head off now," he said, and rolled a fresh sheet of paper into his own machine. As I passed behind him, I saw him type MORRIS-FORD-DORNBERG-1 at the top left as he began to improve my improvements on what Ed had written.

I can't dredge up the name of my driver-guide, so let's call him Fred. "Is that the way the newsroom works?" I asked when we got underway. "I rewrite Ed, and John rewrites me?"

"Yeah, pretty much. But usually it's just the first paragraph or two. You'll get used to it."

We were an hour and a half on the autobahn to Karlsruhe and Stuttgart in Fred's Beetle. I was impressed by the ease of city-to-city travel in Germany, on a divided highway dating back to the 1930s, and amused by the little air-cooled Volkswagen, so rudimentary it didn't have a fuel gauge. There was a lever on the floor that Fred could nudge with his left foot if the engine stuttered, so as to use the last couple liters of gasoline. "And if I forget to nudge it back after filling the tank," he said, "I'll be in trouble the next time I hear the engine burp, because the tank will be dry."

Patch Barracks in Stuttgart was headquarters of the Seventh Army, one hundred and sixty thousand men who defended most of the Iron Curtain. (There were British troops to the north of us, and West German soldiers to the south, along the Austrian border.) Fred introduced me to the Public Information Officer, and after he finished the work that had brought him there – I don't remember what it was – we drove home by way of Kaiserslautern, so I could meet the PIO there.

I soon got the hang of it. Friday I spent on the

phone, calling around in search of story leads. As with the autobahn, I was hugely impressed by Germany's long-distance phone system, which for the most part did away with the women who connected cities in the United States. For Stuttgart, all I had to do was dial 77, which caused a ghastly female voice to come on the line, shrieking "*Stuttgart Stuttgart Stuttgart*" remorselessly and endlessly until I dialed the local number.

Then there was Herr Doktor Naujocks in Dachau – yes, the site of Germany's very first concentration camp, opened less than two months after Adolf Hitler became Reich Chancellor. I first dialed the Munich switchboard, then the extension that gave me "*Dachau Dachau Dachau.*" In all the weeks and months I did this, a little shiver of horror would run through me. Herr Doktor Naujocks collected the Munich newspapers for the week, and if he came up with something worth writing about, I switched him over to Johanna Prym to transcribe and translate the story. Never did anything in the Munich area seem important enough for John Dornberg to approve a trip down to check it out. I would have loved to visit the 10th Special Forces in Bad Tölz, but the Green Berets in Germany seemed always to behave themselves. Or perhaps their misbehavior was classified.

From the leads I developed on Friday, John laid out the assignments for the following week. I became a regular on the Stuttgart and Kaiserslautern run. I left my radio tuned to the Armed Forces station, which in the morning blasted me awake at six o'clock with "The Stars and Stripes Forever." I drank a cup of instant coffee and ate a bowl of Shredded Wheat, washed up, trotted down to the bridge over the Main River, caught a tram to the Bahnhof, and boarded the seven o'clock train to the south. I took my suitcase, since the trial might take two days, and anyhow that gave me the use of my typewriter. On the way down, I'd set the suitcase on end between my knees and try to get five hundred words done on my novel, which was called *The Way Home* and – of course! – featured an American soldier in Paris and a prostitute with a heart of gold named Odette. Our soldier was Stephen Faust, his first name a wink to James Joyce, his surname to Johann Wolfgang von Goethe. (I was by this time reading *Faust* in German, to get the full flavor of it.)

No doubt my typing annoyed the other passengers, but only once did anyone complain. Most Germans in 1958 felt guilty about their part in the Second World War, and I was, after all, an American. No doubt we were hated, but the Germans hid it better than the French had done.

Having lectured about it a couple of times at Coligny Caserne, I regarded the *Uniform Code of Military Justice* as a noble document, based as it was on the Constitution itself. But the little courtroom at Kaiserslautern came as something of a disappointment. It was the size of my Brewster classrooms, with a long plain table at one end, a desk apiece for the prosecution and the defense, and six or eight rows of folding chairs for the rest of us. There were maybe half a dozen spectators, enlisted men who I figured were friends of the defendant. Sergeant Sanchez had supposedly raped a German girl. The *OW* was especially fond of rapes, John Dornberg had explained. Murders were okay, but they were rare and often had nothing to do with sex.

We all stood when the court filed in: six officers, led by a captain with a thick brown volume under his arm. He was the Law Officer, the military's version of a judge. He took the center chair, the five lieutenants took the chairs to either side of him, and we all sat down. There was no *oyez, oyez*, or anything like that. I felt a bit deflated. Here I was, reporting on a trial that could sentence a man to Fort Leavenworth for the rest of his life, and it was all so . . . *ordinary*.

Sergeant Sanchez had a civilian lawyer, who seemed as bored about the trial as the officers at the front of the room. The Army prosecutor was a first lieutenant from the Judge Advocate's office; he did a creditable job of coaxing testimony from the victim, her words translated by a American woman with her hair in a bun. The defense kept objecting, and the Law Officer made a brief show of consulting his manual before denying the objection.

We broke for lunch, but I stayed in the courtroom with my Olivetti portable perched on my suitcase, transcribing my notes while my memory was fresh. (I loved that typewriter, which had cost me forty dollars at the PX in Coligny Caserne. Italian design was charming: Olivetti's Lettera 22, Piaggio's Vespa and, come to think of it, even Fiat's Topolino.)

Then the court reassembled and the defense began. It consisted entirely of enlisted men who had slept with Fraulein Müller and – what was more important – had paid fifty marks for the privilege, or $12.50 at the current rate of exchange. Nobody seemed surprised by this, and after summations by the JAG lieutenant and the civilian lawyer, we again left the room while the Law Officer and the five voting members stayed behind to deliberate. It took about twenty minutes before we were called back. Sergeant Sanchez was acquitted of rape but found guilty of the lesser included charge of adultery. (Of course! He had a wife back home!) The court sentenced him to six years, a dishonorable discharge, and forfeiture of all pay and allowances.

I got an afternoon train back to Frankfurt, somewhat disappointed at not spending the night in Kaiserslautern. I knocked on the door of Harry McGowan, the middle-aged Englishman who rented half of the fourth floor, while I had the attic to myself. Marion had paid the "key money" for the top two floors of 5 Quirinstrasse, effectively leasing them for a big cash payment plus a small monthly rental, which was how German construction was financed in the cash-short years after the War. (Nearly a third of the country's population was homeless when the War ended.) She no doubt made a profit by renting the three apartments to *OW* staffers, plus the lease became more valuable as the economy improved: Germans worked hard, and Frankfurt had done a better job of repairing bomb damage than London or Manchester.

Harry McGowan was our proofreader, an important job because the Linotypists had to work in a foreign language. This was done at the print shop of the *Frankfurter Allgemeine*, the city's rather stuffy daily newspaper, and as far as I know, Harry never set foot in the Overseas Press Club, nor did any of us go to the print shop except a courier named Bodo.

Harry and I went down to our Gasthaus at the foot of Schweizerstrasse and ordered the usual *Lendensteak* and *Bauernsalat*. The little girl of the house left her homework and trotted off to the butcher's, while Harry consoled me over a beer. "Don't worry about your sergeant," he said. "There'll be a big story in the local paper about six years hard labor, and that'll make the locals happy, but when the case gets to the I.G. Farben building" – John pronounced it as the Germans did, *Eee Gay* – "they'll cut the sentence to three or four years, and it'll be cut again back in the States. By the time he's done, he'll have served the six months or a year it takes his case to work through the system, and the poor bastard will be home with the wife and children."

"That's how it works?"

"That's how it works." Harry held up his glass, and I clinked it with mine. He had a big, friendly face, and we'd become drinking buddies though he was years older, having served in the Royal Navy during the War.

~ ~ ~ ~

In February, Jim Dye turned up and moved into the empty Quirinstrasse apartment on the fourth floor. Again we hit it off, and we were now a threesome, though to be honest Jim made me a bit nervous. If I had been hired to replace the reporter who was now the *OW*'s French correspondent, who would Jim replace? When he was in the Air Force, he and a cartoonist friend had published a book called *Mox Nix*, as GIs pronounced *machts nichts*, meaning "it doesn't matter." (Thus the illuminated turn signal that flipped from a Beetle's front door was known to GIs as the Mox Nix Stick, since they believed that German drivers had no idea which way they'd turn.) Jim's book was for sale at every Post Exchange in Europe. That surely topped my clipping from the *Christian Science Monitor*, and Jim spoke a pretty good colloquial German.

We learned much later that he was supposed to replace Ed Morris. But when Marion gave Ed the sack, he talked her out of it. He *couldn't* leave Frankfurt, he explained. His wife was German and wanted their kids to grow up near their grandparents, and anyhow he didn't have the money to take them all to the United States. Marion offered him a salary of twenty-five dollars a week, and he accepted. What else could he do?

In truth, we were all stuck on the expatriate life. John Dornberg had been born in what was now East Germany, but his family had escaped to the United States before that route was closed to Jews. He returned as an American serviceman, and like Ed he married a German girl. Harry McGowan had lived most of his life outside Britain. As a young man he'd sailed to Antarctica on a hare-brained project to harvest ice for British refrigerators; then he became a Berlitz teacher in India, where the War caught up with him. So he joined the Royal Navy, and after 1945 he knocked about Germany until Marion came along and gave him a job. Our sports editor, Vince Mullahy, had landed at Omaha Beach on D-Day and never gone home. Vince had a wife in the U.S.; they couldn't divorce because they were Catholics, so he took up with the American woman who became Marion's secretary. Jim Dye liked to scoff at Germany as "the land of inconvenience," but like me he obviously preferred it to the settled life in the United States.

Finally there was Gloria, the travel editor. She was a handsome woman, maybe thirty years old, and her principal duty at the *Overseas Weekly* turned out to be as Marion's sweetheart. I got my first clue when I made a courtesy call at the Kaiserslautern Public Information Office before Sergeant Sanchez's trial. "Oh," said the PIO captain. "You work for that butch lesbian up in Frankfurt, huh?"

I would hear this again and again as I traveled around the American subculture in West Germany, though of course it was never discussed at the Overseas Press Club. Gloria was a general's daughter and perhaps the reason for Marion's divorce, hence for the newspaper's existence. Oddly, she was the only member of the newspaper staff who got along with both its factions, which Jim Dye had christened the Inner Circle and the Outer Circle, with himself, Ed, Harry, and me as its outermost ring.

I enjoyed Gloria, especially when spring came and she peeked into the dining room one Thursday morning. Jim and I were digging into our hangover breakfast of *Gehactes mit Ei*, a raw egg cracked upon a patty of raw ground beef. In a high clear voice, Gloria cried: "Hooray, hooray, the first of May! Outdoor fucking starts today!" I had never before heard a woman say *fuck*, and from that moment Gloria was my favorite member of the Inner Circle. She was, besides, both pretty and shapely. She was a few years older, but I was hardly in the running, was I? I found that rather liberating.

There were a couple of Lufthansa pilots in the restaurant at the time, and they enjoyed Gloria's apercus as well. Jim and I fell to talking with them. They'd served in RAF Bomber Command during the War, and one of them told us how he'd recently had trouble landing at Tempelhof in a fog, whereupon the voice in the control tower snapped at him, "Haff you never been to Berlin before?"

"I have, actually," the pilot replied to himself in a high-toned English accent. "But I didn't stop."

The two Brits laughed hugely and, when we had worked it out, so did we.

Among his other virtues, Jim brought me news of the American literary scene. If I was to be a writer, he warned me, I could no longer wear my Harris Tweed jacket, which had hitchhiked through Europe with me, gone on passes and furloughs, and sat through so many courts martial. "This is the Beat Generation!" Jim said. "Dirty tee shirts and ripped jeans. Haven't you read *On the Road*?"

I'd never heard of Jack Kerouac or Allen Ginsberg. Their books weren't on display at the Post Exchange newsstands, and naturally the German bookstores didn't stock them either.

~ ~ ~ ~

Marion was ambitious. She wanted to widen her audience, but that would mean giving up the features that made the *Overseas Weekly* so popular among the enlisted men: the cheesecake, scandals, courts martial, and a week's worth of Beetle Bailey comics. The solution was a companion tabloid, the *Overseas Family*, for the wives and children and perhaps the officers. Indeed, she probably was already thinking of a third newspaper, one for tourists. The turbojet engines that had powered fighters and bombers at the end of the War would soon be carrying Americans by the thousands – by the millions, perhaps! – to London and Paris and Rome for a week or two. No more Grand Tours or college students vagabonding in Europe! A two-week vacation would be all that anyone needed to see the wonders of the Old World.

Marion had snared the enlisted men in 1950, and now she was going after the families. And eventually, though we didn't know it at the time, she'd launch the *Overseas Traveler*, to entertain and inform the tourists who nipped to Europe on Boeing's magnificent new 707 jetliner.

For the *Overseas Family*, she didn't need much. She had Gloria to write travel features, Vince Mullahy for sports and, thanks to Ed Morris's desperate need for a job, an actual surplus of reporters. To put the new tabloid together, she hired an upstanding gent named Cecil Neff who, like Gloria when she turned on the charm, could bridge the gulf between Inner and Outer Circles. Even John Dornberg deferred to Cecil. He seemed to have no office of his own, but worked sometimes in the newsroom, sometimes in the lobby with the desks and tables used by the Germans photographers, Gaby and Heinz, by a staff artist whose name I have forgotten, and by Bodo, the twenty-something university student who on his motorcycle rushed our copy down to the *Frankfurter Allgemeine* printshop and brought back the galleys after they'd been proofed by Harry McGowan.

Bodo had been a Hitler Youth during the War, and towards the end been assigned to a flak cannon with others from his squad. They served under an elderly sergeant who promised: "If we don't shoot at them, boys, they won't shoot at us." Or so Bodo told the story. Much the same was true of every German I talked to about the War – he'd served on the Eastern front and, if he'd found himself in France or along the Rhine, why, he fired into the air. It was a mystery to me, in that case who caused all those American and British casualties. As for the Holocaust, well, "*Davon haben wir nichts gewusst*" ("We knew nothing about that"). In 1958, when asked who had started the War, about half of the Federal Republic thought it wasn't Germany; nearly half agreed that, if not for the War, Hitler would have been one of the greatest statesmen of the century; and ninety percent thought that Jews belonged to a different race, while only ten percent said the same thing of the English.

Cecil did add a reporter to his staff, a high-school girl whose name also I have forgotten. I'll call her Ellen for purposes of this story. She lived in Frankfurt, the daughter of a tailor and a teacher, two of the tens of thousands of American civilians catering to the needs and wants of the U.S. military in Europe. Cecil announced that Ellen would write a teen column for the *Overseas Family*, and that I would go along to protect her from randy GIs.

"Jim is taller," I said."She'll be safer with him."

"I'm saving Jim for when we need a German speaker. Besides, you've got that Speed Graphic. You can be her photographer, and if she gets into trouble you can hit the guy over the head with it." He'd had me write a piece arguing the virtues of a press camera over a 35 millimeter, while John Dornberg argued the case for a Leica, though by this time I would happily have swapped my Speed Graphic for something smaller. The only way for me to get color photographs was to put a roll-film adapter on the back of my camera, effectively turning it into a Kodak Brownie with a telephoto lens.

The new setup worked out nicely for me at mid-summer, when SAS, the Scandinavian airline, ran a press tour to Kiruna, above the Arctic Circle, to experience the midnight sun. We saw the sun rise in the west at eleven o'clock, and we had a bowl of reindeer soup at midnight in Kiruna. Alas, *Stars and Stripes* also sent a reporter on the trip, and since *Stripes* was a daily, he was bound to scoop me, so I didn't get a story out of it.

But we did have a layover in Stockholm on the way back, so I took the train to Uppsala and spent the evening with Kai, whom I'd met on the Gedser Ferry the year before. It was quite a surprise to find myself in a city where I didn't know the first word of the language! However, the second man I stopped knew a bit of German, and he pointed me to Kai's apartment. Ryan and Ingrid were happy and living on Long Island, she told me. Indeed, she too would like to go to America, which made me a bit nervous.

John Dornberg didn't mind loaning me to Cecil. He had two reporters in Jim Dye and Ed Morris, and he could always draft me to rewrite their stories on Wednesday, as we put the news pages to bed. Jim and I seldom got home to Quirinstrasse before midnight on Wednesday and could relax with a bottle of schnapps. Some nights indeed it was two o'clock in the morning. That's why we sometimes needed *Gehactes mit Ei* for Thursday breakfast.

To be honest, I was more suited to features for the *Family* than to what the *Overseas Weekly* regarded as hard news, which involved putting quotes into the mouths of the soldiers we interviewed. Now this is done every day by the woke journalists employed by our newspapers, television networks, and especially websites, but in the 1950s it was still considered a sin against the profession of journalism.

Then yet another reporter showed up! He was a skinny ex-sergeant who'd been stationed in Italy. "The plot thickens," Jim said, and together we got the new guy to join us at our favorite Gasthaus on Schweizerstrasse. I don't remember his name; I'll call him Tony. He had a good story to tell: he was drafted in June 1950 but didn't make it to Korea until the following year, when the front had stabilized and the Chinese would launch a human-wave attack to overrun an American position, which the GIs had to take back with the help of bombs, artillery, and tanks. The Chinese had the men, the Americans had the weapons, and the two sides were equally wasteful with what they had. Since Tony was the smallest man in his squad, he was given its Browning Automatic Rifle to carry. This was an infantry tradition: you gave the little guy the big weapon. The BAR weighed twenty pounds unloaded.

"Figure it out," Tony said. "That fucking magazine held twenty rounds, which lasts three seconds if you keep the trigger down. So we carried a *lot* of ammo. And that BAR was so old it had a rope instead of a sling. And because I was the Fucking New Guy, I had to carry everyone's canteen down to the water hole, and I had to carry ten canteens *and* the BAR *and* all that ammo. I like to broke my back, carrying all that shit back up the hill."

He obviously loved to tell this story. "And when the Chinks came over!" he went on. "It all depended on the BAR, you know. I'd shoot that son of a bitch until the barrel got so hot it jammed, and then I'd yell, 'Fuck 'em! Leave 'em to the artillery!' and we'd all run down the hill. Then Div Arty blew the top off the hill, and the Chinks with it. And in the morning we'd go back up and kill anyone who was still alive, and we'd dig out the trenches again."

He took a long draft of beer and got a bit misty-eyed. "I kinda liked it, to tell you the truth. The Korean women especially. When the truce came, I thought I should see some more of the world, so I reupped for three years, and then I was in Japan, and then I told 'em I'd reup again if they sent me to Italy, where my family came from, so that's what they did. I was in Vicenza, and I got the job of putting out the base newspaper, pretty neat, really. I liked it. That's why I decided to try my luck as a civilian with you guys."

"What's Marion paying you?" Jim asked. This was why we'd invited him to join us.

"Twenty-five a week. She said that was the starting wage."

"It's beginning to look that way," Jim said. Sure enough, a few weeks later Marion called Jim into her office and gave him the sack. Harry McGowan and I gave him a fine going-away party. We invited Ed Morris, of course, and Tony and Ellen since they were honorary members of the Outer Circle.

It was a sad day for me when Jim took the train to Bremerhaven for the voyage home. "You won't be long following me," he said in parting, and he was right.

~ ~ ~ ~

In the new way of things, Ed and Tony handled the scandals and the courts martial. It was pretty clear to everyone, including me, that I wasn't the hard-digging investigator that Marion and John needed in the field. Feature stories were my style. Well, and improving Ed's and Tony's stories. I was really good at rewrite. And telephoning – I was good on the phone, too, if dealing with Americans. Much as had happened in France, my command of the language never got beyond the necessities of acquiring a hotel room, a meal, a beer, a train ticket, and a fraulein. And my pronunciation left something to be desired, as Johanna told me when I treated her to my favorite passage from *Faust*. "Ach!" she said. "You haff a terrible American ecksent!" So she handled Herr Doktor Naujocks and other German connections, or Ed Morris did.

I wound up occupying a desk in the lobby, where the German staff worked – the photographers, the artist, and Bodo the courier – and anyone else with a temporary need for a desk or a table, like Ellen and the chubby high-school chum she sometimes brought along with her. Ellen didn't get paid, so Cecil gave her considerable latitude.

The lobby was quieter than the newsroom, and I had my eye on Gaby Beilfuss, who was as good with a Rolleiflex as I was with a typewriter. Gaby was quite the elf. We went out on maneuvers with Third Armored Division one time, big Patton tanks tearing up farmers' fields while a lieutenant followed along behind and handed out deutchmarks to pay for the damage. To get ready for the overnight, Gaby hung the Rollei around her neck, stuffed her pockets with 120 film, and tossed – yes, with a flick of her hand! – a toothbrush into the hood of her duffel coat. "I'm ready," she said.

I was enchanted, but I couldn't get close to Gaby. It seemed that earlier she had fallen into a dalliance with the news editor, causing great Sturm und Drang at the *OW* and also, I suppose, in the Dornberg household. I didn't see why this ruled me out, but Gaby did, so that was that, and I was left with such pickups as I met downtown or on the prowl with Harry McGowan.

Chumming with Harry could be risky, as I discovered one night when I came home late and found him trying to fit the key into the lock of his door while blood ran down his chin. I got him inside and stopped his nosebleed with a washcloth and cold water. Mostly he was just bruised. He'd made a pass at a woman who turned out to be married, and her husband had punched him. John then took a roundhouse swing at the man, but missed and fell down, much as had happened to me the night before graduating from Brewster Academy; and while he was on the floor every man in the place took a kick at him. "Germans are like that," he said. "Even if they don't know why he's on the floor, they'll kick the chap who's down. Churchill said, 'the Hun is either at your throat or at your feet.' And this lot made good use of *their* feet."

I remember only one of my photographer-bodyguard assignments with Ellen, when she interviewed young GIs downtown and at the Special Services club. What did a teenage soldier do for entertainment, since the NCO clubs were off limits to them? I photographed the lads who were agreeable, and fortunately didn't have to hit anyone with my Speed Graphic.

We became good friends on these excursions. In September, Ellen announced that she was going on a school trip to Paris, and why didn't I come too, and show her some the sights their chaperone wouldn't? I still read the Paris *Herald-Trib* most weekdays, so I knew that Charles de Gaulle now ruled France by decree, pending the adoption of a new constitution that would abolish the Fourth Republic and create the Fifth. A national referendum was scheduled for the Sunday Ellen would be there, September 28, so I fell in with her scheme. There had been one big revolution in my lifetime, but I'd never actually *seen* one. I took the train to Paris on Saturday afternoon, and that night I took Ellen for coffee on the Champs and beer at Les Deux Magots. (The chaperone had taken care of the Eiffel Tower, Notre Dame, and the basilica of Sacré Coeur.) Ellen wanted to see Rue Blondel, too, but I demurred, and I got her back to her hotel for her eleven o'clock curfew.

My plan had been to walk the streets all night, as I had sometimes done on my Paris weekends, but at midnight the city shut down. As if a light had been turned off! There were no pedestrians on the street, except me, and at every corner a policeman with a pillbox cap on his head and a sub-machinegun slung by a strap from his right shoulder. It was both unnerving and rather dull. After half an hour I'd had enough of this surreal version of Paris, and I walked to Gare de l'Est and changed my ticket to first class. The train to Frankfurt was already made up, so I climbed aboard, chose a carriage, and went to sleep.

The referendum was a triumph for de Gaulle. Almost 85 percent of metropolitan French turned out to vote, and nearly 80 percent opted for the Fifth

Republic. Within a year this would give France its first president – Charles de Gaulle, of course—who in time withdrew French soldiers from Algeria and evicted American soldiers from France. That should have been a warning to the United States: be careful whom you rescue, because he might decide he's better off without you.

He also stabilized the French franc. There would be no more $2.50 hotel rooms in Paris, such as I had enjoyed on my weekends from Coligny Caserne, nor the easy living that had attracted American artists and writers in the 1920s and again in the 1940s.

~ ~ ~ ~

In October, Private First Class Elvis Presley arrived in Bremerhaven aboard the troopship *General Randall.* Cecil and John Dornberg had a bit of a quarrel about who would cover the event; Cecil won out, and he gave the assignment to Ellen and me. Major Vickery at the 7th Army Public Information Office kindly got us sleeper berths on the southbound troop train – we'd be in the officers' car, no less! Civilians attached to the Army had the honorary grade of major, so little Ellen ranked up there with Vickery and his golden oak leaves.

But we had to make our own way north. We left Frankfurt at one o'clock in the morning, changed in Hannover, and reached Bremerhaven at eight-thirty. Today that would leave me weak, but at twenty-six it was all in the day's work, and we arrived fairly fresh to meet the celebrity when he came down the gangway. Ellen was splendid. She darted through the mob of photographers and gawkers, ran a few steps up the gangway, and offered to help him with his duffel bag. Presley grinned and let her pretend to take half the weight. It made a great photo, though alas it wasn't mine that went out on the Associated

Press wire to the world's press. On our way back to Frankfurt, in the officers' carriage, Ellen told me that the famous PFC was "nice."

"You should say that in your story," I said.

"Really?

"Absolutely."

She put her head on my shoulder and went to sleep.

Cecil was pleased with my photo, anyhow, and ran it on the front page of the *Overseas Family*. It ran big in the *Overseas Weekly* too, headline on the front page, story and photo inside. Predictably, *Stars and Stripes* ignored Presley's arrival, so we had an exclusive.

~ ~ ~ ~

I managed to keep my hands off Ellen for the most part, though she did spend one night in my bed. It came about like this:

One morning in November, I was typing away at my desk in the lobby when Cecil Neff came by. "Pack your stuff and leave," he said. "You're fired." He gave me a pay packet, four hundred and eighty deutschmarks. "Two weeks' pay in lieu of notice," he said. "Count it if you like, but I don't want to see you in this building again. You can keep your apartment until the two weeks are up. Leave the key with Harry McGowan, and he'll get it to us."

That's when I learned what it meant to be stunned. Did my jaw drop? I don't know. I have no idea what I said or what I did, except that I made my way home to Sachsenhausen by foot and by trolley.

News travels fast. Bodo apparently carried it to the *Frankfurter Allgemeine*, because Harry McGowan knocked on my door at six o'clock. We were still working on our first stein of beer at the Gasthaus on Schweizerstrasse when Ed Morris and Tony showed up. It was Tony who solved the mystery: "I heard them talking about you and your girlfriend."

"She's not my girlfriend."

"Well, *they* think so. And they think you told her about Marion and Gloria."

"I'll be a son of a bitch."

"Yeah, that's what Cecil thinks, too." Tony was suspiciously cheerful. Probably he figured this was his chance to get a raise and become a fixture at the *Overseas Weekly*.

Next afternoon I phoned the *OW*, asked for Ellen, and was put through without question. Her voice went to a whisper when she realized who was calling, so I figured that Cecil or another of the Inner Circle was nearby. "Meet me for dinner?" I said, and she would, but where? We agreed that I would meet her at six o'clock at the first trolley stop on my side of the Main River bridge.

She was a bit late but seemed to be thrilled by the adventure. "I told my parents I was spending the night at Trudy's," she said, Trudy being the plump classmate who sometimes kept her company at the *OW*. Once when I was making my Friday round of phone calls, the two of them began to giggle when they heard me say, "I've got a couple of queries here," so for my next call I changed it to "questions," and of course they giggled at that as well. Queries, queeries. They were still in high school, after all. "So can I stay with you?" she asked. "I don't want Trudy to know where I've been. Or my parents. Or Cecil!"

Oh my, what was this? "I've only got the one bed."

"I don't mind!"

Herr Wirt had no problem serving beer to Ellen, but I don't think she noticed that German bartenders weren't as puritanical as those at the NCO Club, and that her teenage GIs could have drunk all the beer they wanted in downtown Frankfurt.

The little girl of the Gasthaus wasn't back yet with her package of steaks before I had the story. Sure enough, Ellen had been chatting with Cecil about homosexuals, then put the question that was on her mind: "Is Marion one of *those*?"

It was wonderful to me, to think that Marion's sex life was talked about at the American High School. But of course it was! It's only the participants in a secret who think that they alone are privy to it. "*Who told you that*?" Cecil said, and in such a tone that Ellen realized she'd made a big mistake.

"Well," she said, and covered her tracks, or so she thought: "Dan Ford is right about one thing. *Integrity* is the most important thing!"

I had to laugh. I couldn't remember when or why I'd said such a thing, but I had no doubt that Ellen was quoting me fairly. I was, in my twenties, given to such pronouncements.

It was a perfect pickle. As far as Cecil and Marion were concerned, Ellen had fingered me as gossiping about something they believed only the Inner Circle knew about. So what if I denied it? "Oh, Marion, every GI in the American Zone knows about you and Kay!" The wider the web, the worse the news. I'd just get Ellen fired as well.

I managed to keep her down to two beers, so we were back at 5 Quirinstrasse by eight o'clock, tiptoeing past Harry McGowan's door and up to my attic apartment, which had a great view of downtown Frankfurt – including, as I had discovered the night of the Fourth of July, the American Embassy in the southeast. The fireworks were spectacular, though my neighbors across the way seemed more concerned than impressed. They put their heads out their windows and craned around, but they were facing away from downtown; they heard the bangs and could see the flashes of light, but not what was causing them, so it must have been uncomfortably like the British night raiders of 1945.

Like Zorba the Greek, I was a man of the 1950s, and though no longer a believer, I agreed that there was one sin that God would not forgive: when a woman calls a man to her bed, and he does not go. That the bed was mine, and that Ellen was more girl than woman, didn't seem to alter anything. (How old was she? At least seventeen, or at least I hope she was.) And I had no couch, and wasn't about to sleep on the floor.

So we turned out the lights, peeled down to our underwear, and crawled between the sheets. We kissed, of course, and I made the expected moves. Not to have done so would have been an insult, or such was the wisdom of the time. Ellen seemed eager enough, and I began to worry about how I was going to find and apply a condom. But when at last I reached for the honeypot, she put her hand on mine. *Stop!*

"I'm having my period," she said.

Clever girl! Or perhaps it was clever Mom, who'd coached Ellen with an excuse I'd be willing to accept.

Much as I'd detested Army life, it did equip me for my career. I'm even wearing my GI field jacket and khaki trousers this day, as Gaby and I play at war with Third Armored Division. The cigarette is an Ernte 23. I will eventually quit, though it will take a few years, and it won't be easy. (Photo: Gaby Beilfuss)

9 - *The Free Lance*

FLYING THE NORTH ATLANTIC in 1958 cost more than the leisurely ocean passage, and I was in no hurry, so I paid $220 for the eight-day voyage on *SS Amerika*, Hamburg to New York by way of Southampton. I don't remember who shared my below-decks cabin, but in the tourist-class dining room I met Charlie Moritz. We quickly established a link. He had earned a master's degree in library science at Rutgers with Norman Stevens, who'd done me the favor of getting B's in Military Science at UNH. Charlie was returning from a European fling before he took up a new job as editor of *Current Biography*, a reference magazine for libraries and journalists. In the blithe way of young people, he asked me to write for the magazine, and naturally I said yes.

Also at our table was a Hungarian named István Bey, which he changed to Stephen at mid-Atlantic. He had slipped through the Iron Curtain by learning Esperanto and getting an invitation to represent his country at a conference in Copenhagen. He bought Zeiss lenses in East Germany, hid them in the buttons of his duffel coat, and sold the contraband after reaching the West. He liked to stand aloof with his hands in his pockets, riding the ship's motion while the rest of us grabbed onto pillars or staggered into the walls. November weather made for a rough passage to New York.

I hailed a taxi for the trip to the Prince George on East 28th Street, a once-grand hotel that by 1958 was one of the city's most affordable. On the way, I saw a billboard advertising the 1959 Chevrolet Impala: "All New! All Over Again!" My heart sank, as the saying goes. The Impala was huge, powerful, flamboyant, and needlessly novel, everything about America that I'd outgrown, sneering at me from a billboard!

How crazy was that? Here I was, glorying in the adventure of being a young American when the dollar was king and everyone either loved us or was afraid of us, except for a few surly Russians and maybe the French. Yet I was depressed at how other Americans chose to celebrate their good fortune.

I spent a few days in the city, looking for a magazine job and having a reunion with Norman Stevens across the river in New Jersey. Jim Dye had said he could find me a job in Long Beach, proofreading the Los Angeles telephone directory, and his couch to sleep on while I looked for a place of my own. I can't believe that I took this possibility seriously, but I did, though I planned to visit friends and my brother Joe before heading West.

Dad's cousin Jere O'Brien lived in Boston's South End. Like the Prince George, Appleton Street was a once-proud institution on its way down. I knocked on Jere's door and asked if he knew where I could stay for a week or two. He did! He and his family occupied the ground floor and basement of number 34, I think it was, renting the two rooms on the second floor. Both those rooms were occupied, but he owned another house a block away with a room for seven dollars a week, including the loan of a hotplate. We shook hands on that. Cleaned up, condominiumized, and with a faux gas lantern outside, Number 77 is now a pretty townhouse with a tall front stoop leading up to what effectively is its second story. I had the front room on the third floor, with a bow window overlooking the street. It was fairly grim, with an iron bedstead, a bureau with a spotted mirror, a face bowl, and an icebox. I capsized the icebox as a table, putting Jere's hotplate on one side and my Olivetti portable on the other.

I had one neighbor, an old man named Beedee with sagging jowls who was convinced that I was a student at Harvard. "Go back to Harvard College!" he would shout at me when I typed late at night. I came to hate him, because he paced, and he had a floorboard that squeaked. Worse, his pacing was irregular, so I was kept in suspense between squeaks. We shared the bath at the end of the hall. There were two other tenants beneath us on the second floor, and a married couple in the half-basement below, which had its own entry beneath the front stoop.

Every afternoon while the weather lasted, I walked down to the Dartmouth Street intersection, bought the *Christian Science Monitor* and a bag of peanuts for a total of ten cents, and brought them back to read and munch on the stoop. This was a white area – Irish, in fact – but many afternoons a lovely black woman walked past, and she was one of the attractions that kept me reading and munching on my step until well into December.

Emma, my classmate and assistant editor on the *New Hampshire*, was working at the *Atlantic Monthly*. I used the pay phone at the corner store to phone her at the office downtown. "I'm married," she cautioned me.

"Again?"

"Yes."

"Well, congratulations again!" Actually, I don't think I'd ever congratulated Emma on the occasion of her first marriage, to Tommy Bennett when I was at the University of Manchester. The new husband, it seemed, was a passionate socialist like herself, and they lived in the North End, the Italian area beyond Scollay Square. He too was a writer, and Emma was the household's main support, just as she'd supported Tommy during his senior year at UNH. I went over to see them that same evening, and they became my only friends in Boston apart from the O'Briens on Appleton Street. The weather stayed fine until Thanksgiving, and I soon gave up my plan of moving to California. There's nothing so pretty as Indian Summer in New England, if we are still permitted to call it that.

It was a curious life I followed that winter. I went to the state unemployment office and got a job at one of the department stores on Tremont Street, setting up Christmas decorations. We worked nights, and we were quite the gang. I especially remember a bewildered sergeant who'd retired after twenty years – necessarily including both the War and the "police action" in Korea, though he never mentioned either – only to find that he couldn't survive on a half-pay pension. Once, as we passed a display of men's wallets, I saw his hand reach out, snag one, and slip it into his pocket. Indeed, there was a lot of small thievery going on as we followed our arty decorator through the empty aisles.

We were laid off for the holidays, but after the New Year I was called back for a daytime job taking inventory at the store's warehouse across the river in Cambridge, until one morning I overslept and forgot to go to work. This was a minimum-wage job, a dollar an hour in 1959, and I figured it was easier to forget about it than to go in and apologize. So after that I made my living with my typewriter.

Current Biography was my standby. I specialized in celebrities, since they required no particular background knowledge. The first one – my trial run – took me a week, working through the *New York Times* index and the *Reader's Guide to Periodical*

Literature at the Boston Public Library on Copley Square. How the wind blew around the BPL! I walked down to the end of my block, turned north on Dartmouth Street, and followed that to the square. An icy blast came from every point of the compass to meet and mingle and make a whirlpool in this block-sized hole in the city – two blocks, counting the low-lying library, the open spaces around it, and the double-wide sprawl of Huntington Ave slanting in from the southwest. I fancied that a New Hampshire-man must be inured to the worst that winter could do, but those December and January days introduced me to a whole new sort of cold. There was no way to avoid it: I had to wait for a green light at St. James Ave, cross over to Copley Square, then wait again for another green light to cross Dartmouth and enter the BPL.

I soon got the job down to two days, the first at the library taking notes, the second in my room, with my Olivetti portable on the capsized icebox that had become my desk. The drill was to type seven double-spaced lines on a slip of *CB* paper which I then turned over and on the back wrote the source of each quote or statement, so the fact-checkers at the H.W. Wilson office in New York could verify it. This, in effect, obliged me to write seven-line paragraphs, though I sometimes varied the routine with a paragraph covering two slips of paper. I then held onto the package for a week or two, in order to free up my days for more congenial work, because Charlie's secretary sent out a new assignment every time a finished one came in. There was no end of celebrities: Efrem Zimbalist Jr. (who lied about his age), Jean Renoir, Marilyn Monroe . . . and Jack Kerouac! Thus I discovered that the *New York Times* had weirdly compared *On the Road* to *The Sun Also*

Rises as the defining novel of a generation. Poor Hemingway! I hoped that he hadn't read that review.

The biographies were often interesting, but they weren't *fun*. My favorite, in the years I did this work, was the jazz pianist Thelonious Monk. Asked about his riffs on the piano, he explained them in the best words I've ever seen about the creative process: "All I know is, for every note there's another note that melts it, and I try to catch it with my hands." Thank you, Mr. Monk! Words are also notes in the air, and when things go well I can catch them with my hands. I don't always succeed, but I try.

While in the BPL that winter, I came across a trove of old books about the White Mountains that I was able to refashion into articles for *New Hampshire Profiles* magazine. I knew the editor from my summer working for the State Park Division. He only paid twenty-five dollars, but the work was more congenial than typing those seven-line pages for *Current Biography*, so I did several articles for Paul. There was also the occasional article or essay for the *Christian Science Monitor*, so what with one thing and another I made it through to spring. Of course I also striving for bigger things – not a novel, I'm afraid, because I needed the money this week or next, or at the very latest, next month. I couldn't wait for the possible and uncertain payout from my novel about Corporal Stephen Faust and the *belle poule*. I was, in short, a hack.

It was not the best of all possible lives. I had a library card at the BPL and borrowed a book from time to time, and if it was a good one – *The Young Lions*, for one! – I sat up all night reading it, refreshing myself with the occasional cup of instant coffee. And I invested fifty cents in the paperback of *On the Road*. I wasn't much impressed, despite the promise on the cover that I was holding "the bible of the 'beat generation' – the explosive best-seller that tells all about today's wild youth." When I researched Jack Kerouac at the BPL, I found that he was born in 1922. So he was thirty-seven, which didn't sound like wild youth to me. And nobody on the cover of that Signet paperback was wearing jeans, ripped or otherwise.

Mostly, though, I read science fiction and other rubbish, which I bought at a convenience store on Tremont Street for ten cents, the covers torn off and returned to the publisher for credit. It was a black-market lending library, in effect, and I would sell them back to the proprietor for a nickel each. In theory this was a research expense: sci-fi seemed an easy field to break into, and there were a lot of magazines that published this stuff in short form. I collected a lot of rejection slips but made no sales.

My other great entertainment was a twenty-five-cent movie theater, also on Tremont. I saw a lot of out-of-date movies there, including one so washed out it was almost colorless. The cinema ran all night, showing the same film over and over, so many of the patrons were homeless men who used it as a place to sleep. If they snored too loudly, the ticket-taker came down the aisle and poked them with a stick.

There were a lot of homeless men in Boston that winter – no women that I ever saw, and of course nobody called them "homeless." They were tramps, bums, vagrants, and in France, *clochards*. They slept on the subway gratings, kept reasonably warm by the vapor rising from below, or they set fire to a trash barrel on the Public Gardens. I sometimes joined them and warmed my hands, but I never managed to strike up a conversation that made any sense. I also hung around the Greyhound bus station on St.

James Avenue, near Copley Square. At three o'clock in the morning, it was just about the only place in Boston to get a cup of coffee. I fancied that this was good research for something on the line of George Orwell's *Down and Out in Paris and London* – embrace all experience! But nothing came of it.

Of an evening, I often walked down to the O'Briens' and watched a bit of television with them. One of their roomers, a middle-aged bachelor named Al, was there every night, as was Mrs. Jope, Kathleen O'Brien's mother. Al peddled dental equipment from town to town, and during the commercials he'd spin tales of his travels. One evening, Jere brought up the subject of the blacks who were beginning to push into the South End, which belonged to the Irish, just as the North End belonged to the Italians. So Al told us how, when he went to a college town, all the girls were mad about the calypso singer Harry Belafonte, who had been my introduction to Bizet's opera of *Carmen*. "Can you imagine?" he said. "A *nigger*?" The O'Briens shook their heads at the wonder of it. Luckily their daughter Ann was studying in her room, since she too was probably a Belafonte fan.

~ ~ ~ ~

Every couple of weeks, I phoned Emma at the *Atlantic Monthly* and got myself invited to dinner, for which I might contribute a cheap bottle of red wine. These evenings could be hard on my ego. Nikko – he was named after the immigrant anarchist Nicola Sacco, executed for murder in 1920 – would tell me about his conversations with the editor of the *Nation*, Carey McWilliams. He rubbed it in by saying how embarrassing it was, to have an article appear alongside an ad for a vanity publisher or a pay-to-play literary agent like Sterling Lord. He also seemed to be a pal of Jay Laughlin, a cousin of Henry, who'd used his share of the Jones & Laughlin fortune to set up his own publishing company, New Directions. "You *must* send your novel to Jay when it's done," Nikko told me. (Emma dutifully used his birth name, but to me "Nicola" sounded feminine, so I toughened it up a bit.)

And Emma recalled how, a year or two earlier, a couple of Hemingway short stories had come to the *Atlantic*. "When Hemingway's agent calls," she said, "you don't quibble. You just publish the stuff!" As a proto-feminist, Emma didn't approve of Ernest Hemingway. "And you pay top rate." I didn't ask what that was. I'd had a few rejection slips from the *Atlantic*, none graced by a handwritten note, never mind an actual letter such as I sometimes received from a sci-fi magazine.

I can't remember ever arguing with Nikko and Emma, though we differed on almost everything from Hemingway's genius to the origins of the war in Korea. Nikko was convinced that South Korea had invaded the North. I contented myself with going to the BPL and reading the *Boston Globe* for June 1950: If the South had been the aggressor, how did North Korean armored units capture Seoul on the third day of fighting? It was so absurd that I didn't bother to report my findings.

I thought of myself as a cynic, but when it came to my country, life had made me a patriot. It was part of the ground I stood upon. I'd seen a lot of England, France, and Germany in the past four years, and toured other lands and cities of men, and I would be forever grateful that Dad had come to America in 1927, and that Mom had followed him. I liked *being* in Europe, but I wouldn't have wanted to be a European. Emma by contrast had grown up in middle-class American affluence and had no use for it. "This lousy country," she wrote to Joe about this time, "I won't give ten cents for it."

But this never darkened our evenings together. I suppose that, like Secondo at Peter Bulkeley School, and Tookie at UNH, Nikko and Emma were testimonials to the remarkable tolerance young people have for one another, if not for the generations that came before them.

~ ~ ~ ~

My name was still on file at the state unemployment office, and by golly I got an offer to write movie scripts for the U.S. Army. I went to Fort Devens for an interview in March, a two-hour bus ride, and waltzed through the process. When I returned to Boston, I was a GS-5 at last. Wouldn't Dad be delighted? I even had a place in a car pool, leaving Copley Square Monday morning at seven. Saturday night, I went to the North End and begged for advice. With me I had checks from *Current Biography*, *Profiles*, and the *Monitor*, eighty-five dollars in total, about two weeks' work; as a GS-5 I'd earn about four thousand dollars a year, and I could at last get back to work on *The Way Home*. What should I do? Nikko, predictably, was certain that I mustn't sell out to the U.S. Army.

I didn't get anything done that Sunday, nor did I sleep Sunday night; I sat up, brewed cups of instant coffee, and suffered until it was too late to pull myself together. Much relieved, I wrote an apology to the good people at Fort Devens, walked down to Dartmouth Street and mailed the letter, and then went to bed.

As spring came, I resumed my afternoon ritual, reading the *Monitor* and munching a bag of peanuts on the stoop at 77 Appleton Street. But the lovely black woman no longer came by, and although I did write the final chapters of *The Way Home*, it didn't seem that I was any closer to a life where I didn't have to spend most of my time on celebrity biographies. So when the next job offer came – from Paul Estaver at *New Hampshire Profiles*, offering part-time work as his assistant editor – I hitchhiked up to Portsmouth to talk about it.

"Do I have to shave?" I asked, for I had restarted my beard after my adventure at Fort Devens. This kept my face warm while walking to Copley Square, as I explained, but in truth it protected me from looking for another job. Paul was okay with the whiskers, and he brought me back to his house for the night, so I could get myself settled in Durham. Debbie Estaver taught at the Durham high school, and she was in the habit of befriending young people and making pets of them – her students, the occasional foster kid, and my brother Joe. While at UNH, he'd written a few articles for Paul, and he became Debbie's particular pet. Every week, she and Paul picked up his laundry and returned it a week later, washed and ironed, and they continued this habit when Joe went to Harvard. Now, though, he was a Congressional Fellow in Washington, and apparently Debbie had drafted me to fill his place.

I said goodbye to the O'Briens and to Nikko and Emma, packed my Army duffel bag, and with that and my Olivetti portable I boarded the bus to Durham. It was a bit of a retreat, but I wasn't sorry to leave the city behind. My new life entailed five or six days' work in the month, at twenty dollars a day, actually an improvement over what I'd earned as an advertising copywriter or at the *Overseas Weekly*. These were the Good Years in America, before our feet got muddied in the paddy fields and rain forests of Vietnam. There was some inflation, but not so much that we paid attention, and life did indeed get better each passing year.

I rented an apartment of sorts, in a long, low building that once served as housing for married soldiers on a military base. The University of New Hampshire acquired it in 1945 to house veterans who had a wife but no children, and when that need passed, sold it to a Durham resident. He moved it to a lot two miles from town, near the Boston & Maine railroad tracks, and called it "the Flats." There were eight small "studios" on each side, facing a parking lot to the south and the railroad tracks to the north. Mine faced the parking lot. It had a living room, a half-kitchen and half-bath, and an overlarge oil stove. For this I paid twenty-seven dollars a month, plus electricity and fuel oil. The previous tenant had left me an Army cot and a rug, so my first night I rolled the rug and used it as a mattress. Over the next month or so, I gradually improved things, borrowing from the Estavers, dump-picking, and buying what I had to.

I also paid two hundred dollars for a little two-cycle Harley Davidson motorcycle, a German design that had been seized as war reparations. The winners had of course looted German technology, especially the Russians. The British and Americans also helped themselves to what might be useful, such as Werner von Braun and his V-2 rocket, since adapted for a missile we could lob into Eastern Europe. The Redstone warhead couldn't reach Moscow, however. Stalin had reshaped Poland and shoved it more than a hundred miles to the west, meanwhile installing a Communist government in the Soviet Zone of Germany. What with one thing and another, the former DKW 125 was now manufactured postwar in five countries: Russia, Britain, the United States, the

Federal Republic of Germany, and the German Democratic Republic, with the last being where the original factory wound up in 1945.

I rode the bike to Portsmouth in good weather, and when it was raining or snowing I hitched a ride with Paul. I didn't have a phone, but he'd swing by the Flats if he thought the weather might keep me off the road that day.

This was more congenial work than counting dinnerware at the warehouse in Cambridge, and indeed more congenial than the *Overseas Weekly*. I was needed mostly toward the middle of the month, while Paul and the advertising manager put together the magazine for two months hence. I wrote photo captions, proofed the galleys, faked up a letter to the editor if we didn't have enough to fill the column, and with Joyce, Paul's secretary, made sure the real estate ads were correct, reading them aloud while she checked them against the original copy. They were mostly along the line of "New England colonial farmhouse with 100 acres, $35,000." I dreamed of owning a hundred acres of New England farmland. I should have acted on the dream, because any one of those properties would now bring a million dollars, maybe two. But in 1959 Joyce and I just rattled them off, one after the other! Some as low as $28,000, some as high as $37,500.

I also researched the occasional celebrity for *Current Biography*, trying to keep it down to a celebrity a month. This was a challenge. Charlie's secretary seemed to sense when I'd finished one, and she tried to force it out of me by sending me a fresh assignment. For this work, the UNH library had a great advantage over the BPL: open stacks! This was a grand new building from the one I had known as a student, built in anticipation of the Baby Boom that was transforming American education. The children of the War veterans would begin to arrive on campus in the fall of 1964, with ever-increasing numbers in the years that followed. The first new building was the library behind Thompson Hall, its front door on the same level as the administration building, with two stories above it and two stories below. It was into these depths that I descended to study bound volumes of the *New York Times, Newsweek, Time, Variety,* and *Scientific American*, and my favorite since childhood, *Life* magazine with its glorious, oversized photographs (and, now that their time had passed, those equally fascinating advertisements). I could lose myself in a copy of *Life* for an hour, turning the pages and marveling at my own yesteryear, where I had been and could never go again, as A.E. Houseman had written:

That is the land of lost content,
I see it shining plain,
The happy highway where I went
And cannot come again.

To be sure, my life was never much of a highway. More like a Boston street, in fact, with cobblestones laid upon a cowpath, and pavement on top of that. And they weren't all happy, of course, though they do seem rather golden in retrospect.

And speaking of time past! Carleton Eldredge from East Hall and the Government Department was now an associate at a law firm in Concord, the state capital. He lived in Exeter and drove to work by way of Durham, so he dropped in from time to time for a cup of coffee at seven-thirty. One day he challenged me to read *Swann's Way*, the 1922 translation by C.K. Scott Moncrieff. He had acquired the book in a small Modern Library edition of the first volume of

Marcel Proust's great novel. This struck me as a splendid idea, but I thought I could do better by acquiring the whole novel at second hand, so I rode my little Harley down to Boston and parked it on the sidewalk outside the Old Corner Bookstore, a wonderful gambrel-roofed building where I'd spent many afternoons when I lived at 77 Appleton Street. I think it was on the second floor that I found it: *Remembrance of Things Past*, as Scott Moncrieff had unfortunately translated *À la recherché du temps perdu*. The seven books were bound into two volumes, and the asking price was seven dollars, which seemed fair enough: a dollar apiece! I paid it, persuaded the clerk to put it in a plastic bag, buckled the package into one of the saddlebags that straddled the Harley's rear wheel, and rode home to begin my search for Proust's lost time, which could also be regarded as time wasted. This would become a lifelong quest, and it still entrances me.

Every Thursday morning thereafter, Carleton showed up at seven-thirty and smoked a cigar while we drank Nescafe and talked about Proust. On the other mornings of the week, he stopped at Johnson's Dairy Bar halfway to Concord and read the book for an hour, still smoking the cigar but drinking a better cup of coffee.

~ ~ ~ ~

My big project in 1959 was revising my story of Corporal Stephen Faust, the good-hearted *belle poule* on the Rue Blondel, and Army life in general. I had a good first draft of *The Way Home* by September, when Joe returned from Washington to become an instructor in the UNH Government Department for five thousand dollars a year. He too was working on a book. He couldn't get tenure without a doctoral degree, and he couldn't get that PhD until his thesis was approved by V.O. Key, his mentor at Harvard. Joe was writing about Teddy Roosevelt's "Bull Moose" campaign for the presidency in 1912, and its lasting effect on New Hampshire politics. The state Republican party had a liberal wing, he believed, including our incumbent Congressman, Perkins Bass, in whose office Joe had worked as a Congressional Fellow. I found this a fascinating notion, but to my shame I never asked him how it was going. Not very well, as matters turned out.

I ignored Nikko's instructions to send my novel to Jay Laughlin in New York. Instead I mailed it to Cousin Henry's publishing company, Houghton Mifflin in Boston. Believing, as I foolishly did, that literature was a matter of merit and not the author's connections, I didn't mention that I'd once pitched hay at the Laughlin Estate on Old River Road. So the manuscript came in "over the transom," as the saying went. But it didn't languish in the slush pile! Indeed, it earned me a cup of coffee and a slice of apple pie at the Parker House in Boston, as a guest of a Houghton Mifflin editor named George Starbuck, who would later emerge as a notable poet and teacher of writing. He wasn't much older than I, but he'd spent his time more profitably: I've just now learned that when I met him, he was taking lessons in poetry from Robert Lowell, and that his fellow students included Sylvia Plath and Anne Sexton.

The Way Home, George told me, wasn't publishable, but I was a good writer and mustn't give up. I thanked him for the encouragement and the snack, put the manuscript in the left saddlebag of my Harley, and rode home in deepest gloom. (Perhaps I should mention that the right saddlebag was given over to a can of Spam, a box of brown rice, and a quart of two-cycle motor oil. These were to get me to

Canada in the event that Eisenhower had another heart attack and Richard Nixon moved into the White House. For a onetime Young Republican, I took a very dim view of the vice-president.)

A few days later, I got a telegram from George Starbuck, inviting me to a cocktail party on Beacon Hill. Like a fool, I demurred. For one thing, I was afraid to risk the awful merges on the Tobin Bridge, going into Boston at night with my Harley's dim headlamp and barely visible taillight – and I've never been comfortable in a room full of strangers. So I wonder now . . . would I have met Sylvia Plath at that party?

~ ~ ~ ~

Carroll Towle by this time was showing signs of senility. Today that affliction is called Alzheimer's disease, but at the time it just seemed an amusing part of growing old. Indeed, I suppose Dr. Towle was well on his way when Emma, Tommy, and I were his students, but as is the way with young people, we just laughed about it, as we would about any foible on the part of our elders. The University had hired a young man named Thomas Williams, whose first novel was published in 1955 and qualified him for tenure in lieu of a PhD. He'd been Dr. Towle's student and now was beginning to take his mentor's place. One night I came back to the Flats and found a note on my door: *I'm told you're back in Durham and serious about writing. I think the serious ones ought to get together, don't you?*

I didn't know it at the time, but Tom Williams was a harbinger of the new routine for American writers. He'd graduated from UNH, enjoyed an expatriate year at the Sorbonne, and attended the Iowa Writer's Workshop on the GI Bill, and now he would be a well-paid professor, with the summers free for his writing. He was far from alone. "After the war," wrote Louis Menand in *The Free World*, "it became a common practice for writers to be trained (and credentialed) in universities after taking courses taught by other writers who had been trained (and credentialed) in universities." At the age of twenty-eight, with my notion of journalism, garrets, and the expatriate life, it seemed that I was a fossil of the 1920s.

A few nights later, Tom came visiting again, on a motorcycle with brighter lights and a bigger engine than my three-horsepower Harley. What's more, he had a six-pack of beer, which we sat and drank while we talked about books. Fortunately I had a paperback of *Ceremony of Love* in my bookshelf (three planks of pine separated by bricks) and could ask him to sign it. There's nothing a writer likes better than to autograph his books.

Tom was five years older than I, so I didn't hold it against him that he had two novels already published and a third ready to go – and, even more enviable, an agent to represent him! I told him about George Starbuck and the novel judged well written but not publishable because it didn't *go* anywhere. Tom didn't offer to read it, but he did promise that when I had another book ready to go, he'd give me the address of his agent, Mavis McIntosh in New York. This was an incredible coup, and I was so excited after he roared off into the night that I stayed up until dawn, drinking coffee and thinking big thoughts, as I used to do at 77 Appleton Street.

~ ~ ~ ~

One of those big thoughts was the awareness that I should make some changes in my life.

I sent *The Way Home* to a few New York publishers before the typescript became dog-eared and coffee-stained, then I retired it rather than spend a week retyping its three hundred pages. I got a few nice letters of rejection, but the language was boiler-plate ("not suitable for our needs at the present time") and without any invitations to coffee, never mind a literary cocktail party. I'd have to start all over again.

So I gave up *Profiles* and went to work for the University of New Hampshire, eight-thirty to noon, writing press releases and such for three thousand dollars a year. (I was replacing a woman who had earned that salary for a full day's work.) I bought a thirty-foot house trailer and moved it onto a private lot on Packer's Falls Road, near Paul Estaver's house in Lee, so I could walk over to Garrity Road of an evening and have dinner with Debbie and Paul and Joe. I forget what I paid for the trailer, except that it just about emptied my bank account. I also bought a weary 1952 Ford sedan from Joe McElroy, an English instructor who in time became a considerable author in his own right, better known today than Tom Williams. (Or me!) The Harley I sold to a student for the same seventy-five dollars I had paid for the car.

I found that working for the University had an interesting perk: I could take a course every semester, tuition free, so I decided to obtain the equivalent of a bachelor's degree in philosophy. I started with the Greeks, falling in love with Democritus, who two thousand years before Einstein understood that everything was made up of "atoms and void." And Heraclitus, who pointed out that I couldn't step twice into the same river because the river kept changing, and so did I. Epicurus followed, and Machiavelli and Nietzsche and Sartre, and on my own time I studied Zen Buddhism, which like Existentialism was a big thing in the 1960s. Jim Dye and I coached one another by mail, torturing the postal service meanwhile by putting the wrong postage on our letters. This started when I received a half-cent stamp in change at the post office. I put a now-obsolete four-cent stamp plus the one-half-center on my next envelope to Long Beach, so Jim received it with half a cent postage due. He retaliated, of course, and after a few rounds of that, I put a Green Stamp on the letter, and it went through to Long Beach, duly canceled. (Green Stamps were also big in the 1960s: we got stamps as a reward when we shopped; we pasted them into a savings book; and when the book was full we went to the Green Stamp store in Portsmouth and exchanged it for pots and tableware and suchlike stuff.)

I got Jim to read *Thus Spoke Zarathustra*, and in turn he got me to read *Existentialism from Dostoevsky to Sartre*. I was amazed to see that the latter had been published in 1956. What I was doing, it seemed, was catching up to all the stuff I had missed during my years abroad, at the University of Manchester, Coligny Caserne, and Sachsenhausen.

I would eventually tackle Hegel, but I didn't finish the dialectic, for reasons I will explain in time. Philosophy could be boring, especially the American variety of the twentieth century – pragmatism! phenomenology! – but my scheme wasn't entirely cockeyed. If the next few years didn't turn out as I hoped, I would join Jim Dye in California and earn a doctorate at UCLA. The academic life suited my brother just fine; it might also work for me. Meanwhile, though, I'd write another novel. I was sure of one thing: the central character wouldn't be named Stephen, he wouldn't be modeled on me, and he wouldn't be searching for the Meaning of Life.

I am amazed, looking back, at how dressy a journalist was expected to be in 1960. I'm still wearing the Harris Tweed jacket I bought in England six years earlier. (Photo: Jack Adams)

One of the great things about living in a college community is the limitless supply of young women. I dated quite a few, from a high-school senior I met through the Estavers to an assistant professor of English whose husband was still in town and happened to be a friend of mine. It was all very complicated, but it worked out okay, at least for me.

The most important of these love affairs was Theodora, as I shall call her after the name she now bears in fiction. Teddie was a wonderful girl, cute and quick and funny. She was divorced and living in Newmarket, which at the time was to Durham what the Prince George was to the hotel industry in New York, a last resort for the thrifty. She probably had a job, but I'm embarrassed to say I don't know what it was. She had two daughters with exotic names and a baby boy named Johnny, and I was charmed by all of them. My Ford sedan could carry the five of us – none in a seatbelt, of course, for seatbelts had only recently become standard equipment. Teddie owned a Hillman Minx, also without seatbelts and, like most English cars, it was small and unreliable. Anyhow I was too proud to be driven around by my girlfriend.

I met her through a gang of twenty-something students and former students who hung around the University, obsessed about the threat of nuclear war, and in a few cases drove fast sports cars. Their center of gravity was a Quonset hut in the woods off Madbury Road. I soon began to write about them, and I did such a thorough job of it that now I can't distinguish between my fictional characters and their real-life counterparts – often enough, two or three people contributed to a single character, or I dragged in bits from my own student days or the Army or the *Overseas Weekly* or nights on the prowl in Frankfurt and Boston.

It was great fun. I wrote the first draft with a Flair pen in my awful longhand, graded "F" by Sister Mary Agnes at St. Aidan's. I bought lined, white, letter-sized pads from the UNH bookstore, and on them I sketched scenes and characters, dialogues and situations. When a pad was full, I detached the pages and stored them in a three-ring binder. The story would be called *Now Comes Theodora*, the title supplied by Carleton Eldredge, who handled a lot of divorce cases for his law firm in Concord. I loved the wording prescribed for the woman's plea: "Now comes Theodora Merchant of Narwich, in the County of Piscataqua, State of New Hampshire, and complains against Colin Merchant of said Narwich and says. . . ."

I broke the habit of a lifetime by sharing the chapters with Teddie. In turn she shared pieces of her life that became part of the story as it developed. It was an exciting time, because for once I wasn't the hero of my own book. For this I'd conscripted a photographer who sometimes worked with me on a story for *Profiles*, and who processed my own photos for a share of the gross.

Of course there was a lot of me in Boris as well. He lived in the Quonset hut off Madbury Road – Boris, I mean, not the real-life photographer – and he hosted the pacifists and anti-warriors who partied there. Their leaders were two competing young men, a pompous fool named Marvin Peabody and a would-be sculptor named Colin Merchant who had a tendency to get young women pregnant. (Colin *was* searching for the Meaning of Life. Marvin was inspired by a young man with three names who when I turned up in Durham said to me: "I understand you believe the Self can be Actualized." I have always been suspicious of men who pronounce their middle names.) It was great fun, and I felt entirely in control of what was going on. Like Thelonious Monk, I threw a note into the air, sensed another note that would melt it, and tried to catch it with my hands. I succeeded more often than not, or thought I did.

In the course of all this, Teddie gave up her life of independence in Newmarket and moved back to Massachusetts to be nearer her parents. I drove down to see her every week or two, along the awful Route 128 circumferential highway that was being doubled in width, so it was a continual traffic jam. I avoided the worst of it by driving down in the early hours of the afternoon and driving home in the early hours of the morning, but that was tiring, and over time my visits became monthly and then occasional. If not for the novel, we would have broken up altogether. But she was as excited about the book as I was.

~ ~ ~ ~

So it came to September of 1962. I was thirty years old, and at a party one time, our hostess said to me: "Any man who reaches the age of thirty without getting married at least once, by way of experiment, must be a pretty cold fish." And I remembered a "piece" I'd written for Carroll Towle ten years earlier. He liked it; it could be part of a novel, he told me in conference. It was about a young man who has just turned thirty, and who looks back upon his life, playing off the notion that a reporter ended a story by typing -30- at the end. To a young journalist, thirty *was* the end. At twenty-one I couldn't imagine myself as thirty years old, but here I was, still single and mostly unattached, with no real prospect whatever – and tasked with writing Dr. Towle's obituary.

There was one bright spot, and that was the White Mountains of New Hampshire. I had discovered them on my Harley, riding the grand route through Crawford Notch, south again through Franconia Notch, and then over the recently opened Kancamagus Highway through what passed in New England for wilderness. I sometimes dismounted and walked a mile or two into the woods on one of the trails maintained by the Appalachian Mountain Club, trusting that no hiker would bother to steal my motorcycle. And as soon as I acquired the trusty Ford sedan, I started spending nights in the mountains, using the same pack and sleeping bag with which I'd hitchhiked through Europe in the spring and summer of 1955.

This was of course a lonely business, so I lured Carleton Eldredge and Horace Lyndes into making a traverse of the Franconia Ridge over the long Labor Day weekend. Horace was a big man, and he was out of shape; his feet got bloody on the final day, coming down from Mt. Lafayette, which the early settlers had called Big Haystack. We'd also gone over the mountains known as Flume, Liberty, Little Haystack, and Lincoln, all qualifying for the Appalachian Mountain Club's list of Four Thousand Footers, a big deal in the eastern United States. Today I see that the traverse "is only recommended for very experienced adventurers," so I suppose it was unkind of me to use it to use it as my friends' introduction to mountain hiking.

But they got their revenge when winter came. Carleton persuaded me to take up skiing, which seemed a logical extension of my warm-weather sport. I bought a pair of wooden Northland skis with cable bindings and screw-on metal edges, along with a no-brand pair of leather ski boots that came, I think, from Yugoslavia. They were sold to me by Ray, my onetime East Hall roommate, now assistant manager of a department store near Portsmouth.

One Sunday in January, Carleton drove me to Cannon Mountain, on the other side of Franconia Notch from our Labor Day trek. Horace was with us, as was Faith, Carleton's wife. Cannon was famously hardscrabble, part of the state park system, with ski trails and lifts that had been developed in the 1930s and not much improved since then. As I no doubt deserved, my friends took me to the snow-rimed summit and skied away on a trail called Upper Cannon. I followed, missed the first turn, and flew off through the trees. I ended with my head downhill and my skis high above, caught between two trees. I couldn't reach the bindings to release them, and I might have died there if a young woman hadn't missed the same turn and crashed into the woods beside me. Her companions were more faithful than mine; they came back for her and kindly freed me from my bindings as well.

I spent the next hour hacking my way down Upper Cannon, Middle Cannon, and Lower Cannon until I came out on the relatively humane Peabody Slopes, where I could make snowplow turns at my leisure. I needed another hour to recover, drinking coffee in the base lodge. My friends didn't apologize for abandoning me. Perhaps they thought they'd done me a favor – and as matters turned out, they had. I was hooked. I rode up with them every Sunday until the snow melted in March, Horace and I taking turns paying for gas. A day ticket cost four dollars and fifty cents, but since I spent most of my time on the Peabody Slopes, learning how to make a decent stem Christie – start a snowplow turn, shift your weight to the uphill ski, bring the other ski up to meet it – I would buy a few single-ride tickets on the lower T-bar for forty-five cents each. That took me nearly halfway up the mountain. I'd then ski down almost to the bottom and wait for an empty bar. There was always one of these coming along, because inevitably a snow bunny missed the bar or fell off before coming this far; I'd catch the empty and let it drag me along until I could get it behind me and ride it securely.

If not for the necessary coffee-and-cigarette breaks, I could have done this all day. At worst, I seldom spent as much as three dollars on tickets from nine o'clock till the mountain fell into shadow. The state of New Hampshire had to make up the difference at the coffee urn, for we didn't buy lunch. Faith Eldredge made sandwiches and brought them along.

~ ~ ~ ~

In time I upgraded to a secondhand pair of Head Standards. These were metal skis, and they were known as Cheaters because they were so easy to turn. And I did finally master the Stem Christie, but I couldn't "break through to parallel," as the saying went in the 1960s. Not with leather boots, and not on the narrow and icy trails of Cannon Mountain.

I also traded my Ford sedan toward a forty-horsepower Volkswagen Beetle, complete with fuel gauge, backup lights, AM radio, and vent quarter-windows in lieu of air conditioning. If I recall correctly, the car cost me $1,760, the equivalent of $15,281 today. But think of the money I'd save on gasoline! Often I'd work a full day at the News Bureau, then take a day off to ski when the slopes were nearly empty.

Nikko and Emma had also moved to New Hampshire and, like me, were climbing the Four Thousand Footers, so we made a threesome on the treks that were new to us. They drove a secondhand Volkswagen van and wore U.S. Army fatigues, which they called "Fidels" in honor of the dictator in Cuba. When I presumed to criticize Castro for letting the Russians set up missiles ninety miles from the coast of Florida, Emma puffed like a pigeon and declared: "I've seen two revolutions in my life," meaning China in 1949 and Cuba in 1958, "and I hope to see a third." It's amazing how many intelligent Americans thought like that – and still do. Immigrants, and the children of immigrants, usually know better.

For several years I dutifully took my Beetle to the VW dealership in Portsmouth for service. So it was that on November 22, 1963, I was sitting in a plastic chair and reading a story in the company magazine *Small World* about a photographer who put a Beetle in a swimming pool and timed it until it sank, which took forty-two minutes. A radio was playing through a loudspeaker, and I heard the announcer say, "his wife Jaqueline." From those three word s, I could reconstruct the ones that preceded them: *Jacqueline . . . Kennedy . . . shots.*

"What he did say?" asked the woman sitting beside me.

"The President has been shot," I said.

America lost its innocence that day, and as with Pearl Harbor on December 7, 1941, and the collapse of the Twin Towers on September 11, 2001, those of us who remember them know exactly where we were and what we were doing when we heard the news.

~ ~ ~ ~

I'd spent most of that year tweaking and smoothing *Now Comes Theodora*. When I was finished, I typed a clean copy on white paper. Then I spent an afternoon feeding dimes into the Xerox machine at the library. This was a costly business: three hundred and fifty pages, thirty-five dollars, nearly three days' pay at the News Bureau. I stacked the still-warm copies into the box the paper had come in, wrapped it in a repurposed grocery bag, and mailed it to Mavis McIntosh in New York. Tom Williams had kindly given me the address on East 27th Street, along with some advice: be patient, don't pester her! Two weeks later, I got an acknowledgment. It wasn't glowing, but neither was it a rejection.

About this time, New Hampshire decided to establish the nation's first state-run lottery, a "Sweepstakes" tied to the racetrack at Salem, New Hampshire. The state had long profited from the fact that the Puritan heritage in Massachusetts now manifested itself mostly in taxes on sin, on drinking and smoking and pari-mutuel betting. The Salem track was only two miles from the state line, so its Massachusetts patrons liked to spend what money they had left on booze and cigarettes, which we priced a bit cheaper than the neighbors did. Why not sell them a lottery ticket as well?

Paul Estaver had tired of editing a magazine for The Little Old Lady in Casa Grande, as he called his subscribers in honor of an Arizona lady who wrote a letter to the editor every few months. He wanted to make the magazine more intellectual and, um, *manly*. I'd already done a story about the Reverse Freedom Riders, black families bussed north by Southern segregationists, as payback for the Northerners (mostly white, but including a few brave blacks) traveling south to agitate for civil rights.

Now Paul wanted me to interview Edward Powers, former head of the FBI's Boston office, who was figuring how to run a lottery in defiance of Federal law. His solution was to match each ticket to a horse entered in a race the following September – the Sweepstakes! So the customer wasn't buying a lottery ticket but betting on the horses, and that was perfectly legal.

While I was at it, I wrote a shorter version and mailed it to the *Reporter*, a magazine I had read and admired since college. Max Ascoli was unique among American intellectuals: an anti-Fascist immigrant who regarded Stalin as a menace like Hitler. Most of the smart people I knew still thought of Stalin as the genial Uncle Joe of wartime propaganda, more sinned against than sinning. They included my brother. And Emma and Nikko, of course.

Well! The *Reporter* sent me a check for two hundred and fifty dollars– ten times what *Profiles* paid, and quicker, too. So I set to work on a follow-up about New Hampshire's first-in-the-nation presidential primary. The *Reporter* bought that story as well; it ran toward the end of February 1964, and a few weeks later I got the longed-for letter from Mavis McIntosh. She had an offer from Doubleday: twenty-five hundred dollars as an advance on royalties for *Now Comes Theodora*, half when I signed the contract and half on publication, and was I interested?

Interested? I was dizzy. I went to a party in Connecticut that weekend, with Carleton Eldredge and Horace Lyndes, at the home of Collis Beck, another pal from East Hall. I had a lot to drink, and I struck up a conversation with a young woman who asked the usual party question: "What do you do?"

And for the first time in my life, I could say it aloud: "I'm a writer." And when she obliged by asking what I'd written, I had an answer to that as well. I don't know if she was impressed, but I certainly was.

10 – The Good Life

IN THE SPRING OF 1964, I happened upon a story in the *Portsmouth Herald* about a helicopter pilot who'd just returned from Vietnam. I still had no phone, so I drove downtown, put a dime in the slot of a pay phone, and dialed zero for the Dover operator. I asked for Willard Boyle in Hampton. She returned my dime and told me to insert a quarter, and while the call went through I reflected on the downside of winning a war. In Frankfurt, I had called Herr Doktor Naujocks by direct-dialing Munich, then Dachau, then his phone number; in the U.S., where the phone system hadn't been destroyed by enemy bombs, I needed operator assistance to reach Captain Boyle eighteen miles away.

He invited me down for a chat, and on the way I bought a six-pack of beer. Hampton, like Durham, was a dry town in those years, and I figured this would lubricate my interview, which it did. When I got home, I typed the first chapter of what I planned as a book of reportage about the war that seemed to be brewing in South Vietnam. Tom Williams had warned me about the Second Book Syndrome: "You think it was hard the first time, but the next one will be tougher. You probably won't make the best-seller list or get a movie contract with your first novel, so the best you can hope for is a paperback edition. That mightn't be enough. You need an *edge*."

My edge would be Vietnam. I talked my boss at the News Bureau into giving me a three-month leave of absence, and I wrote an apologetic note to Professor Moore, with whom I was taking a graduate seminar in Hegel's dialectics. (One of the lads later told me that the final exam had only question: "When Mr. Ford left the class, he said he was sorry not to know how it all turned out. How *did* it all turn out?") And when the check from Mavis McIntosh cleared the bank, I drove to Dover and bought a round-trip ticket to Saigon on Pan American World Airways. It cost $1,276. That was a breathtaking amount of money in the days before the Great Inflation of the 1970s turned our dollars into dimes. For the equivalent amount of money today – $10,756 – I'd expect a lie-flat seat in first class, with a champagne breakfast. At the time, I felt lucky to find an empty row toward the back of the plane, so I could stretch out for the long vault from Honolulu to Guam.

When I woke at dawn and looked out at the endless Pacific, having fallen asleep on May 5 and awakened on May 7, I went into a panic: *What am I doing here?* But I couldn't step off, step back, and retrieve the Wednesday I'd lost to the International Date Line.

My introduction to Saigon was a sinus headache so awful I feared I was having a stroke, until I looked at the guy next to me and saw tears running down his cheek. It seemed that Viet Cong snipers liked to shoot at planes coming in to land at Tan Son Nhut airport, so the Pan Am pilot had positioned us directly above the runway at twenty thousand feet, then spiraled the nearly four miles straight down, to get us on the runway while offering the smallest possible target.

The airport was hot – and raucous – and tawdry. And I loved it! Really, it was a boyhood dream come true, like playing a role in a "Terry and the Pirates" comic strip. I hitched a ride into the city with Mark Diebolt, trained to fly an F-105 Thunderchief, but in

Vietnam reduced to a T-28 "Nomad," a trainer kitted out with machine guns and bomb racks. We not only supplied T-28s to the South Vietnamese but took American pilots out of their supersonic jets and loaned them as well. Captain Diebolt was one of these men. I'd chatted up his wife on the flight from Manila to Saigon, and when I told him where I planned to stay, he said, "Oh no, that place has hot and cold running maids," and delivered me instead to the Hotel Vinh Loi, where he'd booked a room for Bernadette.

Among other features, the Vinh Loi had air-conditioned rooms and an amiable hanger-on who called himself Joe. He offered to show me the city if I helped him improve his English. I was ready for bed but agreed to meet him in the morning, to share a Vietnamese breakfast. It proved to be some kind of fish, inside a pastry like a croissant. Between the smell and the heat – it was an outdoor café – I could only swallow a bite of it. The coffee was good, though, *café au lait* on the Paris model. When we stood up to leave, a small boy dashed between us, grabbed my pastry with both hands, and crammed it into his mouth before the waiter could drive him off.

Welcome to Saigon!

~ ~ ~ ~

But here's the thing: I loved Vietnam – loved the country; loved the people, and especially the women with their delicate faces and flowing *au dai* tunics; loved being in the field with the Vietnamese army and their American advisors, sleeping rough on my plastic poncho. It was like hiking the White Mountains, though in hotter weather, plus mosquitoes and occasional gunfire, and I soon got comfortable with those.

I spent a week at the Vinh Loi, getting a double

set of press credentials, from the U.S. military and from the Vietnamese government. Meanwhile I interviewed nurses and patients at the U.S. Navy Hospital, went to the open-air black market and equipped myself with canned C rations and U.S. Army field gear with the help of Vo Huynh, the cameraman for NBC News, and spent a night on the town with the Diebolts and Lieutenant Cuong Hue, Mark's counterpart in the 518th Fighter Squadron. They wanted to show me the airbase at Binh Hoa, north of the city, but it was closed to the press. The United States wasn't ready to admit that Americans were flying combat missions in South Vietnam. I also photographed the pretty receptionist at the Vinh Loi. I asked Joe about her and found she was married to an American sergeant.

The *Reporter* wasn't interested in my Vietnam adventure, but Carey McWilliams at the *Nation* had offered sixty-five dollars for any article he published "from the combat zone." In truth, I wrote the first one from my air-conditioned room at the Vinh Loi. I mailed the top copy to Mr. McWilliams and a carbon to Paul Estaver, using the U.S. military mail drop and two seven-cent airmail stamps I'd brought from home. I called it "The Wings Tear Off," and it was based on the stories Mark and Lieutenant Cuong told me during our pub crawl, about the T-28 armed trainers used as fighter-bombers in Vietnam, with the unsurprising result that two of them had broken up in combat. Carey McWilliams liked that. Like Emma and Nikko, if the American government was doing it, he was against it. It was like writing for the *Overseas Weekly*, with a different political slant.

I kept a journal, too. Every couple of days, or whenever I was reunited with my Olivetti portable, I would type up my adventures in the form of a book chapter. The original went to Mavis McIntosh, who sent it to Ellin Roberts, my editor at Doubleday. Again I sent the carbon copy to Paul Estaver and, as we had agreed, he mailed a twenty-dollar bill to the return address on the envelope. It took a few weeks, round trip, but the Andy Jackson greenback never failed to catch up with me. I swapped it for a handful of wrinkled bills, twenty thousand piasters, triple the official rate. No doubt the greenbacks found their way to the Viet Cong and eventually to China, which supplied North Vietnam with knockoffs of the Russian AK-47 assault rifle.

My plan was to catch up with the Green Berets, the U.S. Army Special Forces with whom I'd been stationed at Fort Bragg. They were running a splendid little war in the Vietnamese Highlands – real Terry and the Pirates stuff – but I needed to toughen up before tagging along with them. So I went south, to what was known in the U.S. press as the "Viet Cong infested Mekong River Delta." It was great fun, and only occasionally terrifying. I liked the terror, to be honest. At thirty-two I was still young enough to believe I was immortal.

For my first combat reporting, I landed with a troop of Vietnamese armored cavalry against a village that was said to be an arms depot, where North Vietnamese smugglers brought guns and ammunition down by boat, and villagers paddled out and brought the contraband ashore. A T-28 Nomad came down from Bien Hoa and dropped a few bombs on the village before we came ashore. I rode in an armored personnel carrier – an M-59 from my time in the Army, and a far cry from the Patton tanks of the U.S. Third Armored Division. No matter! I was snug inside its steel hull, with a fifty-caliber machine gun rattling away. The American advisor picked up an empty brass cartridge and handed it to me, still warm. "That's ten cents of your money and mine," he said.

Next I went to Can Tho, where I enjoyed a dollar-a-night room in the Bachelor Officers Quarters and twenty-cent vodka tonics in the Officers Club. As in Germany, I was a simulated major. There was an outdoor movie screen, too, showing *Inherit the Wind*. Conveniently for us movie-goers, and also for the Viet Cong, the sun in Southeast Asia sets at seven o'clock and doesn't rise again until seven in the morning, and the nights are very dark. It was at the O Club in Can Tho that I first heard the gag that I came to associate with Vietnam, spoken by a bumptious captain: "It's a lousy war, but it's the only war we've got." There was no glory to be had in South Vietnam, but if he played his cards right, he could earn the Combat Infantryman's Badge, and what was a young officer without the CIB?

After a week of going out on night patrols, visiting watchtowers, tagging along on courier flights, and drinking vodka tonics, I heard that four battalions of South Vietnamese Marines, Rangers, and infantry – say fifteen hundred men – were about to sweep through the U Minh Forest. This was just the sort of exercise that would fit me for traveling with the Green Berets. The Public Information Officer himself was going, and John Sharkey and Vo Huynh came down from Saigon to join us. I liked these men, whom I'd met my first week in Saigon. John had read my articles in the *Reporter*, which is always pleasing to a writer, and Hyunh (pronounced "Win") had taken me shopping for my black-market field gear. They were stringers for NBC News, with John providing the voice and Huynh shooting sixteen-millimeter film that a Pan Am cockpit crew would fly to New York. Hyunh was just my height, and with his long sideburns and Pancho Villa mustache he looked more Mexican than Vietnamese.

It took us two days to catch up with the big operation, and another two days to march (well, *walk* was the better word) through the flooded U Minh Forest, jumping ditches and wading canals, and inspecting the occasional village. Usually there was a shop or two, a suspicious quantity of rice, and a hundred or so women, children, and old men, who assured us that the young men were working somewhere else that day. It was in one of these places that for the first time in my life I saw a man die. He was a Ranger, who had moved a bamboo pole that blocked the door of a hut, pulling the pin from a hand grenade. He had no visible wounds, but blood oozed from his face – from his very pores, it seemed. Two medics put half a coconut shell under his head for a pillow and gently dabbed his face with balls of cotton. When he died, which he did with no fuss at all, the American captain assigned to the battalion radioed for a helicopter without mentioning that the casualty was no longer alive. (I wonder if, like me, the young Ranger had thought himself immortal?)

The other Rangers made torches from rags and dipped them in a jar of kerosene, but nobody had a dry match. John Sharkey was a cigar smoker, and he provided a light with his Zippo. He then stepped aside while Vo Huynh and I photographed the Rangers as they threw their torches onto the hut's thatched roof. The villagers didn't object; they fetched water from the canal and wet their own roofs against the sparks.

After a lovely night under the stars, we walked out to the muddy beaches of the Gulf of Thailand, near what is now the considerable city of Rac Gia, but in 1964 was no more than a name on the map. We expected to be met by landing craft from the Vietnamese Navy but saw only a lone Huey helicopter that swooped in and disgorged three Saigon Commandos, as John Sharkey called them – reporters in white shirts, slacks, and street shoes who turned up at the end of an action to get a few quotes from the American advisor before flying back to the city and filing an eyewitness story. While they went to work, the three of us ambled over to the Huey, climbed into the cabin, and got comfortable on the bench seat at the back. The door gunners nodded hello; the pilot glanced back to make sure we had fastened our seatbelts, then he spooled up the turbine engine. He'd brought three civilians down from Bac Lieu; now he would take three civilians back. What we did there, and what became of the reporters he'd just delivered, was not his concern.

~ ~ ~ ~

After a month of wandering at will around the Mekong River Delta, I caught a hop back to Saigon and asked for a flight to Pleiku in the Highlands, where the Green Berets waged their private war against the Viet Cong and the North Vietnamese infiltrators coming down the Ho Chi Minh Trail (far more infiltrators than anyone realized at the time). At the U.S. military headquarters, I saw a new photo at the top of the command chart: Lieutenant General William Westmoreland. Would Westy be an improvement? I had no idea, and I didn't much care. It was the men in the field who interested me, not the four-star at the top of the food chain.

With my "orders" duly signed and stamped, I took an ancient Renault taxi out to Tan Son Nhut and got in line to board a C-123 transport. The pilot grinned at us and said we had nothing to fear: he wasn't just any pilot, but had flown B-52s for the Strategic Air Command. There was a lot of this stuff going on in 1964, as the U.S. military scaled down from nuclear war to something more like the American Revolution, with us as the British. We sat in canvas seats, thirty on a side, with pallets of supplies stacked in the center aisle. The loadmaster left the yawning cargo ramp open, flushing out the heat and humidity of Saigon. We flew along the coast for two hours before the pilot turned inland. I was impressed by the landscape, which soon after we left the coast became forested mountains, rolling on forever like an endless green sea.

From the moment I left the C-123 at the airfield outside Pleiku, I was enchanted by the Highlands. "Shangri-la!" I rhapsodized in my journal that night. "The land rolls and tumbles like the Scottish moors, and long-horned cattle graze on the hills." (I'd never been to Scotland.) "The valleys are pale green with sprouting rice. There are groves of tough, coarse-needled pine, red flowering trees, and a climbing vine with blossoms the color of lilacs. The sun scorches down, as always in Vietnam, but the altitude blesses Pleiku with a climate like June in New Hampshire, and I can regulate my temperature simply by moving into or out of the shade. . . . Hard to believe that it is in the same country as the waterlogged paddy fields and steaming mangrove swamps of the Mekong Delta."

The Highlands had been my goal since coming to Vietnam – the mountains, their people, and the Green Berets who not only trained the Highlanders but led them in combat. So I'd made it my business to learn what I could about the *Montagnards*, as the French had called them, a word the Americans rendered as "Mountain Yards" and soon shortened to

"Yards." It was a revelation to me, how *new* a nationality the Vietnamese were. The great Red River valley, fanning out behind Hanoi and the port of Haiphong, had a Vietnamese culture three thousand years ago, but was dominated by China until the tenth century. Only then did the Vietnamese move into the skinny coastal plain to their south, displacing the native inhabitants, who retreated into the mountains. The Vietnamese called them *Moi*, which Wikipedia politely translates as "savages," but which I was told meant "wild men" or "baboons." The two cultures lived apart until the French colonized the Indochina peninsula – today's Vietnam, Laos, and Cambodia – in the nineteenth century. The French regarded the Highlands as fertile ground for souls to be saved, forests to be cleared for rubber plantations, and soldiers to be recruited for their colonial army.

I made my way out to Camp Holloway, an American compound on the eastern edge of Pleiku, where the Special Forces B-Team occupied a low-roofed building with three flagpoles in front. From them flew the Stars and Stripes, the red and yellow banner of South Vietnam, and another with the silhouette of a big-antlered stag. "What's with the deer flag?" I asked the clerk-typist at the desk inside.

"Oh, we fly that when Major Buck is in town."

"Like Queen Elizabeth at Windsor Castle?"

"Yeah, I guess."

Major Buck was a stocky man of great enthusiasm and a scar that ran from the corner of his left eye to the corner of his mouth. The effect, when he smiled, was rather sinister. He waved aside my request to visit a Special Forces camp on the Laotian border. Instead, he would send me down to Phu Bon province, where I could see both the old and the new

– what he had inherited, and how he meant to prosecute the war from now on. "There's an auto heading down to Buon Beng tomorrow, so the boys can jump for payday. You can ride along."

"Auto?"

He gave me a skeptical look. "Otter," he said. "De Havilland Otter. It's an airplane."

And so it was. I hitched a ride to the airport in the morning and was directed to a rugged, high-wing, single-engine plane, made in Canada and just the thing for the airstrips of Vietnam. The U.S. Army painted it olive drab and called it the U-1A. I told the pilots that I was bound for Buon Beng. They looked at one another and shrugged. I explained that Major Buck had sent me, and when we were over Cheo Reo they should radio "Barry" and someone would come out to the airfield to pick me up.

"Cheo Reo, yeah, but their call sign is 'Blaze.' It's our first stop. What the hell, hop in."

There were no seats in back, just a pile of parachutes. I sat on one and arranged another as a back rest, and settled down for an hour-long flight through the mountains. At eleven o'clock we landed on a runway made of pierced-steel planking, where a jeep ambulance was parked with three Green Berets perched on its hood. And yes, they were wearing the iconic headgear. But no, they weren't waiting for me, but to make their payday parachute jumps, which they did, and when they were done, they returned the chutes to the Otter and took me along with them. One was the A-Team commander, Captain Charles Judge, so I had been accepted. (An A-Team formed the tip of the Special Forces spear and consisted of twelve Americans. Major Buck and the B-Team in Pleiku had eighteen A-Teams scattered through the Highlands, and of course there was a C-Team in

Saigon for all of South Vietnam, but I stayed away from that.)

Buon Beng proved to be a Highland village inside barbed wire, with pigs and naked children running about, and longhouses on stilts. With five companies and eight hundred "Strikers," Captain Judge told me, this was the largest Strike Force camp in the Highlands – and the oldest, at more than one year. As the men went out on patrol, their families had moved into the longhouses that were their barracks, and in time the camp became a community. Major Buck wanted to move the troops into the boondocks, where the enemy was. But the province chief – an ethnic Vietnamese, like all province chiefs – enjoyed the security and the money that the Americans brought to Cheo Reo. So a compromise was struck: two companies slept at the future camp, now called the Forward Operating Base. Two companies were out on patrol, and the fifth stayed at Buong Beng and kept the province chief happy.

I soon got out to the FOB, sixteen miles southeast, where three hundred Strikers lived in pup tents under the command of Mike Holland and Russ Brooks. They were glad to see me. For one thing, I was a diversion, but even better, I was an American, and the Green Berets had a rule: when they mounted an ambush, one American had to be awake at all times. No matter that I was a civilian! If I went along with him, Russ and I could take turns napping. The supply sergeant at Buon Beng had issued me a Colt pistol, officially the M-1911, adopted that year because it had the power to stop a drug-fueled Moro guerrilla in the Philippines. It was one of the greatest sidearms ever made, and it's still in use today.

Russ and Mike checked me out, firing at a ration can on the bank of a river called the Song Ba. The recoil was awful, but I was happy to carry that horse pistol if it got me out on patrol, which it did that night. Russ carried an M-79 grenade launcher in addition to the pretty Colt rifle that as the M-16 would soon become standard issue for the U.S. military. When we hunkered down beside a trail near the Song Ba, he gave the "Blooper" to me. So now, when he napped, he had a properly armed American to hold the fort.

I really enjoyed these guys. My impression of the Green Berets at Fort Bragg was that they were either very small or very tall – Puerto Ricans or lanky farm boys. Russ, though from Kentucky, fit the little tough-guy role, while Mike was easily a six-footer. They were, respectively, trained as a weapons specialist and a medic, though like every enlisted man in Special Forces, they also had a second specialty, and fundamentally of course they were riflemen. Each was Specialist 5th Class, the equivalent of a three-stripe sergeant. When I was in a Spec 3 at Coligny Caserne, I had no command authority, but here at the FOB, Russ and Mike gave orders to three hundred men. In the infantry, a company was normally commanded by a captain, with a first lieutenant as his executive officer and a few sergeants to keep the troops in line. Here, their only assistant was a grizzled Highlander who took especially good care of me, pointing out a root that might trip me or a thorny branch I mustn't grab. Russ and Mike called him "Corporal Old Man."

Again, I loved the country. The land was mostly open, with runty trees and many dead ones, ash-white on the ground. It was like my notion of Africa, hot and sere and lonely, with an occasional jarring note in the form of a dead Viet Cong. The Highlanders carefully stepped around the corpse and hurried out of its vicinity.

And those Highlanders! I was very fond of Corporal Old Man, as later I would come to admire Cowboy, the handsome but bloodthirsty interpreter. "You have to take the good with the bad," Captain Judge had told me. "And Cowboy is a good interpreter." He came from the Rhade tribe, valued by the French as the most cosmopolitan of the Highlanders, though the Buon Beng Strikers were all Jarai. Cowboy was more or less fluent in all the necessary languages: English, French, Vietnamese, and Jarai, plus his own, though like most Highlanders he detested the Vietnamese and tried to avoid their language.

There was a downside: I was seventy-five miles southeast of Pleiku and two thousand feet lower, so the air was nearly as hot and humid as in Saigon. And except for the Song Ba, there was precious little water. I filled my canteens whenever I could, the one-quart metal one I'd brought from home and the two-quart water bag I'd acquired on the black market, yet I was always thirsty.

~ ~ ~ ~

I find that people get upset when I admit how much I *loved* Vietnam – the country, the people and yes, the war, such as it was in 1964. I especially enjoyed the Highlanders and the Green Berets, and I still think that if we had left the war to them, we'd have come out of there with America's honor intact. "Never fight a land war in Asia," Douglas MacArthur warned John Kennedy in 1961, and I like to think that if our young president hadn't been murdered, he would have avoided the calamitous mistakes made by his successor.

By August I was home and back at the News Bureau, mending my finances from the considerable cost of that ticket to Saigon – so costly, indeed, that the Internal Revenue Service couldn't believe I'd spent so much to earn so little, and it called me in for an audit. Meanwhile a dubious attack on the U.S. destroyers *Maddox* and *Turner Joy* prompted a raid on North Vietnam by U.S. Navy fighter-bombers. One thing led to another, as it usually does, and President Johnson got an effective declaration of war from Congress. More than two million American servicemen would follow me to Vietnam, and more than fifty thousand would die there. Vietnamese fatalities were beyond counting.

So rapidly did things escalate that my journal was outmoded before I could submit it. Ellin Roberts at Doubleday advised me to turn my experience into fiction instead. Meanwhile we tweaked *Now Comes Theodora,* which was duly published and reviewed in the spring of 1965, for the most part generously. A sentence in the *New Yorker* I will treasure always: "The clear-sighted, unangry Mr. Ford will undoubtedly write another novel, which means we all have something to look forward to."

I bought a little house on salt water, which cost me seven thousand dollars. Most of it came from a bank in Dover – the first time I ever borrowed money for anything. But I was confident in my future as a novelist, certain that I'd pay off that mortgage from the sale of my next book. First, of course, I had to write it. Not as easy as it seemed! Mavis McIntosh, alas, had retired, and I was paired with the first in a series of agents, none of whom I got along with. My relationship with Ellin Roberts, meanwhile, seemed golden, so I decided to go it alone, which was no doubt the worst decision I have ever made.

I began to write a Big Book – Stephen Faust growing up in the city, meeting his Gretchen in Germany, and coming to grief in the Highlands of Vietnam. I worked on this for six months or so before ditching the first two parts and starting Stephen off (with a less pretentious surname) as a Green Beret arriving in Vietnam. The story was based on an operation, massive by Vietnamese standards, that took me and the Boun Beng Strikers to a village called Tan Hoa. We were supposed to collect the villagers and take them out to a Strategic Hamlet, so the region could become a "free-fire zone" that could be bombed and blasted without harming the innocent. Or so went the theory.

That second word, Hoa, was pronounced *wah*, which reminded me of how Jack Kennedy had pronounced "war" – like any New Englander, omitting the *r*. We found a rather pretty French cemetery at Tan Hoa, along with some long-ago fighting holes. But there was no village, nor any villagers. It was a ghost town beside a river, which I think was the Song Ba. The stone grave markers had reminded me of lines I'd read in Simonides, about the Spartans who died at Thermopylae in the fifth century B.C.: "Go, stranger, and tell the Spartans that we lie here in obedience to their laws."

Aha! What if we'd been told to reoccupy the old French garrison? Wouldn't the Viet Cong, seeing us move into their territory, try to drive us out? And wouldn't Major Buck in Pleiku then reinforce our garrison, causing the Viet Cong to increase *their* pressure? It would be a good yarn and a clever warning about what even then was happening in Vietnam. I called it *Incident at Muc Wa* – "muck war," get it? – and mailed it off to Doubleday, asking for an advance of five thousand dollars, which I duly received and paid over to the bank, so I now owned my little house free and clear.

What's more, Doubleday sold the rights for a

British hardcover, a Dutch translation, an American paperback and, most thrilling of all, a movie to be scripted and marketed by Wendell Mayes, whom I'd never heard of though it turned out that I had seen many of his films at the Franklin Theater in Durham. When I added it all up, the total was $9,575, plus $30,000 when and if the movie panned out. This was more than I had earned in my life so far – more than a third of a million dollars in today's debauched currency.

What could possibly go wrong?

~ ~ ~ ~

A lot went wrong, of course, especially in Vietnam, where General Westmoreland more or less decided to refight the Second World War, starting with a brigade of Marines, followed by a brigade of Army airborne troops, and finally two full divisions, for a total of 184,314 Americans in-country by the end of 1965. What especially frightened me was seeing those lads on the evening news wearing *steel helmets* instead of the go-to-hell Australian bush hats that most Americans had worn when I was there. Indeed, the Terry and the Pirates adventure we had enjoyed had become a grim affair. Hans Morgenthau, my hard-nosed mentor from *Politics Among Nations*, was among the first to take alarm. "The United States can no more contain Chinese influence in Asia by arming South Vietnam and Thailand," he wrote soon after the Marines landed at Danang, "than China could contain American influence in the Western Hemisphere by arming, say, Nicaragua and Costa Rica." I should have paid more attention to that.

At home, meanwhile, the tumult continued. The black Islamist Malcolm X was murdered in New York City, and the civil rights leader Medgar Evans in Mississippi. Martin Luther King marched for civil rights in Alabama (joined by James Baldwin among others), Students for a Democratic Society marched on Washington, a Quaker set himself on fire outside the Pentagon, President Johnson doubled the draft call to 35,000 men a month, Los Angeles was torn by the Watts riots, the Beatles sang at Shea Stadium, Bob Dylan recorded "Like a Rolling Stone," and the Weathermen bombed the U.S. Capitol, the Pentagon, a courthouse, a New York police headquarters, and finally themselves. Altogether the country seemed, not long after the centennial of the Civil War, to be on the brink of yet another insurrection. This time it involved not just South against North, but young against old.

Among other calamities, Johnson's determination to wage a double war – one to defeat North Vietnam, the other to build a New Society at home – set off the Great Inflation that crashed the stock market and drove interest rates to twenty percent. One consequence was that, when Go *Tell the Spartans*, the movie that Wendell Mayes made from *Incident at Muc Wa*, finally made its debut in 1978, my thirty thousand dollars would have lost most of their value. I would be married by that time, and the father of a little girl. Gosh, how time flies when you're having fun!

~ ~ ~ ~

And indeed I had a wonderful time in my role as a Writer. I got involved with the Committee for Nonviolent Action, a commune in Connecticut that included a lad just back from Vietnam. He joined the Veterans of Foreign Wars and, as was its custom, the local VFW post installed the Fucking New Guy as its commander – actually, as matters turned out, a very good choice. Like my brother, he was a quiet, reliable man who got along with everyone. But the vets discovered that every Sunday their commander picketed the New London submarine base with the CNVA, and they impeached him. I enjoyed this stuff, just as I had enjoyed the pacifists who had congregated at the Quonset Hut on Madbury Road. They were the leading edge of the Sixties, as the decade is called, though in fact much of it took place in the 1970s.

Horace Lyndes now worked in Boston and kept a sailboat at the harborside. One weekend three of us sailed down to Provincetown, where we fell in with a folksinger and his girlfriend and some hangers-on. We brought them out to the boat, drank beer, and listened to Irish ballads, Appalachian laments, and working men's songs from the 1930s. Horace and I thought this was great stuff – I'm not so sure about the third man, a Harvard dropout who lived on royalties from a patent – and the two of us got hooked on folk music. One weekend Horace turned up at my house on Little Bay and announced that he'd just heard the most beautiful voice in the world, and that I must accompany him that very Saturday evening to a bar in Cambridge. So off we went in his Austin Healey. Alas, the tavern when we got there was empty except for a few patrons at the bar. "She's gone to California," the bartender told us, "and she won't be back." This, I discovered later, was Joan Baez, whose songs are indeed some of the prettiest I have ever heard.

I was meanwhile looking for my third novel. I considered going back to Vietnam with the International Voluntary Services, a Quaker-like group that worked with Highlanders and other minorities, but the IVS was a two-year commitment. My boss at the News Bureau demurred – six months perhaps, but two years, no way! – and I wasn't ready to give up what had turned out to be the ideal job.

"Well," said Horace when I told him about my quest, "if I had a winter with nothing to do, I'd go to Aspen and *ski*." He reached for the telephone (I now had a phone, though I kept the number pretty much to myself) and called a friend who cooked at the Mother Lode, next door to the Wheeler Opera House in Aspen. Right away, I liked the idea of a ski resort with an opera house, though by now it was mostly a movie hall.

So I had a plan! In September I'd drive south and west in my Beetle, visiting people in Washington (Paul Estaver, who had swapped *Profiles* for a more manly job at the Justice Department), New Orleans (friends from UNH), Johnson City, Texas (to inspect the president's home town), Tucson (Mom and Dad), and Long Beach (Jim Dye and his girlfriend). And from California I'd double back toward Colorado in time for the first snowfall in Aspen.

When I was in high school, the story was that a gallant lad could hitchhike to Detroit and deliver two automobiles to Alaska, driving one and towing the other, 1,700 miles of gravel road through British Columbia and the Yukon Territory. How true this was, I don't know, but we all believed it, and it had left me with a yearning to drive across the continent. With Don Silva, who taught English to the short-term Aggie students and had access to their machine shop, I adapted the passenger side of my Beetle so the seat slid forward while the backrest flipped down and joined up with the back seat. During the day, my skis would lie here, on top of my sleeping bag; at night, I'd shift the skis to the driver's side and myself lie flat. Incredibly, it worked. I had a tiny one-burner propane stove, and with this I'd cook and make coffee, just as I'd done while bagging the Four Thousand Footers.

My boss at the News Bureau meanwhile found a replacement for me, a certain Sally Paine, just back from California. I knew the name because Phil Paine was a long-time contributor to *Profiles,* though I'd never met him. The timing was tight: she interviewed for the job on my last day, and when we shook hands, I realized that I absolutely must marry this woman. I'd have to move fast: this was Friday, and in the morning I was meeting Nikko and Emma to hike into the Pemigewasset Wilderness and climb Owl's Head – for each of us, our final Four Thousand Footer. We'd saved it out to do together, making a three-day adventure of it. And the very next day, I had to vacate my house so my tenant could move in, and I would set out on my roundabout route to Aspen.

It was already two o'clock on Friday afternoon, so I threw Sally across my saddlebow and wolfed her off to Somersworth, where I had three printing jobs in progress. (Well, the saddlebow is metaphorical: she actually rode in the passenger seat of my Volkswagen Beetle. She wore nylons and a pretty dress of about the same shade of brown as her eyes, and I think she was wearing gloves.) After I'd introduced her to the print-shop owner and explained about the brochures, or catalogs or whatever they were, we went out for coffee and swapped addresses. She gave me the names of friends in San Francisco whom I might visit, and I got her address, the better to send her the occasional postcard on my progress. Toward five o'clock, I mentioned the Owl's Head project and my promise to Nikko and Emma that I would bring champagne for our celebration, so would she mind if we stopped at the state liquor store in Dover? This we did. I collected two bottles of Great Western, and we got in line behind a tall man with a handsome head of gray hair. "Oh, *Daddy!*" Sally said. And that is how I met my future father-in-law.

Without Sally, I doubt I would ever have made it this far. (Photo: Liz Handy)

~ ~ ~ ~

It worked out splendidly. I didn't become a great skier in Aspen, but I became a strong one, and by spring I could ski all of Ajax (as Aspen Mountain was known to the locals) with my skis tucked together and my arms out to the side, in the then-approved Austrian technique. I rented a room in a ski-bum hostel for the same seventy dollars a month I was getting from my tenant; I smoked pot for the first time; and I got up to date with Joan Baez, Bob Dylan, and even the Beatles. (It was Paul McCartney's "Eleanor Rigby" that won me over.) Meanwhile, by mail, Ellin Roberts and I got *Incident at Muc Wa* into shape for spring publication. In February, Sally came out and skied with me for a week. I drove home in April, and we eloped in July. In her shoe, Sally wore the sixpence that had been in the family since her grandmother's wedding, and in my shoe I wore the first handwritten page of *The High Country Illuminator*, set in an enchanted ski town named Avalon. It would, sadly, be my final novel with Doubleday. People didn't know what to make of it; no paperback publisher took up the story; Ellin Roberts retired; and really, I pretty much gave up hope that I could ever make a living as a novelist.

Together, we filled one job at the News Bureau: I worked the morning shift, Sally worked the afternoons. I must tell you one story about the two years we did this, because it completed a process that had begun eighteen years earlier at Brewster Academy:

Someone had the bright idea that we should have a questionnaire for the incoming freshman class. That way, when a student made the dean's list, or scored a touchdown or did something else of note, we'd have the information necessary to fire off a story to his or her local paper. So I made up the questionnaire, and when the first crop of replies came in, I spotted one from Wolfeboro. Come to find out, the young person had the same surname as Ethel, my wanton high-school classmate. What's more, she had been reared by her grandmother, and in the space for her father's name she had innocently written "Unknown."

Oh my goodness. This was Ethel's child from 1950! Should I tell her that her father had earned a Bronze Star for gallantry in Korea? But I didn't really *know* that Gene Edgerly was the name that belonged on that questionnaire. He was only a guess, wasn't he? I tore the freshman's questionnaire into bits and sent it and the whole batch of them to the University heating plant, to incinerate any other revelations that were better left alone.

~ ~ ~ ~

We kept this up until Sally became so pregnant she she no longer wanted to climb the stairs to the News Bureau. Meanwhile we developed a business as editors for whoever might need us, including Paul Estaver at the Justice Department, whenever he needed someone to beat a confusing research project into good enough shape that even a Congressman could understand it. (I had come to think of the typical academic researcher as Ed Morris with a PhD, always in need of a rewrite. Indeed, it was a pity I hadn't put my brother in this category. Joe's adviser had died in 1963, and he didn't have the heart to start the process over again. He never did get his doctorate.) I became a staff writer for *Skiing* magazine, too, and what with one thing and another, we had a comfortable life in our house on Little Bay. I even remodeled it to include a nursery.

Nineteen sixty-eight – what a year for a child to be born! North Korea seized a U.S. Navy vessel. Viet

Cong guerrillas breached the American embassy in Saigon. In South Carolina, police opened fire on youngsters protesting at a segregated bowling alley, killing three and wounding seventeen. President Johnson announced he wouldn't run for reelection. Martin Luther King was murdered, and the nation's capital erupted in looting and burning that took thousands of Marines, soldiers, and National Guardsmen to stop. Then Bobby Kennedy was murdered, just after winning the California primary en route to the presidency. In Chicago, the Democratic National Convention became an anti-war riot in which protesters were clubbed and tear-gassed by police and the National Guard.

Dad of course was strong for Bobby, so when the news of his killing came to our little house, I phoned him in Tucson, something I had never done before. (I suppose the birth of his granddaughter had something to do with that. It ties the generations together.) I asked him who he'd vote for now. "George Wallace," he said. This may seem slightly mad, switching from a man who, for the times, had been a left-wing radical to the one who'd stood in the schoolhouse door, vowing "segregation today . . . segregation forever." But they were actually very similar, two blunt men with sharp elbows. (And four years later, Wallace himself would be shot and left paralyzed from the waist down as he campaigned for president again.)

I have compared the shock of Jack Kennedy's assassination to the Japanese attack on Pearl Harbor. But really, 1968 was like a slow-motion Pearl Harbor, as the impossibilities rocked us, one after another. (And not just the United States! France and Mexico were beset by student riots worse than ours.) It was too much for me, and I followed

Sally's example and quit my job at the News Bureau. We traded my Beetle and her Mustang convertible for a Volkswagen camper-van, and we set out on much the same route I'd followed two years before, and with many of the same stops. We introduced Kate to Paul Estaver and his new wife in Virginia, to my parents in Tucson, to Jim Dye and his girlfriend in Long Beach, and to Sally's San Francisco friends whom I'd neglected to visit on my own trip West. In November, the country elected my *bête noire*, Richard Nixon. I voted for Hubert Humphrey while Sally voted for Nixon, who claimed to have a plan to end the war, which to his credit he eventually did. He had less success quelling the Great Inflation set off by the war, let alone the passions it aroused, especially in the universities. This was the era when a young woman would arrive at college wearing nylons and a dress, and four years later graduate in ripped blue-jeans and without a bra.

In time, those same youngsters became our teachers, journalists, movie makers, celebrities, and politicians, and they in turn reared a generation more radical than they. The United States is still fighting the Vietnam War today.

Among the casualties of Vietnam was my favorite magazine, the *Reporter*. A Cold Warrior to the end, Max Ascoli was deserted by the academics who had been his most reliable subscribers, and in 1968 he folded the magazine. Even *Incident at Muc Wa* was damaged by the general revulsion against a war we couldn't win with half a million troops and more bombs than we'd dropped against Germany and Japan combined. We brought our soldiers home in 1973, and two years later we shamefully abandoned the Saigon regime when North Vietnamese tanks rolled across the border and swept down through the

Highlands I had loved. (And, as I write this, we are doing the same in Afghanistan.)

By this time, Gerald Ford was president, the third man to inherit Jack Kennedy's mess. Wendell Mayes meanwhile had negotiated an annual renewal of his movie option for five hundred dollars a time. Every year, Doubleday took fifty dollars for itself and sent me a check for the balance. I worried that Mr. Mayes had an efficient secretary who without bothering him sent checks each year for his automobile and house insurance and suchlike, including the option. For fear of shutting it off, I never inquired about the progress he was making, though Doubleday did warn me in 1971 that he was encountering "the great antipathy in Hollywood these days against anything having to do with the war."

He finally got financing for his movie in 1978, with some of the money coming from his star, Burt Lancaster. Its title was *Go Tell the Spartans*, after a reference in my story to the Three Hundred who died holding the pass at Thermopylae in 480 B.C. I wish I'd thought of that!

~ ~ ~ ~

And so the years rolled by. I can't say, like Edith Piaff, *je ne regrette rien*, but my regrets are few. I won't trouble you with them, or with the various twists and turns my life has taken since I left the far country of my youth. There's not much to be learned from them. But I did want you to know how I grew up dirt poor in the 1930s and 1940s and how, despite it all, I got an education and found happiness in what was – during my lifetime anyhow – the best place in the world.

In 2014, Sally and I flew to Athens and took the ferry to the island of Amorgas, where we stayed at the Hotel Pagali, high above the sea. One evening I asked our landlady if the German army had gotten this far out into the Aegean during the War. "No," Joanna said. "The Italians were here, but they weren't too bad." (Wasn't that a nice thing to say about an invading army?) She went on to tell how her father-in-law had ruined his health during the War, a young lad rising at four o'clock every morning to stand in the fierce heat of the ovens, baking bread for the village, then climbing into the hills to spend the day herding goats in the chill and damp of winter. Despite this harsh beginning, she marveled, Mr. Vassalos had lived till just last year, when he died at the great age of eighty. In a flash of pride, I said that I had already passed that landmark. Joanna gave me a cool and level look – what our grand-daughters call the Hairy Eyeball. "You had a good life," she pointed out.

She was right, of course. I grew up poor but never went hungry, and I lived close to the brink until well into my thirties, but I never lacked for anything I needed. That was my good fortune as an American, living in the golden years after the War, each year more prosperous than the one before. Europe and much of Asia eventually narrowed the gap – none faster than our defeated enemies, Germany and Japan! – but never, it seems to me, did they quite catch up, in large part because they're taxed so heavily. This blessed state of affairs may be coming to an end, as our government grows ever larger and our freedoms shrink. In the end, the great victors of the Vietnam War were Ho Chi Minh and Bernie Sanders. Vietnam transformed itself along the Chinese model, with a capitalist economy under an authoritarian government, and the United States seems to be heading in the same direction. Mean-while, other authoritarians – China, Russia, Iran,

North Korea, and now Afghanistan – are at war with us, while we defund and demean our armed forces. "The Roman world is falling," St. Jerome wrote in the fourth century, "and yet we hold heads erect." We Americans by contrast go on apology tours, beating our breasts over white privilege and the injustices we have inflicted upon the world, both real and fancied.

I appreciate that this is no longer a popular view. So, with that, I'll sign off with the digits I was taught long ago to signal The End:

- 30 -

Kate (at left) home-schooled our granddaughters as they sailed from New Hampshire to Greenland, Europe, South America, Antarctica, the Pacific islands, and Alaska. They're in college now, Helen (center) a junior and Anna (right) a sophomore. (Photo: Hamish Laird)

Notes & Sources

1 - The Depression

I use the calculator at dollartimes.com to track the ruin of the U.S. dollar in my lifetime. A 1931 greenback had the buying power of $16.18 in today's currency, so I sometimes give the current value of the money I earned and spent along the way.

Zechariah Symmes "followed the call of Divine providence to New England with his family in 1634" to become pastor of the First Church in today's Arlington (Wikipedia, viewed 12/10/20). A descendant bequeathed land for the hospital in 1903. See the housing development that replaced it at livearlington360.com (viewed 11/12/20). Prohibition lasted from 1919 to 1933. Hell's Kitchen, on New York's West Side between 40th and 59th Street, was notorious at the time as "the most dangerous place in America" (Wikipedia 3/5/21).

When my brother died in 2011, I inherited a footlocker of memorabilia, including his memoir of Alton. Some of his recollections (e.g., the Damon Place was "nearly a thousand acres") are certainly off the mark, but I accept his version where it's plausible. I misremembered Dodier's name and the spelling of Messier's, and I quite forgot the house before Dodier's and the one after it. *New Hampshire: A Guide to the Granite State* (Houghton Mifflin 1938) is one of the wonderful WPA state guides. With tuberculosis no longer much of a menace, the Glencliff sanatorium has become a home for the mentally challenged. I still have Dad's Colt pistol, though my hand isn't strong enough to rack the slide as I did as a youngster, whicker-whick! The Damon Place is now a summer camp and conference center called Brookwoods, with a layout very like what it was in the 1930s. The lane leading down to it is Damon Drive. Among the photos I've uploaded to danfordbooks.com (9/11/21) is one of the Gatehouse in the 1930s. It is no longer as pretty (seen 3/17/21).

Michel de Nostredame was a French physician, astrologer, and seer whose *Les Prophéties* was published in 1555 and became famous in English as the *Oracles of Nostradamus*. Dad had the Modern Library edition, a Charles Ward translation first published in 1891.

2 - The War

For Howard Long, see Ray Duckler, "The noose in Laconia tells a story about the last man executed in the state," *Concord Monitor*, 4/14/18. Other details from an article I wrote for *New Hampshire Profiles* in 1960. "Don't Sit Under the Apple Tree" wasn't recorded until 1942, but an earlier version appeared in a 1939 Broadway musical. That must have been where Mrs. Damon encountered it. For her first book, see Bertha Damon, *Grandma Called It Carnal*, Simon & Schuster 1938. My recently acquired copy is from the sixth printing, a truly impressive number for the Great Depression. The story of St. Paul and the hot water bottle, p32. Her playful allusion to Odysseus: "Then she traveled, and much did she see and know: cities of men – Riverbend and Hillsboro and even Brampton which was seven miles distant – and manners, climates, councils, governments" (p163; see Homer, *The Odyssey*, line 4).

Anne Bean of the Taxiarchai Greek Orthodox Church in Laconia educated me about church activities in 1941 (emails 11/20). I drove along Rochester Hill Road recently and was sorry to see that it has become a confusion of houses, apartments, and business establishments. Skyhaven Airport appears to be thriving, but I couldn't find our little house among those that have sprouted along the south side of the road. Perhaps, like Dodier's Camp, it collapsed since we lived there.

I enjoy Donna Leon for her Commissario Brunetti police procedurals set in Venice, Michael Connelley for his implacable Los Angeles detective Harry Bosch, and Mick Herron for Slough House, where British secret agents go when they become troublesome. I also never tire of Daniel Silva's novels about the Israeli spymaster Gabriel Allon. Literary novels, of the sort that enchanted me in my twenties and thirties, I now find tedious, and most of the novelists who excited me in middle age – Stephen King, John Irving, and the like – seem to have lost their touch, or anyhow their ability to touch me.

The 1941 Lincoln Continental "Cabriolet" sold for $2,788 (nadaguides.com 3/9/21). I don't know what the Laughlin Place is worth today, but in 2020 Castle Hyde in Fermoy, County Cork, was offered for nearly $25 million. A previous tenant was Douglas Hyde, first president of the Irish Republic, and a more recent one the Lord of the Dance, Michael Flatley (irishcentral.com 11/17/20).

Bedford Army Air Field is now Hanscom Air Force Base. I find that General Patton's pistols had handgrips of ivory: "Only a New Orleans pimp would carry a pearl-handled gun!" he told a reporter. He carried two handguns, one of them a Colt hammerless like Dad's, though in .38 caliber and outfitted with the ivory handgrips (guns.com 11/17/20).

3 - The City

Starting with this chapter, I modify names and circumstances that might embarrass people or their descendants. I may have underestimated the Right Rev. Msgr. John Thomas Creagh, who had attended Angelicum College in Rome, taught at Catholic University in Washington, and presided over St. Aidan's since 1913. Pope Pius XII named him an honorary Protonotary Apostolic; he died in 1951 at the age of eighty-one (*NY Times* 12/11/51).

For our house at 200 Freeman Street, see *A Guide To*

North Brookline: Five Walking Tours (Brookline Preservation Commission 1982, online at brooklinehistoricalsociety.org, 11/14/20). St. Aidan's is now a housing development and National Historic Site, thanks not to Monsignor Creagh but to Jack Kennedy, who was baptized there. *Veni vidi vici*: "I came, I saw, I conquered," as Julius Caesar supposedly said of his victory in the Battle of Zela, 47 BC. The first building inside the St. Aidan's gate on Pleasant Street is now, oddly, the rectory of St. James Episcopal Church. The narrow park and playground on Still Street is Winthrop Square. The Coolidge Corner branch library is still at 31 Pleasant Street, but the large Stearns House of the 1940s has been replaced by a handsome brick building (Lauren Pistole email 3/18/21). I find that Zane Grey is the author of 103 books, including a suspicious number published after his death. Lew Wetzel was a frontiersman in Ohio (Wikipedia 3/14/21). My more elevated readings were Russell Whelan, *The Flying Tigers*, Viking 1942; Robert L. Scott Jr., *God Is My Co-Pilot*, Scribner's 1943. Again, I conclude that it doesn't matter what a youngster reads, if only he does.

I don't know what became of Danny Kane, but I got a letter from Michael Tobin when *Incident at Muc Wa* was published in 1967, and his son brought the book home from what I fondly hope was the library at 31 Pleasant Street.

4 - The Academy

For Brewster, see brewsteracademy.org (11/18/20). John Brewster was rather Woke for the nineteenth century, specifying that "no restriction shall be placed upon any person desiring to attend and receive instruction from said school or academy on account of his or her age, sex, or color, provided only he or she is of good moral character." It's possible, of course, that "moral character" was meant to discourage Jews and Catholics. Some

2.2 million veterans took advantage of the GI Bill. Tuition, books, and other academic expenses were capped at $500 a year, the equivalent of $7,200 today (GI Bill page on college.cengage.com, 3/21/21). Tuition alone at the Ivies now averages $58,000, and at Brewster it's $39,400.

I'm told that the academic building is of "Greek neo-classical design with its center entrance suggesting a Greek temple with its projecting pediment supported by double Ionic columns" (Nancy Sandberg email 11/20/20). I've always thought it would look well in the District of Columbia, so I'm glad to see it has a place on our state historic register at nh.gov (11/21/20). How Harry Nash came to Brewster: his email 2/11/21. The Academy's enrollment today is 350, not a huge increase over 1946, but the local area is served by a regional high school with more than 700 students. Brewster has about fifty townies in its student body (Suzanne Morrissey email 11/18/20). Also see Robert & Shirley Anderson, *The Brewster Story: A Definitive History of Brewster Academy* (Brewster 2011), including a chapter on Mr. Vaughan as principal and a photo of him among the ex-GIs of 1946 (p124, second row, second from right). "Sing to me" from Robert Fagles tr., *The Odyssey* (Penguin Books 1996, p77). Almost every year, I listen to the Ian McKlellen narration from Penguin Audio, driving to Walmart for groceries or to the mountains to ski. "Holy, holy, holy" from *Congregational Church Hymnal* (Congregational Union of England and Wales 1905, p178).

Life plays its little tricks on us. When I became a regular on the internet, I set up a Google Search for my name, and for the past thirty years it has regularly returned stories about Judge Daniel Ford, sentencing one or another malefactor to prison. He is now retired, but that doesn't stop Google: I just now got the message "Retired Judge Daniel Ford steps down from diocesan task force on clergy abuse" (masslive.com 5/28/21).

Harry Truman declared the War concluded on 12/31/46, so anyone who had signed up before April 1946 – nearly a year after Germany surrendered – qualified for benefits under the GI Bill. These were the "vets" studying at Brewster in my senior year. Abenaki Tower still exists, though it's a newer and taller version, built of steel. It even has a website, from which I learn that the original was built in 1924 by a club that bought the land for $800 and budgeted $400 for its construction. It cost $100 extra, which was paid off by "bridge and whist parties, food sales, and other entertainment" (abenakitower.org 11/20/20).

The wording of the Hurlin plaque seems to have changed since 1950. The *Lincoln Library of Essential Information* was refreshed every second year; the edition Harry bought in 1950 contained 2,000 pages in a single fat volume. It was our generation's version of Wikipedia. Notice that in my photo of Joe standing on Main Street, the A&P sign has two iterations of the boast "Self Service," then a radical notion in rural New Hampshire.

5 - The University

At a UNH reunion many years later, a classmate reported that he'd run into Ted the Greek in Boston. Apparently Ted was doing well in the underworld, for he was wearing a double-breasted gray suit, a white tie, and a black silk shirt. The University in those years had an enrollment of 3,500 when I began and 3,000 when I graduated, as the rabbit of ex-GIs passed through the python of higher education. Ten years later came the Baby Boom. Today the enrollment is about 15,000, from two-year agricultural to PhD in philosophy.

I find that Reading Gaol is now called HM Prison Reading. Can you imagine Oscar Wilde's writing a ballad about *that?* In much the same way, our county courthouse has become the County Administration and Justice Building, as government strives to take the joy out of our lives. Randall Jarrell, "The Death of the Ball Turret Gunner," in John Holmes & Carroll Towle, *Complete College Reader*, Houghton-Mifflin 1950 – another volume from Henry Laughlin! I read this bleak little poem in college, as did my future bride and our future daughter, who in turn would assign it to her home-schooled daughters.

Jack Dunfey managed the coffee shop when I was a freshman, and he'll serve for the rest. He had a grand life, born 1924, died 2020. He was the fifth of twelve children, and like the others began his working life at the family luncheonette in Lowell, Mass. He served in the Army Air Forces in the War, and afterward he and three brothers ran the coffee shop in Durham and a clam shack in Hampton, to support themselves while they went to college, graduating one after another. In time they came to own Omni Hotels International, but kept the corporate headquarters in New Hampshire. Jack gradually turned his energy to philanthropy, and though a lifetime Democrat served as one of Ronald Reagan's founders of the U.S. Institute for Peace. Of the brothers who worked at the Durham coffee shop in 1951-1952, one still lives in the state, as does a sister, who wrote a clan biography: Eleanor Dunfey-Freiburger, *Counter Culture: Clams, Convents and a Circle of Global Citizens* (Peter Randall 2019).

A semester's tuition, for an in-state student at UNH, is now $7,760, nearly five times what I paid in 1951 after adjusting for inflation. "The migrant has no ground to stand on": Salman Rushdie, *Languages of Truth*, Random House 2021, p60. "Struggle for power": Hans Morgenthau, *Politics Among Nations: The Struggle for Power and Peace* (Knopf 1948, p16). Frank Harris, *My Life and Loves* (Obelisk Press 1934). Theodoor Hendrik van de Velde, *Ideal Marriage: Its Physiology and Technique* (Wm. Heinemann 1926).

Joe got his MPA and all-but-doctorate from the Littauer School of Public Administration, now the Kennedy School. His mentor was V.O. Key Jr. (1908-1963), a Texan noted for research that demolished the notion of the "solid South" in American politics: *Southern Politics in State and Nation* (Knopf 1950). When he died, Dr. Key too had an unfinished project, but unlike Joe he had a collaborator, Milton Cummings, who completed *The Responsible Electorate: Rationality in Presidential Voting, 1936-1960* (Harvard 1966), which perhaps should be required reading today. Joe's thesis was that New Hampshire's independent-minded Republicans like four-term Representative Perkins Bass (1912-2011) were the ideological descendants of Theodore Roosevelt's Bull Moose Progressives of 1912.

6 - The Polish Girl

For more, see Daniel Ford, *Poland's Daughter: How I Met Basia, Hitchhiked to Italy, and Learned About Love, War, and Exile* (CreateSpace 2013). "There is a forgotten": attributed to Winston Churchill, though dang if I can find the source. "The other side" etc.: Goethe, *Faust: Part One*, tr. Philip Wayne (Penguin Books 1949, p87), beginning with line 1656. "Embrace all experience": Louis Menand, *The Free World: Art and Thought in the Cold War* (Farrar Strauss 2021, p69). Mr. Menand is quoting Simone de Beauvoir. I am indebted to his book for giving me a framework to understand America's golden years, 1945-1965, in which I ever so slowly became an adult; see Chapter 10. The Welsh name dates to the 1880s and means "St. Mary's Church in the hollow of white hazel near a rapid whirlpool and the Church of St. Tysilio near the red cave" (atlasobscura.com, 6/25/21). It may have been intended as a joke.

Rosalie as waitress: letter from Joe, 10/27/54. The diary entry quoting my letter is dated November 29, a

Sunday, and speaks of my adventures on a weekend in London, so I probably wrote it a week earlier. Joe typed his diary on half-sized sheets of loose-leaf paper and put them in a small six-ring binder. Before and after this page are others recounting his chaste and tormented pursuit of Betsy Warwick. "Watch out for her," he quotes me as writing. "When it comes to wiles I would put my money on the voluptuous heroine of The Weirs. Please don't feel you are getting off to a late start, and thus must have a family ready-made. . . . You find the least Christian babes to pal around with; while I . . . have wound up with a veritable Saint, albeit in unsaintly clothing." If not Basia, I have no idea who I had in mind.

Chabrus is pronounced, more or less, as "habrs." There's some question whether this is actually the Polish term, but I recorded Basia's voice when she confirmed its spelling and pronunciation (interviews at her home near London, June 2011). My notion of the color has always been "Group Portrait of Women with Cornflowers" (1914) by Igor Graber. See his biography on Wikipedia. The women are his wife and sister-in-law, but they're incidental to the stunning blue of the flowers.

See unistrapg.it/en for Perugia and its university. For the scandal and trial, see the Wikipedia articles for "Amanda Knox" and "Murder of Meredith Kercher." Weirdly, the man eventually convicted for the killing was sentenced to sixteen years, ten years less than Knox's sentence. Ms. Knox was separately given three years for "calumny" (slander) but wisely didn't surrender to Italian authorities on that charge.

As a rough measure, every village and town on the *Route d'Italie* has since tripled in size, and every road has tripled in width. In particular, Bardonecchia is not only a considerable town but a major ski resort. When Enrico Piaggio saw the prototype of his redesigned MP6 scooter, he exclaimed, "*Sembra una vespa*!" ("It looks like a wasp!"), thus naming it on the spot (Wikipedia 5/9/21).

The love of Italy, Italians, and the Italian language from 1955 is still with me. Sally and I visit whenever we can, for opera, mountain walks, and the delights of Florence. Indeed, I sometimes think that Italy, as with the mountain town of Aspen, Colorado, is a place where I might have called for time to stop: *Verweile doch, du bist so schön!* (Goethe, *Faust I,* line 1700.)

Henry Laughlin went to England in 1947 to meet Churchill and negotiate the American rights to the yet-unpublished history, with an advance of $250,000, now regarded as the publishing coup of the century. When I was well settled in marriage, home, and life, I gave away the Cheap Edition and acquired a pristine set of Houghton-Mifflin volumes from 1948-1953. Churchill was delighted when he received the first, *The Gathering Storm*. "When I take it in my hands," he said, "it opens like angel's wings" (Henry A. Laughlin, "Glimpses — First Citizen of the World," on winstonchurchill.org, as read to the Massachusetts Historical Society in 1965).

I still have the Hemingway and Fitzgerald books, the latter stamped "Tourist Class SS United States." Madi's name was Maddalena di Carlo. She was about fifty in 1955, and locally famous as a Communist partisan during the War. By 1975, however, the gamine had become a crone and an embarrassment to the good folk of Lerici, who shut the hostel down. When I made a sentim8ental journey with Sally in 2016, the castle was a museum of paleontology, with the fishermen gone, the harbor choked with yachts, and the town choked with tourists. We couldn't find a room at a price we were willing to pay in Lerici, where as a young vagabond I had bedded down for twenty-five cents a night.

"But most of all": Daniel Ford, *Poland's Daughter* (pp181-182). The *Manneken Pis* in Brussels has since been removed to a museum for safekeeping. Similarly,

Karl Marx's grave in Highgate Cemetery is now guarded day and night by video cameras.

7 - The Army

I can't find any evidence that there was ever an anti-personnel round for the bazooka, but I am positive of what we were told in training. (We were also told that there was no recoil when the rocket launcher was fired, but when I pulled the trigger, my glasses were slammed back into my right eye. Fortunately I was wearing my Army-issue shatterproof lenses.) "One day we were born": Samuel Beckett, *Waiting for Godot* (Grove 1954, p58). Also see the Wikipedia biography of Bert Lahr, and Louis Menand, *The Free World* p369.

George Araujo was of Cape Verdean descent. His challenge for the lightweight championship is available on YouTube (CcUpTr3aPbY, 12/6/20). He went back to boxing after Army service, but the layoff had cost him. He won his first three fights but lost the fourth by a unanimous decision and the next by a TKO. He then quit the ring to become a coach, painter, and union and civil rights activist. After his death in 1997, he was inducted into the Rhode Island Heritage Hall of Fame, making him, I suppose, the most consequential man of my acquaintance. I owe that much to the U.S. Army.

Teddy Kennedy was in my high-school generation, and like me was a college freshman in 1950-51, at Harvard, which expelled him for cheating. He joined the Army for four years but thanks to family connections served less than half that time, after which Harvard let him return. He graduated in the middle of his class in June 1956. I was a great fan of Jack Kennedy, but perhaps you understand why I didn't care for Teddy.

Proust at the caserne gate: *The Guermantes Way* in the Penguin translation by Mark Treharne (Viking 2004 p64). In November 1889, the teenaged Proust reported to

Coligny Caserne as a "cadet" in the 76th Infantry Regiment, a privileged alternative to conscription. In his novel, he called the town Doncières. Today, the caserne has become government offices. There's a school nearby named for him, and a Rue Marcel Proust not far away. I should have spent my eighteen months in Orléans reading *À la recherché du temps perdu*!

I see something similar to the caserne's prefab buildings at longlifebuildings.com called the P-Line (12/8/20). Paris today has a thoroughly modern and very ugly main opera house, and Palais Garnier is largely given over to ballet. Not everyone shares my opinion of its beauty: Le Corbusier called it "a décor of the grave." It still boasts the subterranean lake – in reality a reservoir in case of fire – where the *Phantom* lived. The wonderful market at Les Halles was bulldozed in August 1971 while Paris was on vacation, to be replaced by "a soulless concrete carbuncle squatting atop a subterranean rail hub" ("Les Halles de Paris" on flashback.com, 12/9/20). Rue Blondel changes with the times: in the 1920s, famed for *Aux Belles Poules* (The Pretty Chickens) at number 32; in the 1950s, streetwalkers in furs and fishnet stockings; and in the 1990s, at least for a time, muscle-bound men who apparently offered services similar to those of the *poules*. Now, from what I can see on Bing Maps and Google Earth, the sidewalks are mostly empty and gentrification has begun its terrible work, with reputable establishments – a pizza parlor, a Thai restaurant – creeping in from east and west. And I see a Reginald Marsh lithograph for $2,800 (1stdibs.com, "Rue Blondel, No. 2," 12/10/20).

The Captain's Paradise (London Films 1953) actually had Alec Guinness shuttling between Gibraltar and a port on the Atlantic coast of Morocco, a two-day trip rather than the couple of hours it took me to cross to Tangiers. "Dabrowski's Mazurka": YouTube 2nmFHUbVQtA.

8 - The Overseas Weekly

Les Longchamps no longer seems to exist, a pity. "Which didn't take long": my undated letter to Joe. That darling vendor no doubt inspired Jean Seberg's role in *Breathless*, the much-admired but rather irritating film from Jean-Luc Goddard (1960). See the newsgirl in "Women Overseas," *Life* pp69-70 12/23/57. CONUS: Continental United States.

"5 feet 3 inches": *Life* 12/23/57. "Stocky, energetic divorcee": *Time* 06/09/61. For more about Marion and the *OW*, see *Newsweek* 07/18/66; *True* July 1967; *Time* 10/20/67; *NY Times* p50 10/28/69 and p2 9/01/70; *Stanford Daily* 08/12/18; "Marion Woodward von Rospach" on Findagrave; "John Robert Dornberg" on Prabook; "Overseas Weekly" and "Volkswagen Beetle" on Wikipedia (12/11/20). My apartment in Sachsenhausen has since been overlaid by a park, and while Quirinstrasse still exists, it's a few blocks east of its location in 1958.

The U.S. military has been governed by an evolving set of Articles of War since June 1775. "The Uniform Code of Military Justice" was passed by Congress in May 1950, went into effect a year later, and has itself evolved over the years. See *Manual for Courts-Martial United States*, U.S. Department of Defense 2019.

The de Havilland Comet went into service in 1952 but was plagued with accidents and never flew to the United States. Transatlantic jet travel was introduced in October 1958 on the larger, faster, and safer Boeing 707. I can't determine when the *Overseas Traveler* made its debut, but likely in the early 1960s. My Speed Graphic camera took a sheet negative 3.25 by 4.25 inches, but in Europe I used a roll-film adapter that gave me nine smaller images. To use the camera today, I'd have to buy 4x5 sheets of film and cut them to size, and the roll film is no longer manufactured.

“*Davon haben wir nichts*”: Helmut Smith, “Exit the Fatherland” at aon.com (6/09/21). “The Hun is either at your throat”: Churchill to the U.S. Congress, 5/19/43. The quote is disputed, but it can be heard on YouTube bOgiD3fVujU (05/29/21). Elvis Presley not only became a specialist but a sergeant, a rare accomplishment by a peacetime conscript. And when he went home to be mustered out, his manager provided him with a tailored dress uniform with *four* stripes on the sleeves. This must have annoyed Sergeant Brown at Coligny Caserne, who’d earned his stripes walking back from Frozen Chosin in December 1950, while the Chinese sniped at him from the high ground on either side of the road.

“God has a very big heart, but there is one sin He will not forgive. If a woman calls a man to her bed and he will not go.” Nikos Kazantakis (tr. Carl Wildman), *Zorba the Greek*, Simon & Schuster 1953. I remember it best, however, as spoken by Anthony Quinn in the 1964 film from Twentieth Century-Fox.

9 - The Free Lance

I can find no trace of *SS Amerika* in 1958, but I am positive of my passage from Bremerhaven. The original German liner of that name was seized by the United States in 1917 and used as a troopship; it was, in fact, scrapped at the Bethlehem steel works while I was working in Frankfurt. Norman Stevens and Charles Moritz each got a master’s degree from Rutgers in 1957. Norman died in 2018 after a stellar career in library administration, leaving a wonderfully long-tailed family, even to a great-granddaughter.

The Prince George went further downhill after I stayed there, eventually becoming indigent housing for the city. See its page on daytoninmanhattan.blogspot.com (12/27/20). My room on Appleton Street in Boston, by contrast, has now been joined with Beedee’s and our shared bath to make a 537 square foot “studio” with a Zillow rental value of $2,300 a month. Jere O'Brien's monthly income from this floor was about $60, and he supplied heat and electricity and occasionally cleaned the bathroom, or Kathleen his wife did.

Irwin Shaw, *The Young Lions*, Random House 1948. Shaw lived off and on in Paris, but almost certainly in a neighborhood too pricey for me. "This lousy country": undated letter to my brother, March 1958, in which Emma scolds Joe for being a Congressional Fellow. *Carmen Jones* filmed by Otto Preminger 1954, based on the musical by Oscar Hammerstein, based on the opera by Charles Bizet. "Bible of the beat generation": Jack Kerouac, *On the Road,* Signet 1958. The *Times* review: Gilbert Millstein, "Books of the Times," NYT 09/05/57. As published, my Thelonious Monk biography didn't include his lovely notion of catching notes with his hands. Evidently Charlie Moritz didn't share my fondness for the metaphor. My thanks to Kathrine Aydelott at UNH and Mel Johnson at the University of Maine for that information.

"That is the land of lost content": A.E. Houseman, *A Shropshire Lad* 40, 1896. Marcel Proust (tr. C.K. Scott Moncrieff and Frederick Blossom), *Remembrance of Things Past*, Random House 1934. Foolishly, I sold that boxed set when I bought the three-volume edition of 1981, updated to include the latest French scholarship, and I sold *that* when it was revised yet again as *In Search of Lost Time* in 1992. For more about this private passion, see readingproust.com. I attribute the website to one of my fictional characters, to make the point that, far from being a scholar, I'm still a student of Proust, who reads his great novel only in its various English translations.

Thomas Williams, *Ceremony of Love*, Bobbs-Merrill 1955; *Town Burning*, Macmillan 1959; and *The Night of Trees*, Macmillan 1961. See his Wikipedia biography and his entry on prabook.com (seen 4/30/21). We met about 1960. Tom's first success was *The Hair of Harold Roux*,

Random House 1974. He was an important figure in the 1970s but isn't much read today, a fate that came to most writers of the era, especially those who were white, heterosexual, male, and, as Tom liked to say, serious. "After the war": Louis Menand, *The Free World*, p455.

Friedrich Nietzsche (tr. Thomas Common), *Thus Spake Zarathustra*, Modern Library (undated). Walter Kaufmann ed., *Existentialism from Dostoevsky to Sartre*, Meridian Books 1956. Kaufmann also translated *Thus Spoke Zarathustra* in 1954, and savaged Mr. Common's version. New Hampshire's "Puritan Sweepstakes," as the *Reporter* titled my article, was a spectacular success. Nearly two million tickets were sold at $3 each, with the top winner taking home $50,000. These were substantial sums in 1964, in a state with 600,000 residents and a per capita income of $15,000 a year. See Kevin Flynn, *American Sweepstakes: How One Small State Bucked the Church, the Feds, and the Mob to Usher in the Lottery Age*, University Press of New England 2015. I'm sorry to say that Mr. Flynn didn't cite my pioneering articles.

10 – The Good Life

Saigon is now called Ho Chi Minh City, and the airport is Tan Son Nhat. In 1965, NBC sent its own reporters to Saigon, putting John Sharkey out of a job, but Vo Huynh continued as NBC cameraman. He won an Emmy for the documentary "Same Mud, Same Blood," available on YouTube at Rk97G6DhVmQ (1/4/21). When American combat troops were withdrawn in 1973, Huynh became NBC's reporter, too, providing voice-over for his film. He fled to the U.S. when the Saigon regime collapsed in 1975.

By the time I was home in August 1964, we were bombing North Vietnam, with ground troops committed soon after Lyndon Johnson was elected president in his own right. It was no longer the Terry and the Pirates adventure I had witnessed, and not until the new century did my journal see print: *The Only War We've Got: Early Days in South Vietnam*, Warbird Books 2012. I also wrote about Cowboy, born Y Kdruin Mlo but known to the foreigners as Philippe Drouin: *Cowboy: The Interpreter Who Became a Soldier, a Warlord, and One More Casualty of Our War in Vietnam*, Warbird Books 2018. "The Wings Tear Off," *Nation* 7/13/64. MAC-V: Military Assistance Command, Vietnam.

Now Comes Theodora, Doubleday 1965, Avon 1966, Warbird Books 2018. "Clear-sighted, unangry": *New Yorker*, 6/26/65. When I bought that house, Dad sent me his toolbox by Railway Express, and I got pretty handy myself. I don't think there's any gene for this stuff. If you think you can do a job, and you have the tools, you just go ahead and do it. "The United States can no more contain": Hans Morgenthau, "We Are Deluding Ourselves in Vietnam," *NYT Magazine* 4/18/65. For his honesty, he was fired from his consulting job at the Defense Department.

Go, stranger, and tell the Spartans: The epitaph to the Three Hundred is my translation of a poetic fragment from Simonides, who was about sixty-four at the time of the battle. A more traditional version is "Go tell the Spartans, stranger passing by / That here obedient to their laws we lie." *Incident at Muc Wa*, Doubleday 1967, Wm. Heineman 1968, Pyramid 1968, Arend 1973 (in Dutch), Warbird Books 2012; as *Go Tell the Spartans*, an Avco-Embassy film and Jove paperback 1978. Mr. Mayes also wrote screenplays for *The Spirit of St. Louis*, *Anatomy of a Murder*, *Von Ryan's Express*, and *The Poseidon Adventure*, all of which I had seen at the Franklin Theatre in Durham. "Great antipathy": letter from Diane Matthews 6/21/72. Formally, the *Reporter* merged with *Harper's Magazine* in 1968, but that was really just a purchase of the smaller magazine's mailing list. Harper's made good on the subscriptions and probably picked up some new subscribers. Max Ascoli died ten years later.

In 1931, the United States had a Gross Domestic Product of $748 per person, the equivalent of $11,328 in current dollars. Ninety years later, each American's share of GDP is $34,103, for a tripling of wealth in my lifetime. And, on the average, we have added twenty years in which to spend it. "The Roman world is falling": F.A. Wright tr., *Select Letters of Saint Jerome*, Loeb Classical Library 1933, letter 60. "I shudder when I think of the catastrophes of our time," wrote Jerome in the same epistle. "For twenty years and more the blood of Romans has been shed daily between Constantinople and the Julian Alps." Well, enough of that!

Made in the USA
Las Vegas, NV
16 May 2022